Thursdays

Aretha Wilson

Writer's note

The narrative of my memoirs is structured around music. Each chapter is named for a song. Every song I chose has lyrics that I identified with during specific times in my life. I want you to have an opportunity to hear what helped me cope through some of my greatest challenges. The best way to share our thoughts and feelings is through books and music. These two forms of creative expression are humanity's most relatable connections, and it's a way to help keep us all on the same page.

Out of respect for all characters that are mentioned in my story, I use pseudonyms in lieu of their real names. I do this so as to not commit anyone else to my journey, as they may not see things exactly the same way I did. Besides, we've all got a story to tell, and I'd bet that each adventure is accompanied by a great soundtrack.

Contents

Introduction

Being a guy's girl, by the age of 15, there was only one item throughout my life I ever purchased that was pink. It was the album *Hounds of Love* by Kate Bush. The song "Make a Deal with God." told us that she would be running up that road, if she could swap places; meaning she wishes to switch places with the boys, in order to better understand how the other feels.

She would also teach me the importance of what it means to be "Cloudbusting" while directing me through my life's very own "Wuthering Heights". Between divulging secrets with little coercion, and her ability to swoon like a bird while dancing interpretively through her emotions, I'm convinced that she's an Earthly angel. And I still believe every word she sings.

The courage to take back my name comes from the group The Alan Parsons Project who will sing they are the "Eye In The Sky", to any critics or pundits who will have anything to say, so am I. No one is going to be better at being or knowing me than me, and I accept the challenge, these days happily. Thanks to Modest Mouse who will sing "Float On" and so will I.

Gratitude

To Thom, Colin, Jonny, Philp and Ed, along with all the other musicians/DJ's that are mentioned, it's official; I would've never made it through this life, without hearing about it from you. In my world, you are all musical Ministers. For that, I am eternally grateful.

For Jono, thank you for creating the perfect *Hideaway*.

Dedicated to my family, my Sky being the foremost. Nala, George, Nino and Gwop.

I MIGHT BE WRONG

WOULD I HAVE gotten in the car that night, if I had known the decision was going to change my life irrevocably? Would I have done it, if I had known I would never look at myself the same way again?

Probably not. But we don't get the benefit of hindsight when we're making decisions in the present. And yet, I can't regret the way it turned out, because it set my life on the course it has taken, and I wouldn't alter that now; even if I could.

"*Road rage*" is probably the best way to describe what started the chain of events that set my life on this new course. The night started out innocently enough: some friends and I were going to a restaurant, after we had been out clubbing. I was driving along, minding my own business, when I got cut off by a cab driver.

It happens all the time.

But that night (instead of ignoring it like I was taught when I learned how to drive), I leaned on the horn. The cab driver made a quick U-turn and started following us. My heart started to pound.

He pulled up beside the car and rolled down his window, yelling at us. To hear what he was saying, Clark (my son's father and my boyfriend at the time), rolled down the passenger window. We all shouted back.

It wasn't a good idea. I can see that in retrospect. At the time, we were too riled up to think about the consequences.

We drove a few blocks this way, windows down and hollering. Soon, we were on a bridge, still side by side with the cab. By this time, the enraged driver was done using his words. Instead, he turned his car into a weapon. He sped up, cut his wheel left and headed straight into my lane. To avoid him, I swerved into oncoming traffic.

A car seemingly appeared out of nowhere, suddenly in front of me. Before I could even react, we smashed into it; almost head-on. Our car spun across the road, while I tried desperately to control it. After a few revolutions, we came to a stop in a patch of grass on the other side of the bridge. The cab driver continued full speed ahead, fleeing the scene.

God only knows where I got the energy to jump out of the car and spring into action. I guess it was an adrenaline rush. My first instinct was to make sure Clark and the girl we brought with us weren't injured. I wasn't feeling any pain. I totally focused on them.

Right away, I looked at Clark. "Are you okay?"

He looked back at me in shock. His eyes completely fixated on my face, like he'd just seen a ghost. "Aretha… Please… You need to lie down."

I couldn't figure out why, but I did as he said, lying on the ground. Boy, was it ever cold! I felt like I was on an ice rink with my body temperature rapidly decreasing, even though I could feel warm blood running down my face. All I could think was that I wished I had a hat to cover my freezing ears.

I said to Clark, who was still staring at me with that bereaved look on his face, "I'm so cold…"

The other girl came over. She took one glance at me and began to scream. Beyond her cries, I heard the distant sirens of an ambulance. Then, I lost consciousness.

***

Thursdays are special for me.

I've discovered that these are the days when I make some of my most life-altering decisions. By the time Friday rolls in, I'm left questioning all the choices I made the day before, and I find myself headed in directions I'd never imagined.

These experiences—sometimes good, sometimes bad—have transformed me into a survivor of intense challenges. I wanted to write about those days. How I managed. Who I am. What I've become. When honesty leads to a path where I can reconcile with the past, you'll see why the truth sets me free.

December 2, 1993, was one of those special Thursdays. It began with me on the phone, speaking with my son's godmother. She agreed to babysit my sixteen-month-old son, Scion, as I planned to head out for the evening. A friend of mine, Lock, had a weekend pass from a Kingston penitentiary, and he'd asked me and Clark to join him for one of his two days of freedom.

It had been two years since I'd last seen Lock. He had been incarcerated for a serious offense, and I only visited a few times. I never understood the details of his case, nor did I judge him. I didn't even ask about it. All I knew was, by the time everything was over, he received a seven-year sentence—a long time for any Canadian. One that feels especially long for someone who is only twenty-five years old.

I moved out to be on my own at nineteen, and at twenty-three, I would describe myself as a young woman living on the surface of life, never going very deep, moving through each day basically the same way as the day before. I headed in one direction, calling it the future, with little or no idea of where I was going—aside from pondering an educational upgrade at my job, where I was the receptionist at an investment firm.

I did the best I could to be a decent mother. I would wake up and go to work so I could keep my son fed, clothed, and with a roof over his head. I played with him, cared for him, and sometimes took him to the park to feed the squirrels. On weekends, I would make time to meet up with friends, usually at a restaurant, bar, or club, to let loose and crack a few jokes. Like most people, I loved being in the company of others and listening to music. Even when I wanted to be alone, I was usually listening to a good track. Music is my greatest comfort, and it's always there when I need it.

On the night that changed everything, four of us were heading out from my place: me, Clark, Lock, and a girl called DK. I expected we would get together at a local restaurant with a few of our old neighborhood friends. We would reminisce about the good times we'd had growing up in the same area and going to the same all-ages clubs. I envisioned a laid-back evening, just talking and enjoying ourselves.

We made plans to meet up at my place at 8:30 p.m., but Lock didn't show up until 10. He arrived in a car he'd borrowed from someone I didn't know. I suppose this was his way of making sure Clark and I didn't miss out on whatever it was he had planned. After being in jail for several years, with no participation in society, it appeared he was still ready to go. His idea of a good time was going to a crowded bar. We suggested a few other places, but he was adamant we headed to a specific bar in Scarborough. It was far from where I lived, closer to downtown Toronto, so we needed a ride.

I felt like the night was heading toward obligation, rather than pleasure, when he asked me to drive the car he'd borrowed. But not knowing what state his driver's license was in, and not wanting to ask what freedoms his forty-eight-hour pass included, I agreed; I believed we would be safer if I drove.

It was an extremely cold night, but no snow covered the ground.

It was unusual for that time of year in Toronto. Usually, the roads were filled with muddy slush, while the lakes were on their way to becoming sheets of ice. It was the time of year when my fingertips burned, my ears ached, and shivers racked my body. The cold was deadly.

Driving to the bar wasn't the problem. Anyone who knows me will tell you that I love going out, regardless of the weather, with or without a hat and mittens. I know many people throughout the city, but I didn't care for the bar we were going to. Other places within walking distance would have been just as much fun.

All the decisions made up to that point had changed, which made me uncomfortable. I felt a twinge as soon as we diverged from our initial plans. My instinct produced a slight, uneasy pang in my chest. But I ignored it, as we are too often likely to do, and went along with what Lock wanted. It was his night of freedom, after all.

When we got to the bar, it was already filled with maybe two hundred people. It was noisy, and not just because of the music. Most of the patrons looked like they were already four or five drinks in and three sheets to the wind, yelling at the top of their lungs, so they could be heard by their companions. I didn't recognize a single soul; other than the people I came with. The bar was gigantic, with people walking in every direction. Others danced around wherever they wanted, spilling their half-filled glasses.

As we wound our way through the crowd, the gummy residue of alcohol and pop made my shoes stick to the floor with each step. It was as if we had wandered into an overcrowded frat party.

Being in that type of environment was not new to me. I went to my first all-ages club at fifteen. Right after I discovered it, my mother made a standing arrangement with my best friend's dad to pick us up when it closed. Since then, I showed up every Friday and Saturday night to a place called Club Z. They served pop from 10 p.m. until 6 a.m., and I spent most of my time out on the floor, trying to figure out how to dance to songs like New Order's "Temptation," regardless of how sticky the ground was.

Once we'd made our way to the coat check through the hordes of jocks and cheerleaders, Lock drifted off into the crowd. DK disappeared in the other direction, leaving Clark and I behind.

I figured Lock had gone off to mingle with the free people he hadn't been around in years, so I decided I'd give him some space. I couldn't help wondering why he had asked us along if he just wanted to hang out with strangers. On our way there, he'd told us he wanted to make the most of the next forty-eight hours by letting loose. All he had to do was show up on Sunday morning to get transported back to the penitentiary. At that moment, it seemed to be the only thing he cared about.

I had no jail experience, so I couldn't imagine what it was like to be locked up for so long and then return to society for just two days, only to go back to prison for several more years. What I did know was that Lock would only get a pass from jail based on good behavior. From what I could see, all he wanted to do was have fun with people who were free. I still wasn't sure if this forty-eight-hour pass included all the liberties of going to a crowded bar, but it wasn't my problem.

Since we knew no one, Clark and I did our best to entertain ourselves by chatting with people standing around us. However, we were having a tough time trying to talk over the music and voices.

Not that I wasn't used to a lot of hollering or loud music. I grew up in a four-bedroom house, with three older sisters who would all attempt to sing a cappella at once, while my two older brothers provided accompaniment by clapping and stomping their feet. For the record, only my second oldest sister sings with an angelic voice.

With each one of them having different musical tastes, I was raised on a steady diet of America, The B 52's, Led Zeppelin, Queen, Zapp, and Roger, alongside Gospel Sundays on a radio station called WBLK. All of us would be singing anything from ELO to "I.G.Y.", and everything in between.

At five, I had my first crush: all things musical. I would sneak downstairs to my eldest brother's room, so I could listen to his massive record collection with no one watching. The double album by Stevie Wonder, Songs in the Key of Life, was the one I played most. For whatever reason, at that young age, my favorite song on it was "As." I listened to it countless times, dancing and singing as if my life depended on it. Further, both of my parents were involved in the music industry. My stepfather was the owner of a guitar repair shop, which attracted Canadian artists like Geddy Lee. My mother was the backup for a well-known singer, after whom she'd proudly named me.

Unfortunately, having an undying love for all things musical wasn't going to save me from having a mediocre time that night at the bar. After being there for over an hour, with no sign of Lock, I got the itch to leave. We had a long drive home, and I had to be up early for work the next morning. Even earlier for Scion.

Clark and I began looking for him. I felt it was my obligation to find Lock, seeing how I was the one who'd driven us all, and I still had the keys. We searched the entire bar, hampered by trying to maneuver through the crush of people. By that point, most of them were stumbling around, looking for the coat check, and then making their way to the exit. We bumped into DK, who said she hadn't seen Lock since we arrived. We couldn't find him anywhere.

It was late, and I decided it was time to call my son's godmother to let her know we would be late. I told her how we'd lost Lock and were waiting to see if he would show up. Something told me the possibility of that happening was minimal. She agreed to stay at home until we returned, but she suggested we try checking if he went to The Real Jerk.

Earlier that day, I'd recommended we go there since they had a good crowd on Thursday nights. Not only did they have a bar, but a decent restaurant as well. I'd believed going there would have made more sense, since it was much closer. It was too bad we ended up in Scarborough.

The three of us left the bar. After only a few moments of standing outside, I began to feel my ears freezing in the icy air. We got into the car to turn on the heat and escape the bitter cold. After a brief discussion about what to do next, we all agreed we would head over to The Real Jerk, hoping to find Lock there. Having cell phones really would've helped us out, but at the time they were big, clunky, and expensive. Most normal people didn't own a cell phone, and a person on a two-day pass from Joyceville Penitentiary certainly wouldn't have one.

The fastest route to get downtown from the bar was to take Danforth Road to Danforth Avenue, which I followed west toward the center of the city. Danforth turned into Bloor Street. Soon, we were right in the heart of Toronto. It was about a forty-five-minute drive, which gave me plenty of time to think.

I was upset with my friend. Not only had he abandoned us at the bar, but he'd also left me with the keys to someone's car. I had no clue who owned it! Little did I know, being disgruntled with him would not compare to the nightmare about to unfold.

I was only about ten minutes away from the restaurant when the accident with the cab happened. My new destination became the Toronto Western Hospital. By then, I was no longer the one who was driving, and I would later wake up as an entirely different person.

I became aware of my dire situation when they placed me onto a gurney and lifted me into an ambulance. I overheard the attendant seated beside me say to his partner, "Don't take her to St. Michael's Hospital. Let's take her to Western. They've got better plastics there."

"Okay, sounds good."

And then it hit me: something must be terribly wrong with my face. I was aware enough to understand that plastics meant plastic surgeons, meaning my face must be badly injured. The suggestion to redirect us to another hospital meant it was severe, even though I couldn't feel a thing. After hearing their back and forth, I passed out. Not because of the pain, which would eventually come. Perhaps from the loss of blood, which I could still feel dripping down my face.

***

The next time I woke up, it was to the voices of the emergency staff in the hospital room where they'd brought me. Still in a daze, I could hear strangers calling out my name, like an echo: "Aretha… Aretha… Aretha…" Sometimes it sounded loud. Sometimes it seemed far away.

One of them was attaching an intravenous line into my left arm, and I could feel someone cutting off my clothing. Vaguely, as I came to, I could see the jeans I had put on earlier covered with blood. By that point, I knew it was all mine.

The nurse standing on the right side of me said, "Aretha… you're going to have to be awake for this, okay? Stay with me…" She paused for a moment before she added, "You've been through a lot."

It began with a frenzy of needles injecting anesthetic deeply throughout my nose. The needles going into my face produced a pain I didn't believe could exist in this world. It was excruciating. On top of that, not knowing how I would look afterward caused a panicky dread inside me.

I didn't know if I wanted to cry or scream. I took short breaths of air in anticipation of the next injection, and then I would grunt through each pierce, as though it were my only escape, making noises I had never made before.

I passed out again, and the same nurse woke me right back up. For some reason, I had to remain awake, as the surgeon began sewing a multitude of stitches in and out of my face. She said the reason, but I didn't process it. With the amount of pain I was in, I don't believe I cared. Last, they put my left eyeball back into its socket, stitching my eyelid back together. Sewing up this part of my face seemed to take forever.

Doctors, attendants, and surgeons worked on me for hours, and then transferred me to another room. With all the pain I had gone through during the surgery, coupled with the horror and terror of what I had endured, all I wanted to do was sleep the rest of that painful Friday away. I drifted off, but was abruptly awoken again in what felt like seconds later.

The door to my room was frantically opened by the youngest of my three older sisters. She would be the first person to see what I looked like after the doctors had done what they could. I had no idea what sort of reaction to expect. She stepped into the room without letting go of the door, peeking around it as if frightened of what she might see. Then she looked me dead straight in the face. After a few seconds of staring, she started screaming. Without hesitation, she ran straight back out of the room. I knew then that my face must be truly horrific.

My sister's reaction wasn't helping me feel better about what had happened. Then again, how could I blame her? When you're screaming, there is no room for words.

Next, my mom came in. She seemed more prepared, entering with a smile. As in most situations, my mother was calm. The way she looked at me reminded me of when I had been a little girl, and I got hurt. My mom has a way of turning situations around, using phrases to ensure that I don't worry and convincing me that whatever pain I was feeling would magically disappear soon.

She would say things like, "Here today, gone tomorrow," and, "Smile and you're bound to bear it!" Combined with her confident and reassuring smile, these phrases usually worked, although, this time it might not be that easy. Somehow, I knew my emotional wounds, and the change I was lined up for, would go way deeper than the mere cuts and scrapes I'd received in childhood.

After saying what she could to lift my spirits, she told me to rest and left. But by that point, there was no way I could sleep. I wondered what I looked like, as I lay in the hospital bed.

My mind pictured the angry face of the cab driver, right before he'd cut us off the second time. All of this had started because of the noise of a horn and a few words. Now it was over, and I was permanently damaged for life.

Later, I learned that everyone else in both cars had come out practically unscathed. Even if I had been severely injured, the one bit of relief I had was knowing that no one else had been. I had gone through the driver's side window—or I should say the left side of my face did—right after my head had broken the massively thick glass. As for the car I'd smashed into, the driver hadn't seen us coming, either. It had happened so fast.

The room was cold, and I felt chilled. I glanced over at the window, realizing it was covered in frost. I guessed it must have snowed while I was being sewn back together. As I continued to look around, I noticed there wasn't a restroom, so I found the call button and pressed it to get the nurse.

As soon as she walked in, her expression showed she felt sorry for me. I could tell as she tilted her head with sorrowful eyes. I thought if her face could speak, it would say something like, "You poor thing. You don't look good."

My only question was, "Can you tell me where the bathroom is?"

She turned away, saying, "I'm going to go grab you a bedpan." This was another sign that I was in terrible shape.

Abruptly, I said, "No, no. I'm sure there's nothing wrong with my legs." I'm not exactly certain why I was so determined to see myself in the mirror. I guess maybe, I needed to know how bad it was.

I paused for a moment, while she stared at me. Then I asked her to please take me to the bathroom. She helped me up, and we walked down the hallway to the restroom. I avoided all eye contact with people. I didn't want anyone else to tell me about my appearance with those same looks on their faces. I'd had quite enough of that already.

When we got to the door, the nurse gently swung me around, so we were looking at each other. She stood staring at me intensely for a moment. I could tell she was preparing to say something difficult—something she thought I didn't want to hear. She took a deep breath, and then said, "Listen, Aretha. There's a mirror in there. Whatever you do, take it easy on yourself."

I shrugged my shoulders and said, "Okay."

All I knew was a bunch of stitches were sewn through the left side of my face, and I only had one good eye to see them with.

I anxiously walked in and looked into the mirror.

I saw my image in the bathroom mirror for the first time and my breath got caught in my throat. I stared at all the black thread sewn in and out of my face. The stitches tightly held my sliced skin back together.

It didn't look like me. My face was twice its normal size, with my complexion different shades of purple, yellow, and blue. My contagious and confident smile (much like my mother's) was gone. It took no more than a second for the overly swollen left side of my lip to send a message to my brain, advising me not to attempt it. Compared to the right side, it appeared as though that side was in 3D.

I gently touched my wound to see if it was real, even though I could still feel it throbbing as if it had its own heartbeat. Then, I traced all the stitches with the tip of my finger. I noticed they started on the left side of my ear and were sewn straight across my cheek to the corner of my mouth. Another set went up from the inside of my lip; along the side of my nose, to about a half of an inch from my left eye.

I noticed the stitches in my eyelid were much smaller and neatly sewn, as if to keep my eyeball safe in the socket. My left nostril looked like it had been torn clean off, and then sewn back on. I was too scared to touch that part of my face. To hold it in a natural position, two more sets of stitches went in different directions.

I could never have imagined a disfiguration so extreme that I couldn't recognize myself. I'd never been disfigured before; I'd hadn't even suffered from bad acne growing up. Then again, I suppose any person would have had a hard time waking up to almost a hundred stitches sewn into their face.

They would need to create a new word in the dictionary for me to describe how my appearance had transformed between Thursday night and Friday morning. Even the words marred or maimed wouldn't cut it. Now I could see why my sister had screamed when she'd seen me. No one could have prepared me for this.

Suddenly, as I tried to process what I was looking at, I heard my inner voice speak:

You're going to be okay.

Hearing those words gave me the courage to look in the mirror and say out loud, "It will get better. It's just going to take some time."

God only knows where I got the strength to say those words while looking at the new me. I figured it must have been His voice in my head. I didn't believe there was any way I could say those words on my own.

After staring at myself for a few more moments, I took a deep breath, opened the door, and walked out toward the waiting nurse. I forced a smile through the throbbing pain, to let her know I was okay, and we walked back to my bed. I got back in bed while the nurse adjusted my intravenous line.

Then she said, "We've got you on a morphine drip. It will help with the pain. Let me know if you need more." With that, she left the room.

I pulled the sheets up over my body. The room seemed even colder than before. Lying in a fetal position, with my mind going in circles, I began to cry. I thought about all the things that had led up to the night before, and how I'd ended up this way.

I tried my best to listen to the voice I'd heard earlier. It was already forcing me to accept what had happened. I heard it speak again, in my mind:

Embrace it. You can't erase it.

Finally, the pain medication kicked in, and I fell asleep.

The next day, I woke up with Clark in my room. He told me he had gone to five different hospitals looking for me.

He thought they'd taken me to St. Michael's Hospital until my mother had contacted him. He hadn't brought our son just yet as he wanted to make sure I felt well enough. We decided it would be best to bring him the following morning.

I noticed while we were talking that he would look down at the floor and then around the room as if he was having a hard time looking directly at me. When I told him about the severity of my pain, and what the doctors had had to do, he cried.

He spent a little more time with me, and after kissing my forehead, he left to go back home to our son. Seeing the mother of his child looking the way I did must have been difficult for him. I didn't look like the person he had been with the night before; never mind the person he had known for years.

I first met Clark briefly when I was eighteen, at a party one night. A few days later, he moved to Newfoundland to stay with his parents. A year later, and within a week of him returning to Toronto, we bumped into each other at a club called The Government. Within two weeks of that, we'd already begun to make plans to get a place together, even though we'd never once spoken on the phone while he'd been away. I suppose this would be a case of love at second sight, considering we became the proud parents of Scion within a year of happily living together. Four years later, as a young couple, we were struggling to figure out who we were individually, and we were uncertain if we were destined to remain together. We took a break twice, for a couple months each time. For the sake of our son, we still tried to make it work, and as a young man, Clark was doing his best to be a super dad, because of this and based off his real name, I refer to him as Clark

After having disappeared for over twenty-four hours, Lock finally showed up, bursting into the room like a bat out of hell. He shook his head in disbelief, saying nothing. Like Clark, I could see it was hard for him to keep his eyes on me.

For someone who thought they were going to have a lot to talk about with an old friend, I didn't know what to say. I no longer had any desire to talk about the way we used to go pool hopping when we were twelve.

He began pleading his case, telling me he hadn't left the bar. He claimed he'd searched up and down. I wasn't sure if what he was saying was true. He said it hadn't been until he'd gotten ahold of the other girl who'd been with us, DK, that he'd learned of the accident. Like Clark, he'd had a hard time finding me. He told me he wanted to make sure he saw me before he turned himself back in.

I still wondered how we could have missed each other the night before and why he took off. However, I said nothing. I didn't want him to return to the penitentiary feeling bad or that my accident was his fault. He could never have expected things to turn out the way they had.

He said sorry one more time and left.

We never spoke much after that day, even after he was released. I read an article in the newspaper about another arrest, but I don't have a clue where he is now. It was as if everything he'd gone through up to that point in his life had led him to his primary purpose in my life: to give me the keys to the car that night.

A few of my other friends came by the hospital to visit me, which I appreciated. But repeating the story of the accident, combined with the looks on their faces, took its toll on me. After a while, all I wanted to do was get some rest and prepare for my son to see me in the morning.

Based on the response I was getting from most people, I worried about what he might say. My son had begun to speak when he was quite young, and he'd already been forming sentences by the time he was sixteen months old. I'm also aware that children can be brutally honest without skipping a beat. So, no doubt, I was nervous. My primary concern was that the way I looked would scare him. I thought perhaps it would be best for us to meet in the waiting area, where it was more public. There would be other things for him to focus on.

The next morning when his dad took him to the hospital, I picked him up and held him in my arms. Instantly, it made me feel better. It was the first time we had been away from each other for that long, and I had missed him. He looked at my face, noticing the difference right away, and slowly his eyes opened wider, as if he was wondering why my left eye was sewn up.

He looked deeper at me for a moment, and then touched my face, running his little fingers alongside the stitches, ever so gently. He said, "Mommy, you have an owie." Then he smiled at me and looked away, as we continued to walk toward the visiting room couches.

Something else caught his attention, and after a couple more steps, I put him down, watching as he ran to a small play area. He showed no fear of me. It only took him a few seconds to decide all I had was an "owie", and that was the end of that.

***

At the time of the accident, I was working as the head receptionist at an investment firm. For four and a half years, I was the first face everyone saw. By the time of my accident, the people I worked with had become like family.

One of the phone calls I got while in the hospital was from Partner A of the firm where I worked. He had expected me to be at work on the Friday morning after my accident. Once I explained what had happened to me, he assured me that he and the other two partners wanted to provide all the help I needed, so I could get back to work and my regular life.

Hardly a week after the accident, they released me from the hospital with raw scars that I knew everyone would see. I was deeply concerned. No matter how much I told myself it would get better and that time heals all wounds, I was still afraid of what other people would think. Whether they would wonder how I ended up looking the way I now did.

We live in a judgmental society where kind children—who only see a person's heart—rub elbows with some very cruel adults. The kind who can be harsh in their criticism of someone's appearance.

For the first few weeks, I refused to leave my apartment, not wanting to face anyone. While my son was at daycare, I would spend a good majority of my time crying in the bathroom, staring in the mirror, and contemplating my existence, while trying to figure out if there was makeup that I could wear to cover the scars. I felt as though some force of nature had taken over my life, causing this enormous change, and I didn't understand why. A longing to know the reason such a thing had happened to me only fueled my tears and frustration. At the same time, I told myself, "It will get better. It's just going to take some time."

While I hid at home, different family members dropped in and kept a close watch on me. My manager from the office would call, sometimes two or three times during the day. She made it clear she would not stop until I got back to work. She wanted to make sure I wasn't sinking into depression or embarrassed to be in public. I liked her for that, and she was right. I didn't want to get stuck staring in the mirror, waiting for permanent scars to somehow magically disappear.

Eventually, my manager convinced me it was time to go back to what she called everyday life. So, four weeks after the accident, and with the new year just beginning, I was once again sitting at my desk as the head receptionist. Though the desk and office were exactly the way I remembered them, I couldn't say the same about my own face. It was sporting a new permanent disfigurement.

My coworkers couldn't help but look at me like I was someone else. Watching them walk into the office one by one, I would say the word grief best described the emotion on their faces, as they exchanged pleasantries with me. I knew the partners had probably made an announcement, warning everyone as best they could.

At the office, I answered the phones and greeted clients and other visitors. The company employed sixty brokers, twenty administrative staff, and three head partners. I knew each person I worked with and their families.

Sometimes the partners would bring their kids into the office. This meant they were usually coming in to spend the day with me. Partner C brought his children in more often than the other two partners. He told me it was because his girls said they thought I was pretty, and they always had fun even though I put them to work.

Though his daughters looked like little angels, they were also armed with the brutal truth and usually had no qualms speaking it. I was petrified when Partner C said he was going to bring his daughters in for a visit when I hadn't even been back to work for a week. What if they got scared and started screaming like my sister?

When I got home from work in the evening, all I kept thinking about was that when his daughters saw me the next day, they would think I was a monster. No longer the pretty woman they had known.

The left side of my face was swollen with slowly dissolving stitches. My eyelid was still sewn shut. If I didn't look like a monster, I certainly looked as though one had attacked me. For children, that might be just as horrifying.

I could only fall asleep by telling myself that even if they thought I looked like a monster, as long as I dared to face them, then perhaps they would know I wasn't one. Besides, most children believe monsters are hiding under their bed at home, they're not out in the world, and especially are not at their father's workplace.

At 9 a.m. sharp, I was at my desk. I looked up and saw Partner C and his two girls standing in front of me. The children didn't hesitate, but they stared directly at my face.

It was as if the girls were trying to get a read on me and how I may have felt so they would know how to respond. For a moment, I gazed back, thinking about Clark and Lock with his two days of freedom. Two grown men who couldn't look at me for more than a split second.

However, at ages of five and seven, these two had no problems. I smiled as much as I could, and then I winked at both of them, as if to assure them they would be safe with me once their dad left.

After a brief exchange of goodbyes and kisses from his daughters, Partner C left for his second-floor office. I had the girls (Seven and Five) on either side of me, acting as though nothing had changed.

I usually allowed them to assist me with my duties, pretending they were my little helpers. So, like normal, I gave them their instructions. I handed them some empty envelopes, and they began stuffing them with the letters I'd folded before they'd come in.

We spent the rest of the day like it was any other, as I continued giving them odd jobs to do. Like most children, the two of them bombarded me with questions, followed by the cutest statements.

The reactions I got from the girls and my son made it easier for me to accept my new appearance. I realized they were more focused on the person I was on the inside, and that their perspective was true. I wasn't different on the inside. However, the world can be very cruel. I knew that at some point, I would probably face some adults who couldn't handle how I looked, and who would be purposefully mean to me. I steeled myself against this by thinking about how good it felt when the children accepted me as though nothing had changed.

At one point during the day, I looked over and noticed Seven staring straight at me again. She had her arms folded across her chest, and her head was tilted, like a question stuck in her head was puzzling her. Then she adjusted her mouth into a grin and started smiling at me, as if she had just figured it out. I smiled back at her, feeling the stitches stretching out across my face and triggering a sharp pain.

"My daddy told us you were in a bad car accident," she said thoughtfully, "but you don't seem any different to me."

Then her little sister smiled at me, as if to put a stamp on what her older sister had said. Just like with my son, that was the end of it. Life went on. They returned to their work without hesitation, and as much as it hurt, I couldn't help but smile even wider.

Chapter Two

WEIRD FISHES/ARPEGGI

IT WAS THE woman's voice that reached my ears first, "Doctor, she's a disaster."

For a moment, there was silence. All I could hear was my heart as it beat harder in my chest.

A man's voice mumbled something, followed by a brief pause.

Then the lady spoke again, "It looks horrible." Her voice was loud and clear.

My heart was racing now. I could feel it jumping up toward my throat, like it wanted to leave my body.

I would soon find out it was the voice of one of the assisting nurses for Dr Lastname. She must have seen me when I'd first checked in at the main reception area. I had noticed a few of the assisting nurses standing around when I'd announced myself. After verifying my appointment, without so much as a nod or a friendly word, one lady asked me to take a seat.

I sat down, facing their direction. Huddled in a circle, I could see them chatting. Then, one by one, they would look over at me with somber and blank faces.

I supposed this one didn't realize that I could hear her from where I was waiting for Dr. Lastname.

That's what I looked like to her? A disaster?

To top it off, she used the word it. As though my injury made me less of a human. This was the absolute last thing I would ever expect to overhear in a doctor's office, a professional environment. I tried desperately to swallow everything I heard, along with the lump in my throat.

I couldn't help but feel as though I didn't belong, and this woman's comment made me feel like I was some kind of alien. I swallowed again, trying to calm down.

One of the best lessons I'd learned from my mother was, "Sticks and stones may break my bones, but words will never hurt me, come bitter or sweet." But the words she said were piercing, and I heard all of them.

Sometimes, even when we aren't trying to use them in a harmful way, our words can be the most dangerous weapons we possess. We each carry them with us all the time. With one word, you can change a person's energy. Words can also be magic wands. When we use them to express kindness, they can create the feeling we call love. On the other hand, even a gun is a word before it's a weapon. There is usually some dialogue before a gun goes off.

I tried not to let the bad words hurt me because I needed some control. My heart slid back into place, although, I could still feel it thumping through my shirt.

Breathe, Aretha.

Suddenly, the door opened. It was clear from both of their expressions that they realized I had overheard everything they said.

Immediately, I blurted out the first words that crossed my mind, "I look like a disaster to you?"

It was Dr. Lastname who responded, even though I wasn't talking to him, "No, Aretha, you don't."

I could tell he was caught off guard by my appearance, although he'd been thoroughly warned.

I spent the next few moments glaring at the assistant, waiting for her to make eye contact with me. Finally, I said, "Hopefully, one day, you'll learn to use your words better."

Her response was a weak, "I'm sorry you had to hear that," and she walked away without looking at me. After all my high hopes for this appointment, it wasn't exactly off to an auspicious start.

***

My son's father and I were in an on-again, off-again relationship. At the time of the accident, he had been visiting from Newfoundland, where he'd been living with his parents. A couple of weeks after I got out of the hospital, he left to go back East. So, Scion and I were back to being on our own, but now we were on a whole new schedule.

I had so many medical and legal appointments, it was hard to keep up with work, take care of my son, and go to a chiropractor three times a week. Somehow, I managed.

The only appointment I had been looking forward to was my first follow-up with an out-care plastic surgeon. It was at another hospital in Toronto, with a top doctor in his field.

I had thought this would be a delightful conversation centered on reconstructive surgery, with encouragement for a speedy recovery. Unfortunately, it turned out to be the beginning of the cruel treatment I would receive at the hands of society's judgmental adults. We can be very cruel, even when we're not trying to be.

And this appointment would be the hardest I ever attended.

***

After touching, poking, and probing my face, the doctor told me his thoughts. The stitches were dissolving, but even after a month, I flinched as he touched me. It reminded me that I would forever have to protect this part of my body, even when a doctor came near it. He told me my healing would be a long road, especially with all the nerve damage, and he mentioned something about whistling being out of the question. He told me that I'd most likely lose feeling on the left side of my face, even though I could feel everything he touched.

I was stunned.

Nothing he said was what I hoped to hear. If I had known this was what I was in for, I certainly wouldn't have shown up early. Maybe I wouldn't have shown up at all.

The only real information he could give me was that there were still fragments of glass in my face. On the night of my accident, they couldn't remove it all because the surgeons at the hospital had to stitch me up as soon as I got there. With my face sliced open, my nerves had been exposed. That could cause facial paralysis and the loss of sensation in my face.

Some glass, still left inside, could eventually make its way to the surface, appearing as pimples. This had something to do with the body's reaction to foreign objects, and how the body rejects what doesn't belong. He said that when it happened, I should use tweezers to slide the slivers out. The thought of it made me cringe.

Finally, he recommended that I have no reconstructive surgery. Or at least that he could foresee at that time. I was flabbergasted. No reconstructive surgery at all? That couldn't be right.

I sat in mute dismay as he explained that the consequences of reconstructive surgery would outweigh the overall benefit. Adults don't heal as fast as children. Because I was twenty-three, I could end up with more of a visual impairment as time healed, repaired, and re-healed.

At that point, I wasn't sure if he was saying my face would be more visually impaired for him or for me. He meant that I might come out looking more damaged. Then, he proceeded to explain how lucky I was to still have the use of my left eye, marveling at the delicate vertical stitching that had been used to reattach my eyelid.

Don't get me wrong, I was extremely glad to still have the use of my eye, but at that moment, I couldn't appreciate it.

I was drowning in disappointment.

He was right about the fragments of glass. I pulled slivers out of my face over the following months. As a matter of fact, I can still feel pieces in there today.

I made my way out of the hospital with a heavy heart. What a difference from how happy and hopeful I had felt when I'd walked in sixty minutes earlier. As I went through the main waiting area, going through the corridors and standing in the elevator, I couldn't help but look into the eyes of those that met mine, wanting to see what their expressions would be.

Some people's reactions seemed to come from a skewed point of view. Maybe, they thought that I had done this to myself. Or perhaps they believed that if they touched me, they might catch what I had.

The expressions on their faces seemed to speak to me, saying, "Ew, that looks awful," or "Glad I'm not her." I mused that if I was a man, I might be viewed as some type of warrior. Though, if the treatment of men with disfigurements in books and movies is correct, maybe they face just as much prejudice as women.

I only went to see Dr Lastname a couple more times after that day. I never saw his harsh assistant again. After a while, I could see no reason to go back. I simply needed to let time take its course and allow the natural elements on Earth to heal me; not only the skin on my face, but also my mental state. As for the public and how they might view me, that would be something I would have to learn to deal with. Starting with my very own family.

***

I'm the youngest of seven children, but before I was born, one of my sisters died a crib death. This left me with five older brothers and sisters, being raised by my mother and stepfather. They were typical siblings, who (when given the chance), would scold me as if they knew more than I ever could. But they also protected me from bullies and anything negative thrown my way. I appreciated that, but since I was the youngest, it was hard for them to let me grow up. When I was in my twenties, even though I was a mother, they still treated me like I was sixteen and didn't know anything.

After the crash, strangely enough, it was still the same. Even though none of my brothers or sisters had any experience dealing with what I was going through, some of them still thought they knew better than me. I could tell they felt sorry for me, although, most of them tried their best to treat me like nothing was different about the way I looked.

My mother was my saving grace, continually using her words of wisdom. Always comforting, her way of dealing with how I looked was the calmest of all of them. We have a large extended family, with many aunts, uncles, countless cousins, and a flock of nephews and nieces. We were connected to one of the oldest families in Canada, who had arrived in the late 1700s.

With my mother being the eldest girl in her family, she learned how to take the good and the not-so-good with equanimity. I tried to draw from her strength; especially when it came to my oldest sister.

She was the most difficult to deal with, and her way of showing me sympathy certainly didn't make me feel any better. Her reaction seemed to be sorrow at my plight mixed up with the constant need to remind me of what I looked like. After the accident, her reactions to me were never good. Within a few seconds of seeing me, she would always mournfully make her usual statement: "I can't believe this happened to you." Then she would add, "And the way you look now!" Then she'd shake her head, like she was wondering how I could possibly make it through life looking the way I did now.

It wouldn't matter where I saw her. It might be at a family function or when she would show up at my house uninvited. Though, oddly, she never once said it to me when we talked on the phone.

I don't think she realized how odd it was for me to hear what she was saying, speaking as though she was the one who had been wronged. I was the one who was wearing permanent scars on my face. She had nothing to worry about. I got the feeling she didn't understand why I accepted what happened so easily. It was like she thought that I didn't feel bad enough about it. She seemed to think I ought to be weeping and wailing about my predicament, instead of getting on with my life.

Or, that's how it was until I confronted her about it.

One day, she showed up at my place unannounced as I was taking out the garbage. I turned around to face her in the hallway, stunned by her gall to just show up at my house with no notice. This time, she was already shaking her head. She came to a stop, and then folded her arms in front of me. She faked a smile and then began, "I can't believe what—"

I interrupted her in mid-sentence and took a tone much louder than hers, one that she had never heard from me before, "Why are you acting more traumatized than I am?" I demanded. "I'm the one who had a car accident. It's like you expect me to feel bad about the way I look, and I don't want to!"

I had to let her know how I felt, considering she kept acting like she knew how I ought to feel. I walked around her and took out my garbage. I walked slowly, giving myself time to cool off and gather myself. She entered my apartment and after a few moments, I walked in behind her. I said nothing else about it, and after that day, she never spoke to me that way again.

***

How people responded to me became easier as time went on. And yet, I did begin to question my faith in God. I began to wonder why I would do this more so during bad times instead of the good times which I would usually chalk up as luck, and then sometimes only thanking God for it. Then I started to believe, it seemed like the head and tail of the same coin. I mean, after all, where does luck come from? Where does that dwell?

One night while I was out, I had a dispute with a girl I knew. The next day, when I came home from work, I found that she had left a message on my answering machine saying, "God struck you for a reason, Aretha. If you don't change, your son will be next."

She was referring to the scars on my face. I didn't take it as a threat, since I knew it was her way of trying to hurt me with words. I'm certain I hurt her with the things I'd said the night before. Even though I was aware of how powerful our words are, I must admit, I've said a few very mean things when I was angry.

I tried to dismiss her words. And yet, I couldn't help but think that maybe this really was God's way of trying to tell me something. That's when the deeper questions started.

My biological father, whom I've never met, was Scottish Canadian. I only know this thanks to his brother and his wife, my Loving Native Aunt, (who could see the beauty and honesty in every child she came across). She had done her best to keep me close while taking me to Sunday School throughout the first eight years of my life. For some reason or another we had lost all contact with them after moving away further from the city when I was nine. Essentially, I had been raised by a German Protestant stepfather and a Canadian Baptist mother. It was my mother who'd taught me what she believed. All of her teachings were reinforced by my grandmother, who was well-known as one of the most devout Christians to ever walk the Earth. As with everyone else in my family, she too loved music. Only her favorite song was "Jesus Is Love" by The Commodores. She would use it as a lullaby for her grandchildren, great-grandchildren, and great-great-grandchildren.

She taught my mother many lessons that my mother passed on to me. One that kept coming back to me was that if you do something bad, God may punish you. But he only does this to bless you with a moral lesson. That led me to thinking about all the things I could have done to deserve what had happened to me, and what the lesson might be in this.

Frankly, I couldn't think of anything that would justify a punishment like this, one that would keep me from ever looking in the mirror again. I also didn't want to believe in a vengeful God.

Finally, I got up enough courage to ask a woman at work who I thought could give me another point of view. She certainly differed from the average person. I had no doubt that she would give me an alternative viewpoint.

I had worked with her for five years at the brokerage firm, although, she had been guarding her post in the mailroom long before I arrived at the company. She had a soft-spoken voice and a kind-hearted demeanor. She always seemed to be willing to help.

When you looked at this woman, right off the bat you could tell she was different. She purposely made sure she stood out. Five days a week, she showed up at work with a ton of makeup on, making it impossible not to wonder what she was aiming for. She would cover her face with a thick layer of foundation that was a shade or two off her natural color. You could clearly see where it ended, and where her real skin tone started. Her eyeshadow covered her eyelids, and she brushed it from the bottom of her eyebrows to the tip of her eyelids. The blush on her cheeks was a fire engine red, accompanied by hot pink lipstick. All of it was topped off by teasing her blonde hair as high as she could, which made it shoot out in every direction. Each day, she wore high-cut skirts, with blouse combinations worn so tightly you'd think she might burst out of them.

You would never have guessed, but not only did she deliver the mail, she also delivered herself to the Lord's house four times a week.

And that was just on weekdays.

Aside from my grandmother, she was the only other woman I

knew who completely dedicated herself to the Lord. And boy, did she ever know Him.

That morning, when she came to my desk to drop off some envelopes, I just outright asked her, "Do you think God struck me, because He's mad at me?"

She took two steps away from the desk I was sitting at, as if to say that was the furthest thing from the truth possible. Then she smiled at me, slowly taking the steps back toward me. "Aretha, God doesn't strike us, and He isn't mad. It wouldn't happen to you or anyone else."

I listened intently, as she continued talking in her soft voice, telling me about how His purpose is to pick us up when we fall. How His word gives us the strength to get back up.

Then, in her softest voice, she said, "Please never think God is mad, Aretha."

I thought to myself that this was way more comforting than what other people had led me to believe about God. Somehow, deep down inside, I already knew what she was saying was true, and I liked the idea. She was onto something, and she was good with her words. I thanked her for what she'd said, and she placed the envelopes she had for me on my desk. We smiled at each other.

I stared at her for a moment longer, and something changed as I gazed at her. Suddenly, the makeup she was wearing seemed to blend in nicely. Then, I realized her lipstick fused perfectly with her smile.

I thought to myself it didn't matter how high she teased her hair, or what makeup she wore. She was happy with herself, and that's probably because the Lord wasn't mad at her for anything. It reminded me of what Seven had said. Then it occurred to me that she was also beautiful—because she was comfortable with herself.

It was what I wanted for myself, rather desperately.

She grabbed the trolley and squeaked back down the hallway to continue her daily route. As the day went on, I put what she said in the back of my head and continued with my normal routine, almost forgetting the Sunday school lesson I'd just learned. But it wouldn't be long before it would come back to me.

It was like God was throwing it at me again, as though He wanted me to learn it well.

***

A few hours later, I went out on my lunch break, heading toward the deli I usually went to, right around the corner from the office. The deli is also beside The Real Jerk restaurant, the place we'd been headed to, before I ended up in the accident. Go figure.

After grabbing a roast beef sandwich, I waved goodbye to the deli owner and left, taking a shortcut through the alley behind The Real Jerk to get back to work.

Out of nowhere a man came toward me, someone I had never seen before. He walked right up to me. "I know you," he declared, without any preamble.

I wondered how he could know me, considering I'd never seen him before that moment. I wondered if this was some weird pickup line. Then I thought, wait until he sees the other side of my face. He'll change his mind about trying to pick me up. He had approached me on my right side, and I didn't think he'd gotten a full look at my scars.

Before I could turn to look at him head-on, he continued speaking. "I was there on the night of your car accident."

I was facing him now, staring at him in shock. I waited for a second, trying to wrap my head around his words. "From what I was told, there were no witnesses, aside from the people directly involved," I told him.

He looked at me, and his smile grew.

On the night of the accident, no other cars had been on the road. I was also told no one came forward as a witness. This made sense, because it was so late in the evening. I got excited at the thought that I might actually have a witness, which would help me pursue legal action against the cab driver.

A month earlier, I'd begun a civil suit against the company the cab driver represented, with very little to go on other than our word against his.

But now…

Now I had a witness.

It was fantastic news. My lawyer was going to love this guy. Excitedly, I said, "I'm going to need your name and number. I was told there were no witnesses, and as you can clearly see, I'm going to need one."

The smile grew bigger across his face. After another moment he replied, "All I can say is Jesus was with you that night."

I smiled back. "Yeah, that's nice to hear, but I need your help as a witness."

"Like I said, Jesus was with you that night, and that's the only thing I can say as a witness." Then he turned and walked away, back toward wherever he came from. I was left standing speechless behind The Real Jerk restaurant. He quickly disappeared into the crowd of people walking on the street, never once looking back at me.

I turned around and started walking in the other direction, down the alley toward my office.

As I got closer to work, I kept wondering why this man wouldn't want to help me. I turned back around to look for him again. Standing there in the empty alley, I thought to myself that there must be a reason I'd bumped into this strange man. There must be a reason why he'd said what he had.

Then it hit me.

I thought about what Different had taught me earlier in the day. Perhaps, seeing this man was a way to reconfirm that God wasn't mad at me. If Jesus was with me that night, then it was a miracle that I was still alive.

All of a sudden, I wondered how it was that I had met that particular man in that particular alley, out of all the thousands walking the streets that day. How had he recognized me? The accident had happened in the dark and, well, if he'd seen me after the accident, then there was no way he could have recognized me now.

Had he been an angel?

Had the man been sent to help me accept my appearance now?

To help me realize that the accident contained a blessing?

I had known before that day that I needed to put my best foot forward. I needed to search for the blessings my mom and grandmother had always talked about, which seemed to still be in disguise. But I hadn't really believed that the injury was a miracle or a blessing. Of course, I appreciated that I was still alive. But on the whole, it seemed more like a curse, than a gift from God.

But this man had made me see things differently. Made me think differently. It was the beginning of the healing of my mind.

***

After I stopped seeing Dr. Lastname, I searched for a homeopathic practitioner for treatment,. He would be my last hope, after the last doctor had left me none.

The practitioner suggested a remedy consisting of just two elements: saltwater and hot, dry sun.

He said it would be the best way to heal my scars. The rest, he told me, was up to time. Considering there wasn't much hot, dry sun in Toronto, and no saltwater whatsoever, I began making plans to go away.

I planned my first trip a few months after the accident. I headed for Cancun, Mexico, which turned out to be a huge culture shock. It was my first time in a country that was of a single nationality, aside from the hordes of college kids and other tourists (primarily from the United States), who were on vacation.

Prior to going to Mexico, I had gone to New York, to the Bahamas, and to Las Vegas twice. Then there was the one time I'd driven from Las Vegas to Hollywood, California, just to stay for three days. I had also traveled to Montreal and Winnipeg, and to Nova Scotia once to visit my grandparents. I have five generations of family there, where it seems gospel hymns are a household requirement, and country music rules all of the land. You'd almost believe Charlie Pride was king and Anne Marie was queen.

That trip was traumatic. I had been five years old when I went. It had been the first time I'd ever left my mother, who had sent me to spend the summer with her parents while she stayed at home. I had cried practically the entire time, which only ended up lasting about forty-eight hours.

The weeping had started as soon as I'd gotten off the train, and overheard the adults talking about passengers whose luggage had been left behind in Ontario, mine included. All that did was give me an excuse to whine. Then, once I'd realized how long the summer really was, I'd bawled.

It had only gotten worse once I'd arrived at my family's homestead, and I learned some people up there were still using outhouses; I'd never seen or heard of these before. I'd also had no intention of using one myself. My sobbing had been so bad that the next day, my favorite aunt and uncle had had to put me in their car and drive me for twenty hours back home to my mom in Ontario. It would be another thirty-one years before I went back there.

I did not understand what it meant to be in Mexico during Spring Break. Cancun becomes jammed with countless college-age Americans fighting to get their piece of the dry, hot Mexican sun and let loose by drinking copious amounts of alcohol.

I was going on the trip with five stunning women, but I only knew one of them: Roller. I had known her for thirteen years, after meeting her when I was eleven at a local roller-skating rink.

Even though I know many people in Toronto, I have to admit I am a guy's girl and have always hung out with guys more than girls. It probably started because my mom nominated the youngest of my brothers to look out for me. With the record player always on, spinning tracks like Teena Marie's "Square Biz", or any song by his favorite band (The S.O.S.), steadily he would bounce his head up and down, while counting beats with his feet. He taught me how to play games like five rocks, crazy eights, rummy five hundred, poker, and gin. I had been convinced he was a musical mathematician. He'd also given me useful advice, like how it wasn't cool to be a rat. From the sage youngest of my brothers, I learned to keep my word because no one likes a tattletale. All of his teachings would eventually come in handy for his sister with beat-counting feet and scars.

I'd only had a few girl friends from junior kindergarten until grade five. My two best friends had been redheaded British brothers, whose house I ate lunch at almost every day while they spoke in their thick English accents. After lunch, we would make time to climb the trees in their backyard, usually to sing anything by Elton John. The two of them had spent a lot of time swearing at each other and bickering about what song to sing. Then, they would scream for their mother's help. It had been more than entertaining to me, considering it was the sort of thing I'd never witnessed in my own household.

Since I hadn't had even one girl friend through junior high and high-school, going away with a bunch of women was going to be a novel experience for me. I also knew I would stand out because of my appearance, although I knew Roller had warned the others of my state.

Being new to the group, I tried to keep things lighthearted. I nominated myself as the group comedian among the six of us. I kept the jokes mainly about myself, telling them about the funny experiences I'd had.

Of course, jokes are not funny when they're at another person's expense. But they can be hilarious when it's the truth, and it's about you.

It was my way of showing them I would not focus on the way

I looked, even though I'm sure it was impossible for them not to wonder how I felt walking around with scars like mine.

I thought that maybe if I didn't draw attention to my face, no one else would either. Eventually, whatever they were thinking would fade away. Who can care, if you don't? Besides, by that point, I saw my scar as a painting. One that always comes with a story. I was determined that mine would be one of survival.

Out of all the women, I was the only one of mixed descent. If not for the advice of the homeopathic practitioner, I'd be the last one trying to get a tan.

As for the other five, they'd begun burning at tanning salons weeks before we even left for Mexico. Roller said it had something to do with them wanting a base to attract the sun to their skin. She said, by doing this, they believed it would eventually give them that prized bronze look.

On the flight, all they talked about was how they couldn't wait to get to the beach and soak up the actual sun. My hope was to get into that salty ocean and absorb the sun's rays. I hoped that the sun and sea would heal my new fresh scars, just like my homeopathic practitioner had said they would.

***

When I was younger, my mother had made sure her kids took part in recreational sports. We all went to the Mid-Scarborough Community Centre, where they had a rink, and I learned how to ice skate and roller skate. On Sundays, we went to Kitchener Park Baptist Church. Once a week, I had to go to piano lessons with a lady who lived on our street. I also played the violin and clarinet. The two instruments I picked up in school.

My mother always had us participating in extracurricular activities, like the other children did in our area. It was her way of making sure we were all on the same playing fields.

Importantly, my mother made sure we were all excellent swimmers, sending us at least two to three times a week to Midland Collegiate, where they had a pool with Olympic-style lanes. That's where we swam for hours, playing Marco Polo. I was swimming in the deep end by the time I was nine.

Aside from my mother's need to make sure we learned what she thought was an important life skill, I also believed that because of my astrological sign, I'd been born with the ability to swim like a fish.

Even though I thought I was an excellent swimmer, no one can really prepare you for the ocean. Even though I had been in Lake Ontario, I truly did not understand the endless power of the Caribbean Sea. As beautiful as it is to look at, it can be extremely terrifying to be in, if you've never experienced it. Then again, you could be the best surfer in the world, or the top scientist from The National Oceanic and Atmospheric Association, but when a tsunami hits, no human can control a body of water. I suppose, if I'm to really consider its power, nothing on Earth could exist without it.

We arrived in Cancun, Mexico, on Thursday. After quickly checking into our hotel rooms, we all met back up in the lobby and headed straight to the beach. It was located just seventy-five feet off the back of our resort. We couldn't have asked for it to be more perfect.

After making our way through the crowds of people scattered everywhere, we found a spot close to the water. That's where I placed my towel down on the hot sand. I removed my headphones. After listening to A Tribe Called Quest's The Low End Theory, I put the Walkman in my bag and set it on top of my towel. I looked around for a moment and stared out at the water; an incredibly beautiful green coastline that turned into a blue body of water, which seemed to stretch all the way to the sky.

Suddenly, it felt as though the bottoms of my feet were on fire. I'd never stood on sand that hot before. My immediate instinct was to run. With no hesitation, I ran full force straight for the ocean and dove in. Then, I allowed the current to carry me out farther, as if I was part of the ocean. Swimming around in the waves, the song "Once in a Lifetime" by Talking Heads played in my mind. It seemed to fit the setting perfectly.

I flipped to my back and spent some time looking up at the sky, noticing that it was a clear blue without a cloud in sight. It reminded me of my son, fittingly, for his name.

I lay there, floating and gazing, not aware that I had drifted off far away from the coastline, and the hundreds of people on the beach.

Suddenly, the water got much colder. The ocean was no longer green but a cold dark blue. It became frigid, and my fingertips had shriveled up and started to go numb. I looked back toward the resort, realizing I could barely see the people on the beach. They looked like ants, which meant they probably couldn't see me. I got nervous realizing how far out I had floated. Suddenly, I wanted nothing more than to be back on shore.

I decided to ride a wave, thinking it could give me a boost back toward the beach. I thought it would be faster than if I simply swam. Turns out, it wasn't such a good idea. But I knew nothing of the ocean and its currents.

As soon as I had the chance, I dove on the upsurge of a wave, which ended up dragging me down below the water's surface. As I tried to swim back up, the water held me down. It was terrifying.

The next thing I knew, it was as if the water had grown hands that began pulling on my feet. It yanked me down deeper, pulling me further below the surface. It was the most terrifying natural force I had ever encountered.

As I tried to break away, it only got stronger. As I went deeper, the water became much colder. Struggling, I didn't know where this force was taking me, or how it would end. In a situation like that, you quickly come to believe that there's nothing left to do except die. I couldn't reason with a force of nature. Another moment, and there was no doubt it was going to be over for me.

Then, out of nowhere, I told myself that I couldn't let those women believe I didn't know how to swim, never mind what they thought about the raw scars on my face.

I fought back harder, my arms flapping and my feet kicking. With every attempted stroke, I tried desperately to reach for the sky.

I knew, dead or alive, this force would eventually have to let me go. Until then, I didn't want to give up. Then, finally, it did. For whatever reason, at that very second, the water let me win the fight, releasing me from its icy grip.

I turned into a dolphin. One who could have beaten the best swimmer in the world on my way back up to the surface. Although, I probably appeared more like a fish flopping about in dire need of air.

Once the oxygen hit my lungs, I opened up my eyes to see if anyone had seen what happened. No one had. I guess you could say I got the ride I needed. I was much closer to shore than I had expected to be.

I swam to the beach, put my Walkman back on, and never said a word to any of the other women about what happened. It would take another twenty-four years before any of them might find out what happened, and that's only because I'm writing about it now.

With no compassion, that wave had almost taken my life.

And that changed me. I'd almost lost my life again.

It was as though I had been given another reminder of the preciousness of life. Had I not been paying enough attention the first time? I couldn't help but wonder.

I made it a point to jump into the Caribbean Sea every chance I got while in Mexico, even going in once at night. It was my way of making sure I wouldn't be afraid of the ocean after it had taught me such an important lesson.

I later found out that the hands in the water that had grabbed onto my feet were the ocean's undertow currents. The same currents that have taken the lives of more than one unsuspecting swimmer.

A simple decision to go into the ocean on a Thursday had led me to the possibility of not being alive on Friday. It was a sobering thought. I was understandably alarmed. Yet another close call, following closely on the heels of my near-fatal car accident.

I returned home to Canada with an even broader point of view. I told myself that I would live my life differently knowing that I'd already had two near misses. It was another reminder that I had to make significant changes in my life.

However, hands down, the next notable Thursday is one for the books. Pun intended. It was so life-altering that drowning in Mexico didn't seem so startling.

I'll admit, there might have been some moments after that Thursday when, for just a second, I wanted everything to stop. Strangely enough, when every liberty is taken away, even that freedom—the freedom to end it all—is no longer an option. I found that out the hard way.

If someone had warned me of what was to come, I would have done anything I could to change my life's course. And my tussle with the ocean had been mere child's play compared with the struggle that was looming on my horizon.

Chapter Three

DON'T YOU WORRY BOUT A THING

AFTER WORKING AT the brokerage for nearly six years, I decided that being a receptionist would no longer cut it. Not as a single mother. Not if I wanted to provide a better life for my son.

It was the starting point on my way up the ladder. I wanted to become a stockbroker, so I quit my job in the spring of 1996 to go back to school. I studied for the Canadian Securities Course, also known as the CSC.

Back then, that was the only way to get your license to become, what we would call, an investment adviser today. I can tell you this: whoever was in charge made sure that it wouldn't be easy. The course included two full assignments, due by a certain date. Then you had to mail them in to a random facilitator who checked them.

Funnily enough, some people believed that correspondence courses were just plain easy, but now I know better. With no teacher to help, and no ability to share ideas in a classroom setting, it was a lot harder than I'd expected.

The final exam had several versions. It was known for having a first-time failure rate of over 98 percent, no matter which one they handed you. This also meant, if you knew anyone who took it, most likely they wouldn't be able to help you. All the brokers I spoke to before I enrolled told me they'd had to write the exam three or four times before they'd passed it. I even knew some who had given up after their first written attempt.

Over 99 percent of the information we studied for, and got tested on, we never used. I never once had a client call me and ask for a company's working capital ratio.

The brokerage profession was really in demand. Knowing this, I believe whoever was in charge at The Canadian Securities Institute had designed the course to be unreasonably challenging on purpose.

Difficult or not, it's one of the highest-paying occupations a person can get. For a woman, it's one of the few professions where we tend to make more than our male counterparts.

Six months after quitting my job, I passed my CSC and completed my Canadian Practice Handbook course at the same time. I was so very proud of myself. The CPH is an exam for a broker, ensuring we know who to sell to and why. It's not as complicated as the CSC, but what you learn from it is more widely used.

I had done it.

I'd gone back to school and successfully graduated.

I was on my way.

***

By the following January (of 1997), I was a junior account executive and back working for the same firm, but no longer a receptionist. Not bad for a girl who dropped out of high school!

My success was immediate. Within my first year as a junior broker, I made over $125,000, which was $100,000 more than my yearly salary had been as a receptionist.

About a month after I began working as a junior broker, I got my first real commission check for $8,700. The difference between making $400 a week compared to what I was making as a stockbroker was ridiculous. I now received more money than I had ever dreamed of. I spent it just as fast as I got it, giving a lot of it away. The sharing part seemed to be the most fun.

However, the good money I was making didn't last long, for good reason. I believe pride comes when you're able to put a real smile on someone else's face, and money seems to do that every single time. I realized within that same year that selling penny stocks would not cut it for me. Their worth would not make me or my clients truly happy

I added up the cost of living, right down to the money I could make. I felt, as a woman, getting paid a commission from the win or the losses of another human could turn all that pride into an ego that I didn't need.

I quit working at the firm, and this time it was for good, although, that wasn't all I was leaving.

One of the most significant changes I knew I had to make was to break off my romantic relationship with Clark. Scion's best chance at happiness would be for his parents to be just friends. We'd both realized our intimate relationship was long over. If we were going to raise our son properly, we would have to commit to an amicable platonic relationship with each other.

I believe falling in and out of love is a force of nature. Knowing this allowed me to turn our breakup into one of my best goodbyes. This way, I guaranteed that my son's father would always be a part of our lives. Besides, saying goodbye should always be made good, otherwise, we would just say "bad-bye" to each other. With the forewarning that the good times you had will soon become regrets of the past.

I also wanted to broaden my horizons, and by that point, I knew I wasn't just leaving the brokerage firm or my son's father. I wanted to physically leave Toronto. That's when I convinced myself that I wanted to live outside of Canada. I knew, as a female broker, I would be in demand, at least, for any firm where a woman's voice on the phone was more valuable than a man's.

That meant I could get a job anywhere in North America, although Mexico was out of the equation since I'd never learned to speak Spanish. The way I saw it, my only option without leaving the continent was the United States.

Breakfast in America by Supertramp was the first album I'd ever purchased, when I was nine years old. I think I chose it after hearing "The Logical Song". Turns out "Goodbye Stranger" and "Take the Long Road Home", songs on the same album, will help set the pace. Like many others, I found myself starving to discover America.

To put this plan into motion, I began to travel more on the weekends. I left my son with his dad and his godfather. Knowing he would be in the best care made me feel good about exploring my options and checking out new places.

I got a house with a girl friend who was also a single mother. Instantly, she became like my own sister. We did everything together, even raising her daughter and my son.

I went away more, going to New York for the weekend some-times, trying to decide whether that's where I wanted to be. That went on for about six months, but it didn't take long for me to real-ize that I didn't want to swim with sharks disguised as investment advisers. I was also warned that brokers in New York don't like any competition. Being a woman would only make matters worse.

Even though I had worked at the same firm as a receptionist for six years, one of the first things I'd experienced when I became a junior broker was that some of the men I had worked with for years now seemed to see me as a threat. If not to their bank accounts, then to their egos. It's hard to work in an environment where everyone looks at everyone else like an enemy.

What I knew for sure was that I wanted my son and I to live somewhere I thought would be upbeat. Somewhere forward-thinking. A place that would be fresh and new, where a broker would be welcomed by her peers. I wanted to move to a state where I could successfully make people money. I wanted to be somewhere where I could experience the hot, dry sun and the ocean. Somewhere like Mexico, minus the almost-drowning experience. That way, I could follow the homeopathic practitioner's advice. And his energy remedy, which, combined with my courage, I believed had already begun to work.

Back then, I only had a couple of women whom I would consider my good friends, aside from Instant Sister. One woman I knew from before the car accident. She had been the first one of my girlfriends to visit me in the hospital, which convinced me she was a genuine friend. Even though I had a facial disfigurement, Genuine never treated me any differently. She always encouraged me.

She filled my head with stories about all the great times she had living in the US for five years when she had been younger. She told me that if it were up to her, she would move right back.

She described the beaches. According to her, where she'd lived had the most beautiful coastline. She said, if I liked Mexico, this would be the next best thing. Finally, she told me that because I was a licensed broker, climbing the corporate ladder would be a breeze.

I couldn't help but think that moving to the US would mean leaving all the unwanted things in my life in the past. I convinced myself I wanted to live in California. By the time I finished talking myself into it, my scars had become eighty-seven stitches of confidence. I decided I was going to be the hero that Esthero sings about in her song named for "That Girl."

***

The first time I flew to California was right after I met two American guys visiting Toronto. I ran into them at a club, and after a night of dancing, talking, and some drinking, the three of us became fast friends. That night, we exchanged numbers. This led to several long-distance phone calls, where they told me how much fun it was to live in California, and how it was the best place to be in the entire country.

I ended up staying with them for a week every couple of months while they taught me the basics of what it's like to live in a place like Los Angeles.

The two of them were roommates. They lived in an area called San Fernando Valley, which was a few miles away from Hollywood. Even though it was far from where I thought I wanted to be staying, living with them was nothing short of amazing.

One time when I went to stay with them, they had what they called their annual "Leo Party" to celebrate all their friends who shared the same astrological sign. On the day of the party, even before they'd turned on the grill, there had to have been at least a hundred people in their backyard. By the time the sun set, more people had come. As the night went on, most of them were dancing.

People were playing triangles, cowbells, and bongos, while others were sitting in circles smoking weed and whatnot. No doubt they were having conversations that they thought were strangely significant. Not one person was unhappy, myself included.

It was the first time an army of what I could only call flower children had surrounded me. They were high on life. It was like a scene out of Woodstock.

The party went on all night long. By the next afternoon, a whole slew of others came, and it all started right back up again. I couldn't be happier being with people playing guitars, and banging on bongos, and makeshift drums. Humming along to The Rolling Stones, CCR, Janis Joplin, and the Beatles. I was in my element.

Thanks to my two friends, that night I met a nice girl who had come there by herself. I couldn't help but notice that she had the prettiest green eyes I'd ever seen. At the end of the evening, she suggested that the next time I came to visit I should stay with her and her brother.

Green Eyes, my kind friend, eventually introduced me to two of her other good friends. Within days, they were friends of mine. They offered me the loft space in their condo, and for my next trip back, I was going to stay with them. The best part was, it was on what some people call the right side of the hill.

After some fairly easy negotiations, the two women, Generous and Gracious, gave me the extra room, charging me a mere $300 a month for a place that was right smack in the heart of LA. I was so close that, if I wanted to, I could throw a rock and hit the Hollywood sign. Okay, maybe not exactly, but I was much closer than I had ever thought I might be.

Without hesitation, I took them up on their generous offer. The decision was simple once I knew I could maintain a place in LA and still have a place in Toronto where Instant Sister would always welcome me back. Just as Genuine promised, not only was the weather warm in California, but everyone I'd met so far had had personalities to match.

***

While I was in LA, I would spend the days learning more about the American financial industry and looking for a job in my field. Anytime I found a company that I thought would be a suitable match, I set up a meeting.

I believed being a Canadian in the US would encourage the hiring organization to take me more seriously. I was banking on the fact that my experience, and the credentials of my CSC, would help land me a job in finance.

One good thing was that Generous and Gracious each had their own car. They would take turns driving me to any appointments. In the evenings, we'd all go out to different parties, restaurants, and bars to meet up with some of their other friends.

The weeks that I would fly back home to Toronto to be with

my son and spend time with my family were great, too. I constantly missed them all when I was away.

I also needed to be back in the country as much as I could in order to focus on the civil suit filed against the cab company because of my accident.

When I found out my lawyer was purposely working slowly and not paying any attention to my case, I knew I had to be around and follow up with him if I wanted the case to go anywhere.

I understood my case was a civil attorney's dream, especially since I had visible permanent damage. It was right there on my face, proving the harm that had been done. According to my lawyer, all I had to do was walk into the courtroom and I would be showered with money.

And yet, I saw no money.

The only thing my lawyer seemed to be good at was putting my case off to some future date. I had to take it upon myself to do my own research. I had to identify the reinsurance company for the cab driver, which had already been ordered to pay me a large sum of money, the same one my lawyer had said he couldn't find.

Lies.

It only took me two days to provide him with the information he needed. By that point, I didn't care about the money. Especially after I discovered that my lawyer was intentionally stalling my case so he could justify a higher fee. It was more than clear that he didn't care about the scars on my face. And the fact remained that no amount of money was going to make them go away.

The whole lawsuit just forced me to relive the terrible memory of an accident I wanted to forget. It guaranteed that I would have to be thinking back to that time. I finally got to a point where, as much as I loved my city, I only wanted to escape back to California. When I was in LA, I could focus on building a new life for Scion and me.

***

As soon as my case was resolved, I returned to LA. This time, I went with even more reason to establish myself in the US. Trying to find a job would be the key to moving to Los Angeles permanently, so I stayed away for longer periods. And even though I knew my son was safe with his father when I wasn't with him, I missed him terribly.

He was the most untroubled person I'd ever been around. Like my mother, Scion took most situations with the greatest of ease. It didn't matter if it was me leaving him with his father, or the times he left his father to stay with me, it was his parents who had the hardest time saying goodbye, not him.

Eventually, Clark's mother (whom our son called Nan'J), moved from Newfoundland to Toronto so she could help take care of him while I was away, and his father worked.

He loved being with her. Ever since he was two years old, he had gone to visit his grandparents every summer in Gander Bay, Newfoundland. My son was thrilled when we found out she was moving to Toronto.

Nan'J woke up every morning to make his breakfast, pack his lunch for school, and would find out exactly what he wanted to eat for dinner. Sometimes, she would walk with him to school or wait for him at the corner until he finished. She was honestly the perfect grandmother, baking fresh cookies at a moment's notice, keeping him company, and making sure he felt safe. Always.

His aunts and uncles on both sides, along with his godfather's family, were always tremendously supportive. Everyone pitched in to make sure our son had a solid foundation whenever I went away to build our new life in California.

***

The condo my roommates and I lived in in LA was beautiful and designed with two different levels; some points of the ceiling reaching as high as sixteen feet. It had two bedrooms, each with a full bathroom and large windows that made it naturally bright. A good-sized kitchen, combined with a large combined dining and living room space, made the house feel open and comfortable. At the back of the living area, there was a metal winding staircase that led to the loft, which had a view that overlooked the entire apartment.

I liked the place a lot. It reminded me of a show I used to watch called Melrose Place, where the complex is a square surrounded by three-story buildings, like a small gated community.

Sectioned in the middle of the surrounding condos was a pool surrounded by a courtyard, nicely tucked away from the outside world, a place where all the neighbors would meet to gossip. We took advantage of it. Sometimes late at night, my two roommates and I would invite our friends to come over, and we all went swimming, while playing every type of music as loud as we wanted. Sometimes, we splashed around until 4:00 a.m.

On some occasions, the day after a late-night get-together, I would make a point of taking advantage of the barbeques on the patio. I always made extra for my neighbors, just in case I had kept them up the night before. I wanted to avoid bearing the brunt of their whispered conversations. Regardless, we never once got a complaint.

Another advantage of the location was that I only had to walk about a third of a mile to go see performances by Radiohead, Sade, Erykah Badu, and The Agape International Choir at the Hollywood Bowl. For someone whose first love is music, the place I was living couldn't have been any more perfect.

Eventually, Generous moved out. That left me with the other bedroom in a condo that had about 1000 square feet, which also left us with an unoccupied loft space. This allowed me to invite my nephews, nieces, friends, and other family members to come to visit. My remaining roommate, Gracious, had been born in Canada and was of mixed descent like me, with a Christian mother just like mine. We got along very well.

As much as my son and family came to visit and I went back there, whenever I was in LA, I would call home continuously, mainly to talk to my son. I would call him before and after school, and then once again during the evening, just to say goodnight.

It was my way of making sure he didn't forget my voice, and to reassure him I wasn't forgetting about him just because I was far away. I would fill him in on the things I was doing to become more established, as well as the people I was meeting, and all the interesting places I was going. Then we talked about what and how he was doing at school. Of course, no conversation would be complete if he didn't tell me about basketball. He played it every day.

I always ended the call by saying to him, "I love you forever and a day." I'd picked up the phrase from "Always and Forever" by Heatwave. It was one of the many songs that we listened to together, and it seemed to be the perfect metaphor for my relationship with him.

***

By December 1998, I believed my life was heading in a better direction. I was doing my best not to live in the past, or make the memory of my accident any part of my future. It was the first time I felt like I was living during the moment, doing my best to look at life from a different angle, just like I'd promised myself I would.

I had a magnificent apartment. When my son wasn't with me, I knew he was safe at home with his father. This also gave me an opportunity to rediscover myself in a whole new scene, and it took no time before I was back to having a social life much like the one I'd had in Toronto prior to my accident. Living in LA didn't hinder me one bit. It didn't seem like anyone cared about my scars. Right away, I fit right in. I made a lot of new friends.

Although I would never have guessed I would wind up in a relationship so soon, it wasn't long before I was dating someone.

I landed him before I'd even landed a job.

My new boyfriend, Last, was the person I focused on the most. We met through a mutual friend one night when I was out at a bar in Hollywood. By the end of the night, we were cracking a bunch of jokes in the parking lot after spending most of the night at a place called Dublin's.

Back then, that was the best place to be on a Monday night in Hollywood. It didn't take long for both of us to realize we had a lot in common. After that, he asked for my number, making it clear he wanted to take me out on a date.

I didn't give him my number that night. Instead, I left and went straight home. I knew I would see him again, and I did, a couple of weeks later at a house party. He showed up with some of his friends. This time, we spent the night laughing at the host of the party, who had frantically tried to shift us out of the hallway as soon as we'd all came in.

He had been acting as though he was expecting somebody famous to walk across his marble floors and, just in case, he wanted to keep the entrance clear. That is, until we convinced him that one guy with us was a famous actor on his way to winning an Oscar. The host ate it up. He spent most of the night running back and forth between us and his guests, apologizing profusely for not knowing who this guy was before. The third time he ran over, he tripped over his own feet.

As much as we made a joke out of the host thinking our friend was a superstar, I thought it was odd to see a person act like such a fool simply because they were told someone was famous.

He had never seen or heard of our friend before, but that didn't stop him from treating us like royalty. By the end of the night, he finally figured it out. But only because we couldn't stop laughing whenever he came over. I realized it wasn't just my soon-to-be-boyfriend who was hilarious, but his friends were also a lot of fun to be around. That night, I gave my future boyfriend my number with no hesitation. Instantly, I knew this was a relationship that I was going to make last for as long as he would let me.

***

Later that week, we planned to go to the movies at Universal Studios. When the movie was over, we still wanted to hang out and ended up at a restaurant on the theme park grounds. That's where he told me I had a smile he would never forget, and that I made him laugh like no other girl before. It was the first time I felt as though someone new was seeing me beyond my scars.

I was on another path, only this time I was on my way to falling in love.

Most of my nights in LA were spent with Last. During the daytime, while he was at work, I would continue on the job hunt, sending out my resume and then following up with interviews.

That changed when an opportunity sort of fell in my lap. It centered on negotiations for a contract to raise capital for a private placement company. It was the perfect job, since it allowed me to travel to Toronto whenever I wanted. Plus, for the first time in my life (at twenty-eight years old), I was on my way to being my own boss.

This also meant I could come and go as I pleased, as long as I had my cell phone with me. Another perk of the job was that it came with a company car! At that age, I could go out three times a week without missing a beat. With all the friends I had made, it didn't take long before I was going out to some of the best parties in LA.

If you're wondering whether it's hard to get into those parties, the answer is an emphatic yes. Getting into any party comes down to who you know, and what you look like.

Luckily, I became friends with a woman in Hollywood, Real, who guarded the velvet rope for some of the best places. She controlled access to the kinds of parties that most people could only dream about.

The kinds of events that Real worked at drew the attention of all the young, rich, and famous people throughout the city. And some of them even got shamelessly turned away. What I liked about her was that if she said "No," she meant it. To her, it didn't matter if you were a superstar, astronaut, or otherwise.

She was always keeping it real, and that's more than I can say about some of the people she let inside. The good thing was that

Real never said no to me. Whenever she was at the door, I got in. This allowed me to go out—up to four times a week, if I wanted—to places that most people couldn't get into on their best night.

Anybody who wanted to be a part of the Hollywood scene showed up at all the parties she had. Back then, the only event that could beat hers was a party for the Oscars. Although, if I remember correctly, she was hired to do some of those events as well.

Not me, though. Real never refused me once, and with the extra special parties, she would call me up and ask, "Aretha, how many people can you bring out tonight?"

One night, she might as well have given me my own guest list for a party she hosted at the Playboy mansion. I assembled twelve girls to go with me so we could reap the benefits of a party that I was sure we would never forget. Without a doubt, it was something to see. Incredible, really.

The mansion rested on a luxurious property that captured any nature lover's attention. As soon as we got there, I took a peek inside the house. That's where I saw HH lounging around in the front room with a host of at least twenty of his playmates, some of them, sporting their famous bunny outfits.

Outside the house, we walked straight into a paradise filled with freshly trimmed hedges and lush green lawns surrounded by a forest of trees. It was the first time I had ever been on a property that had a sanctuary of monkeys and a well-kept zoo. It hosted a plethora of birds: peacocks, flamingos, toucans, and other types were flying freely and wandering around.

I followed a peacock and found a building containing a full-sized arcade. Adults were inside playing pinball and old video games, such as Centipede, while reminiscing about their youth. Seeing as no one else was on it, I played Galaga.

That night at the mansion, the band Limp Bizkit was having a party for their record release, and there had to be a few hundred people there, including a good number of celebrities walking around. Some people ventured into the main house, while most of the festivities took place on the back of the property.

Guests were already jumping in and going for a swim, and I couldn't blame them. The water looked gorgeous. Caves and waterfalls encircled a sprawling pool, so big it looked like it belonged in a theme park. Naked women adorned the water as well, looking as beautiful as their surroundings.

None of the women I came with opted to go for a swim. Even though there were a ton of celebrities at the party, we had more fun looking at the monkeys. They were more approachable than the stars.

Real never treated me differently from any celebrity she knew, whether it was inviting me to go to the Playboy mansion or to a private party for Prince. Sometimes, as soon as she saw me coming into one of her parties, she would remove the velvet rope, even before I got across the street, already prepared to let me in. Then she'd yell out, "Aretha, who you with?"

I usually waited until I got right in front of her to let her know. That way, I could look through the crowds of people lined up, grabbing anyone I could that I thought wouldn't make it in.

I trusted Real, especially knowing she had been around a bunch of celebrities. Even with them she knew when they were acting or pretending to be someone else. She could see right through anyone, right down to the real person beneath.

***

One Saturday morning, we went out on a shopping spree. After that, Real took me out for lunch to a restaurant on Sunset Boulevard. Once we were seated, we ordered drinks and an appetizer. She followed that up with an six-ounce T-bone steak, and this was all at 1:00 p.m..

I was amazed, until she told me that she hadn't eaten since the day before because she had been busy getting ready for a party. That's the kind of person she was, staying up late at a party, and then showing up bright and early the next morning to help me through the weekend.

I had broken up with Last.

And I had become a mess.

It was the middle of July 2001, it was the week I refer to as Portishead, because I listened to the band's album Dummy nonstop. Last and I had been a couple for quite some time. Between me going back and forth to Toronto from LA, we had been together for over two years. It was the first time we had ever broken up.

When we were dating, we were hardly ever apart. After the breakup, I began to experience separation anxiety. I felt as though I was in the beginning stages of a heart attack. I had been constantly with him and his friends over the years. I had developed good relationships with most of them. Losing him (and them) so suddenly when we broke up left a big hole in my life that I didn't know how to fill.

Real asked me about it while we had lunch. She wanted to know what was going on, and why we'd split up. I eagerly answered her, hoping to hear something that would make me feel better.

After we'd committed to being with each other, I'd seen him practically every day. Since he lived with his parents, I'd spent a good amount of time with his family as well. I had gone to church with his sister-in-law. Other times, I had taken his nephew and niece on outings with Scion.

I'd even started a side business with his sister. It had been an easy decision, after realizing how committed she was to her church. I liked every one of his family members. They were all people who set a good example for my son and I.

All I wanted was for Real to tell me that he would come back, and that she thought we still had a chance.

Right off the bat, she said she thought we had a great relationship. And she saw us out together all the time, so she had a pretty good idea. Then she added, "Don't worry about it. I'm sure the two of you will be back together in no time." That was all I wanted to hear. Then, she told me some things she thought I needed to hear. She started asking me about one of his friends. "You do realize who he hangs around with, right?"

Of course, I knew who she was talking about. Like I said, I hung out with all his friends. Despite it all, I wasn't expecting her to say some of the things she did, considering she was speaking about one of the world's leading actors. Unlike Last's other friend, who had pretended to be an actor, this guy was a real actor, a wildly famous one.

That's when she gave me advice about something that could affect my future. She told me that in Hollywood, when you hang around a person who is that famous, it gets a lot of notice. Sometimes, when the attention is drawn away from that celebrity, it could prove to be difficult for those less-famous people.

She was skirting around the issue, but I thought I understood her warning. I never expected that it would turn out the way it did, though.

Everything she said reconfirmed my belief that she liked me. Our relationship wasn't just based on getting into a club. She shared personal stories about stars that even my boyfriend wouldn't have known about. The fact that they came with more warnings proved to me that she cared.

***

And behold! Didn't her prediction come true!

Three days later, Last and I got back together, just like she'd said we would. The two of us ended up bumping into each other at another of Real's parties. As usual, he showed up with all of his friends. It didn't take long for all of us to get back on track.

More good news was heading my way. The cab company responsible for my car accident finally awarded me a settlement after eight years of fighting. Although it was helpful, the money wasn't as important as being able to look in the mirror every day, no longer being forced to relive that night while my lawyer took his sweet time.

The quickest thing he ever did was get me to his office a few days after the last judgment to try convincing me I should pay him over 50% of the money I was to receive. The amount he was requesting was much higher than the 15–25% we'd originally agreed on.

This proved to me that the disfigurement I would have to wear for the rest of my life, and the changes I had to go through, had never been a concern for my lawyer, especially after he made sure to get his money before I even did.

But that was all over now, and I couldn't be happier. I was so thrilled that I would never have to walk into another courtroom or pay another lawyer.

Or, so I thought. I immediately wanted to invest the money they'd awarded me from my lawsuit. Upon returning to LA, I transferred it into an investment account and started my own personal trading account. By that point, I was no longer consulting for the private placement company, and I had already returned the company car. This meant if I wanted to get anywhere, I would have to get my own vehicle.

I was eyeing an older model 850 BMW, but I ended up buying a Lexus SC that I loved for its rare indigo blue color.

Life was good. The money was great because it meant not having to commit to a regular full-time job. This freedom allowed me to discover a new life in LA, and to take Scion traveling.

We flew everywhere: Chicago, New York, Las Vegas, San Francisco, and a lot of places in between. I even took a trip down to Mexico and rented a villa in Rosarito, visiting Baja Malibu with Scion, my nephew, my niece, and Last.

***

One of the first things I noticed when we got to Mexico was that most of the areas had the same names as so many of the cities and boroughs I was familiar with in and around Los Angeles. Soon after, I learned that California used to belong to Mexico, and that in 1848, the US got awarded the land in (what seemed to me as) an unfair deal.

It was no wonder Genuine said being in California might as well be the same as being in Mexico. After all, California used to be a part of Mexico. California has the largest population of Latino Americans living in the country: 14 million in a state that has a total population of less than 40 million.

Being in Mexico would also bring out another side of Scion, once he saw what true poverty was. It was the first time he had ever actually seen people who looked like society had abandoned them. Grief-stricken would be the best way to describe the expression on his face, when the locals started asking him for money in a language he didn't understand.

It wasn't that he hadn't witnessed poverty before. We come from a country where, in the winter, there are people who have nowhere to keep warm. But my son was ten, and this was the first time he had ever been approached by kids, who were barely old enough to walk, begging him for money. These were children that had nothing to eat and nowhere to go. I wasn't sure how to make him feel better, or how I could construct something good out of what he was seeing.

After walking around watching three-legged dogs dart aimlessly across the streets, I decided I would take him into the market area, where we could buy some trinkets to remember our trip. I handed him twenty dollars to take his mind off the impoverished children and unwanted animals that were wandering about.

After taking the money from me, he asked if we could go somewhere to get it changed, which we quickly did into single dollar bills. Then he asked if we could go back outside. As much as I would like to say I taught my son the importance of sharing, I believe the true gift of giving has to come from a person's own heart.

So, I was not entirely surprised he started handing money out to anyone who asked, giving it all away with a gigantic smile on his face. He didn't even consider keeping any of that money for himself. It was enough for him to know, the world had disregarded these people, and he wanted to help.

Scion's experience with poverty in Mexico brought out the best in him. The look on his face was one that I would expect to see on a grown man buying a sports car. He was so gratified and happy to be able to actually do something to help. So much so, that after handing all the money out, he started begging me to give him some more bills, so he could do it again.

On this trip, I would discover more about the person my son was by seeing how he responded to the children who had less than he did. He was on his way to becoming a truly good person. It made me realize that these were the big moments that I was missing whenever I left him behind with his father.

After our trip to Mexico, we all returned to California. That's when I decided I was going to make it official and have my son stay with me more permanently. I sent him back home to Canada with his cousins so he could spend a little more time with his dad, and then we began to make all the arrangements. I thought to myself that this would be the final piece of the puzzle to my new life. I needed my son with me. Then things would be perfect.

All the changes I thought I needed to make were working out in my favor. I believed California was allowing me to see the world the way I wanted to, from a different point of view. I was on a better path now, and I was doing whatever I could to leave any bad memories behind.

Although, I must admit, whenever I checked in on my feelings for the future, instinctively I could feel something was off. It was as though the same voice from the hospital was back. Only this time, it was telling me some type of storm was brewing, and I needed to turn back.

But I ignored the voice, not able to imagine how anything bad could happen now. Everything was going so well. I continued to believe I was living in the moment, thinking whatever the intuition was it would eventually go away.

It didn't. That eerie feeling I had kept coming back. It was a warning that I would ignore, until it was too late. But at that time, I couldn't have done anything else except push it aside, and try hard to live by the motto Scion and I shared:

Don't you worry 'bout a thing.

If only that could have saved me from what was coming.

Chapter Four

ARE FRIENDS ELECTRIC?

ASIDE FROM THE one time we broke up for less than a week, Last and I got along exceptionally well. The people who knew us admired our relationship.

I have countless memories of us laughing. Although laughter was the key to our hearts, music was embedded in our souls; we spent a lot of time listening to it together. We would play everything from The Roots, Buju Banton, The Smiths, Cody Chesnutt, and of course two of my favorites, Stevie Wonder and Radiohead.

Because I've always been a guy's girl, without a doubt, some of the best times in my life were with Last and his friends. On weekends, we would go to his friend's house; well technically, it was his friend's parents' house. That's where we would go swimming, have barbeques, and discuss the weekend's events. Unlike the comedian or Leading Actor, there was no question that this guy was the coolest of his friends.

His father, who was a doctor, would cook for us for hours

while schooling us with his music. He was always willing to provide answers for any questions we had about life. With this father and son, I don't think the apple fell far from the tree. They both had a cool, calm, and collected attitude. To me, they both resembled Jimi Hendrix, which was funny because that's the artist his dad often played. All of us got along really well. Spending time with them was as natural as breathing.

Eventually, Last and I took a trip to Toronto together, where he met some more of my family, including Clark and many of my close friends. Even my favorite aunt and uncle had a barbeque in honor of his first visit to Canada, so they could meet the man I had been spending so much time with.

The last and most important purchase I made with the money I'd received from the lawsuit, was the condo in LA where I lived. This was after my landlord presented me with an offer that no one in their right mind would refuse.

I got so excited, the first thing I did was ask Last if he or his dad wanted to be partners with me, so we could buy it together. It was going to be a great purchase. My landlord was offering it to me for $100,000 less than current market value, when LA real estate had nowhere else to go but up. I offered the opportunity to the two of them so they could also reap the rewards of a great buy. Even though I had enough money to make the purchase on my own, sharing the opportunity felt better to me.

My landlord had to leave the country, which was his reason for offering me the place for a steal. Within sixty days, Last and I were the proud owners of the condo. His dad had decided to opt out, saying he wanted to give us an opportunity to build a life together.

Unfortunately, it turned out that Last had other plans.

***

Shortly after we bought the condo, Gracious got married and moved out. But my boyfriend never moved in. Aside from the eight hours a day when he was at work, and an hour during which he would drop by his dad's place, the rest of the day he spent at the condo with me, which he still called my place.

After a short while, he convinced me to move out and find another place for Scion and I to live, so I went along with it. Our mortgage was affordable enough that we could rent it out, and at the end of the month, we would still have a little left over to cover any additional expenses. All of it seemed like a good idea at the time.

It didn't take long for us to find tenants to rent the condo. As we expected, it guaranteed us a mortgage payment and covered all of our expenses. My problem was finding another place for my son and I to move into. Unfortunately, trying to get my own apartment in LA wasn't as easy as I'd thought.

I returned home to Toronto so I could prepare my son for starting his first school year in California. But since I hadn't been able to secure another apartment, we ended up moving back in with Gracious when we returned to Los Angeles.

She was living on her own, after splitting up with her husband of less than six months. As for Last, he still hadn't given any sign he was going to move in after getting me to give up my condo, even though that was what we'd originally planned.

He promised that he would still help me find a place, and when we did, he said we would put it in his name. It sounded like a good deal, considering I didn't have an established credit history for myself in the US. In order for us to get a mortgage, we had to put the new condo in his name.

For the time being, I would have to stay with Gracious. Thankfully, she let us live with her over the summer months. I spent the time looking for another apartment, and my goal was to get settled in before the school year began. After a couple of weeks, I was getting nervous because I still hadn't found a place to live.

In 2003, as September got closer, things shifted. For the first time since coming to LA, I felt like everything that had been going great was slowly slipping away. That eerie, instinctive feeling was coming back, and the struggle to find a place only made it worse. With the leaves changing as the calendar rushed toward the fall, I could sense a figurative change coming in the weather of my life.

I believe relationships are like seasons: they come and go. Often, we can feel the transformations as they're happening. After four years of good times with Last, our relationship was about to shift.

It was during a phone conversation that we had one Saturday evening, which led to a disagreement on whether we should go out that night. I ended the call by saying, "Maybe we should take a break."

The next morning, he said the same thing to me on the phone. Even though we were only taking a break, he declared that the obligation to help my son and I find a place was no longer his.

This time, I knew the breakup was serious.

When someone you care about promises you one thing, and then leaves you hanging when you need their help, you know that they're the furthest thing from a friend. Despite the seasons I had spent with Last, his attitude then changed faster than fall turning to winter, and he became colder than any season I had ever known.

What we said was let's just take a break. But that soon turned into let's just be friends. And then suddenly, we weren't friends anymore. That's when he turned into someone I don't think I ever really knew at all.

Unlike when my son's father and I fell out of love, with Last it seemed more like we were both tripping out of it into a faceplant.

What had started off as a strong relationship soon turned into one filled with mind games, which I had no experience playing. It didn't take long for most of his friends to follow his lead. The guys who I'd thought were my friends turned into wolves, and it's never fair when you're one person against a pack. Unfortunately, this would become a case where we should have said "bad-bye" to each other. Not just for me to Last, but to most of them.

As difficult as it was, the only thing I could do was move on and tell myself that Last hadn't been the reason I'd initially wanted to come to LA. Perhaps, even though we weren't getting along, eventually he would remember the good times we had. Maybe we could even end up as friends again in the future.

By the end of that summer, I found a place for my son and me, with no help from Last. I continued to stay in LA. I had developed many other friendships, and I still had property that I owned. Therefore, I figured there was no reason for me not to continue doing everything my son and I had originally planned.

I enrolled him in school, and I used my free time to start a T-shirt company, wanting to do something different from finance. By that point, I'd realized that, when it came right down to it, the emotional cost of the job was greater than I wanted to pay.

The T-shirt company I started with Instant Sister and another lady was called Lost in Lingo. As soon as we secured a reputation in California (thanks to our tenacity and constant promotion of the brand), it took off.

The concept was to put phrases on T-shirts written in dead or foreign languages. We chose languages that we knew most people in North America wouldn't understand. Those phrases were already premade, with punchlines depending on which of the ten different phrases you were wearing.

The person bold enough to ask what the words on your shirt meant often found themselves starring in a joke of our making. We used the Swahili phrase, "Kwanini unapenda unachokiona?" If someone were to ask you what your T-shirt says, the translation of the words on the shirt is, "Why? Do you like what you see?" All ten of the phrases usually gave everyone who wore or read them a hearty laugh.

We manufactured the shirts in LA, and we had buyers arranged in the US and Canada. Once again, this gave Scion and I the opportunity to go back and forth to Canada whenever we wanted, and that's exactly what we did. Even though I'd told myself I wanted to have a life in Los Angeles, Toronto kept calling me back.

No doubt, I missed my ex-boyfriend, although having my son with me made it easier. Especially after he presented me with a handmade card for Mother's Day. He drew a big shiny sun on it, with only five words that said "Mommy you are all yellow." Then he told me he'd gotten the idea from a song by Coldplay. I figured it was because I couldn't stop playing their album Parachutes.

The card he made reminded me of the tribute that Bono pays to his own mother with a video and a song called "Lemon". I challenged my son by making Mary J. Blige's song "Everything" as my anthem to him.

This type of inspiration coming from each other lead us forward. We kept ourselves busy by going on as many adventures as we could. We would go to basketball games making sure not to miss the Raptors whenever they were in LA. Or, if they played the Lakers in Toronto, we would rush to get back home.

We discovered places like the Getty Museum. This was where my son decided that out of all the paintings, drawings, sculptures, illuminated manuscripts, and decorative arts, his favorite piece was "The Doubting of Thomas." He said it was because the faces of the disciples looking at Jesus's wound looked very real.

Most importantly, we always made time for him to play basketball. Between LA and Toronto, we had him on three different teams. I always had a great time watching him play in his tournaments, but the best part was the three hours we spent driving back and forth between practices.

We were always listening to radio in the background with shows that included Rodney Bingenheimer on KROQ 106.7 through Big Boy's Neighborhood on 105.9. These moments together would give us the best opportunity to learn more about each other.

Even though we always made it a point to go back home (to make sure he knew the people in Toronto were never too far), one time I surprised him by flying his dad to LA. Both Clark and my Instant Sister came to visit us in Los Angeles for Scion's thirteenth birthday party, an event we all planned in secret. Clark loved LA. So much so, he was back again within months to celebrate my birthday. That time, he came with my mother and my closest niece. Scion's Godfather came once with his new wife, on their way to Las Vegas to celebrate their honeymoon. My second oldest sister had actually been born in LA. She flew in like the angel that she is, and she kept us entertained by singing whenever anyone would listen. Everyone was pitching in to make sure Scion understood he always had a solid foundation of support, wherever we were.

I have to admit that being single in LA was a whole new experience. Even though I missed Last, the sudden change in him made me realize it was important for me to work on myself. I thought that maybe I could try another path, and perhaps get some questions answered. I also thought it was important to provide my son with an opportunity to decide on his own beliefs, so he would have something to follow.

And just like that, I started going to church.

***

In order to give my son an overview of a few different religions, we sampled a church buffet. We went to different congregations and denominations to see what they all had to say.

On Saturdays, we checked out kabbalah classes. On Sundays, we would choose one of the three churches that had become our favorites. One was The Agape International Spiritual Center, where I happened to purchase one of the most influential books I would ever read, The Power of the Spoken Word by Florence Scovel Shinn.

The other two that we enjoyed were McClendon Ministries and The First AME.

The First AME was where we chose to first get baptized. The pastor sprinkled a few drops of water on our foreheads.

The second time we were baptized, we actually jumped in the water. This was at the request of a man I like to call my deacon brother, who went to Christ Temple Apostolic Pentecostal church. That's a denomination where they submerge you in the water, hoping you come up and speak in a different language. He insisted that we be baptized again, after I couldn't remember if the pastor at the First AME had blessed us in the name of The Son, The Father, and The Ghost…or The Holy Spirit.

I said I would consider it, though I thought that one baptism was probably enough. Then he promised me his one-year-old toy Pomeranian, if we came to his church and got baptized again.

You want to talk about going to see a man about a dog? We practically dove into that water, and mysteriously, I began talking in tongues.

Getting baptized twice in less than three months was more than worth it. Our new dog daughter would stay with us for fifteen years. We weren't able to go back to that church, but that was only because it was too far from where we lived in Beverlywood, a three-hour drive away.

Aside from that, I enjoyed going to all of them. Not just because they usually offered a positive message (all except the kabbalah classes), but all of them had those uplifting gospel choirs that anyone could sing and dance along with.

Even though I was going to church looking for answers, I don't know if I was finding them. I still continued to go to the clubs at night, like I was searching for something else. Even so, meeting someone new was the last thing on my mind. I just believed going out, listening to music, and being able to dance your worries away was a great escape, whether you did so in a club or in a church.

The only problem was every time I went out, I kept bumping into my ex-boyfriend and his friends, who by that point, were no longer my friends. Seeing some of them after the breakup was becoming more and more of a challenge. Particularly because some of them treated me as if I'd become their sworn enemy.

Guy's girl or not, one thing was for sure: I was not one of the boys in that group. By that point, I couldn't even make small talk with Last without one of his friends saying something snarky. I'm not exactly sure why they did it, although, I suppose sometimes when people break up, it's treated as a betrayal. This was their way of protecting their friend.

But it was completely unnecessary. I didn't mean Last any harm. The only thing I was guilty of was missing him. The best way to describe how they treated me was mean, mean, and mean.

***

It was February 2004. I was stuck on the song "Maps", which had come out in 2003 and described how I felt in those moments. The Yeah Yeah Yeahs couldn't have come at a better time. I almost believed the song had been written solely for me. I still missed Last and our friendship, but his boys kept pulling him farther away. Then I tuned into Interpol's album Turn on The Bright Lights. I realized I'd become more like their song "Obstacle 1". Along with the constant moments where I would have to succumb to their "P.D.A" and Last always had a different girl.

I suppose I should've known what would happen with his friends. I'd hung around those boys for years and witnessed how some of them had treated their exes: effectively banishing them from the village.

After a bunch of run-ins with them that never ended well, I thought it would be best if we sold the property that we still owned together to sever all of our remaining ties.

The same way he'd convinced me to rent out the condo, I convinced him we needed to sell it. After only eighteen months of ownership, we sold it for almost twice the amount we'd originally paid. I took pride in the investment, and I was happy that Last and I had made a lot of money, even though we were struggling to get along.

I started focusing more on the other relationships I had. Since I didn't have Last's friends to hang around with anymore, for the first time in my life, I surrounded myself with a bunch of women.

Each one of them seemed to serve a different purpose. I had an American girl friend born in LA who was a bartender. She was usually with me whenever I went out. On the nights when she worked at the bar, she would reserve the VIP table for me, whether I was with ten friends or alone.

I had a Chinese girl friend raised with a Jewish father, who gave me the best advice for starting my T-shirt company. She told me I didn't need to use a sledgehammer to crack open a nut. Some other good advice she offered was, "You can't change people, but you can change yourself, which will change how people respond to you."

Vraie, my favorite French Canadian, was my truest friend and usually the person who looked after my son whenever I went out. She was also his favorite. She, too, was a young mother, and I had the opportunity to look after her son as well. He was the most content baby I'd ever watched. It only took a few lyrics from his favorite lullaby, and he'd be sound asleep. Vraie once told me no one is ugly and that we're all equally different. I've always loved her for that.

I had another friend, an Australian woman, who introduced me to The Agape Church. She was the only person I ever trusted in LA to watch our dog. She had aspirations of directing, producing, and writing her own movie that she was going to star in, which eventually she accomplished.

One thing these ladies had in common was each one was there for me, coaching me through my breakup. Sometimes, all I did was talk about how sad I was. Because it was the first time I'd experienced that kind of heartbreak, I asked them for advice nonstop.

It appeared I had every type of girl friend. Like my hairdresser, who didn't hesitate to invite me over to her house so we could rock out to our favorite band. And the two Canadian women who would come to stay with me during pilot season, looking to land roles in TV shows.

Going out to some of the hottest spots in LA became a regular thing. Even though I could go where I wanted, after a while it became the same old thing, over and over.

So, one night, I decided that this would be the last night I would go out. I knew that in the coming days, my son and I would be leaving to go back home to Toronto.

The school year was almost over, which meant it was time for us to go back to Canada. Only this time, Scion and I thought it would be best if we picked a high school for him to attend in Toronto. That way, he could pursue his aspirations of playing basketball. Also, at that point, I got diagnosed with a medical condition which was getting serious enough that I had to have surgery back in Canada. Nothing was tying us to LA after selling the condo, and I knew I could run the T-shirt company from anywhere.

I thought about all the friendships I had built, and the women who were there for me, but I also knew bumping into one of Last's friends was never fun. This would be the best way to avoid any more of that.

When it came down to it, staying in LA was no longer appealing to us. After all the years of going back and forth, I suppose The Eagles were right. I felt as though I was staying at "Hotel California." And it was time to check out.

Therefore, it made sense to go out that Thursday night, have a couple drinks, dance a bit, have a laugh, and say goodbye to LA for a while.

Chapter Five

THIS PLACE HOTEL

THE CLUB WE went to was on La Cienega Boulevard in Hollywood. Not that it's ever been my favorite club, but back then, it was the best place to be on a Thursday night in 2005.

I'd originally made plans to go with this woman I had just met, named Recent. It had been her idea to go there, and since I knew that I would be leaving for a while, I also invited Vraie and another woman, too. I thought the four of us would have a good night out as I said goodbye to California.

The club was always scorching hot, and as soon as we walked in, I remembered that was one reason I didn't care much for it. Inside were countless people moving around. Getting anywhere felt like pushing through a herd of cattle.

I've been to clubs in the cities of Canada, America, England, Ireland, and Mexico. (aside from Canada, Ireland is my favorite), but some places in LA always seemed strange to me. Mainly because most people were busy doing the opposite of what you usually do at a club. As packed as this place was, nobody there was dancing, even though the DJs were always great.

They used the dance floor in this place for standing conversations. That's because most of the people who live in LA do what many like to call networking. Eventually, this leads to conversations that include name-dropping, and soon after, the key question, "What can you do for me?"

Of course, this all adds up to star jocking. In a place like LA, people will do anything to get close to a celebrity.

Together, the four of us headed toward the bar, maneuvering through what felt like thousands of people, in a place that should have held a couple hundred.

As we tried to make our way around, we were forced to walk alongside the VIP lounge. Toward the middle, the railing opened up to a small entrance. To get into it, you needed to take four to five steps up and away from the regular crowd.

You also have to be invited.

I always wondered why clubs have these VIP sections that seem to have everything except a dance floor. You can find tables, bottles, railings, even star jockers in there, but really it's just a place for some people to look down on others. As far as I could tell, the VIP section was only there to install a separation of class. Or, at least, the illusion of it.

Tonight, I looked up and saw Last. This was his regular spot on a Thursday night, and of course, he was in the VIP section.

I looked up at him, and he looked down at me. He smiled and waved hello. The good thing was, I didn't see any of his boys around him. Usually, when he was on his own, things weren't as tense.

I remembered the last time I'd come to this place, about a year before. Last had been here with his friends and something had happened.

That night last year, Leading Actor had seemed to lose his mind, because I hadn't greeted him quickly enough. Then I'd watched in confusion while Last got scolded for continuing to talk to me. Leading Actor had wagged his finger at Last and said, "If you ever talk to her again, so help me God," as if he were Last's dad.

I suppose, maybe I don't understand the dynamics of hanging around with a famous person. In this case, it's not bros before hos, it's more like bros before anything, which included me.

Back when Last and I had been together, and we were all still friends, it had always seemed odd to me for grown men to come running whenever Leading Actor beckoned.

Sometimes, Last and I would be with Leading Actor out in public. I'd watch as grown adults tripped over each other, pushing their own children out of the way just to get a look at him. I have to admit, it was weird watching people change like that as if they were looking at a god, while they confessed their undying love, simply because they'd seen him in a movie. I'm more than certain, most people don't have a clue who he really is, or what he's really like.

I thanked God that Leading Actor wasn't there at the club with Last that night. Although, I will admit, the last few times I had seen his friends, they hadn't been as bad as they had been before. So, as I walked by the VIP lounge, I smiled at Last, thinking it would be a long time until I saw any of them again.

I walked to the bar with Recent, while the other two ladies stopped to say hi to Last. I didn't blame them. At one point all of us had been good friends, and the reason I'd stayed with him for all of those years was because I knew he was a great guy. Even though we were no longer together, I was still aware of that fact, and I missed him a lot.

The night got better as soon as Vraie came back up to me. She reported that Last had nothing but good things to say, and it was all about me. Most of all, she said he told her he missed being my friend. It felt good to hear. It made me happy to know that our friendship meant something to him, too. After that, we got our drinks and headed straight for the dance floor for some fun.

That was the best time I ever had at that club. The four of us ended up having a great evening together, just as I'd hoped we would. So much so, in fact, that we ended up staying until closing time.

I noticed Last was still there when I was leaving, and this time as I walked by, I did my best not to make any eye contact. Less was more, as far as I was concerned. Besides, I was happy enough to hear what he had told Vraie, and I figured the best way to leave was on a pleasant note.

Once we were outside, as usual after leaving the club, there were always people still hanging around in the parking lot. After a brief discussion of what to do next, we decided on getting something to eat and then heading straight home. Recent rushed back up to us, and asked if I wanted to go somewhere else with her.

She said a friend of hers had invited her to another party up in the hills, and she assured me that the owner had the best house parties.

At first, when I thought about it, I didn't want to go. Since the night of my accident, I had tried to make it a point not to drive to another party right after leaving one, but for whatever reason, I said yes.

As we drove up the dark winding roads, it felt as though something was off. It was that eerie feeling; my instinct told me that something wasn't right, and not knowing where we were going didn't help. Aside from going to the Playboy mansion a few times, I didn't go to a lot of house parties in LA. Although, the party with the host who was tripping over his own guests was the best one I'd been to.

We got to the front gate and soon the huge door opened. We walked up the driveway and to the front door. No one came to the door to greet us. We only heard a faceless voice, which opened the entrance for us, and we walked right in. According to Recent the owner wasn't even home, apparently, they had lent the house out to one of their friends for the night.

Inside, I noticed how big the house was. The room I was in led out to a huge terrace overlooking the Hollywood hills. Always a beautiful view of LA. I walked over to the large window beside the terrace door. It felt as though the house was mainly on one level, with a few thousand square feet of space throughout. For a moment, I just stood there by myself, looking around and enjoying the view.

Recent had disappeared the moment we both walked in, perhaps looking for some of her other friends. The house felt big, bland, and almost empty. It was as if the owner had moved only a few of his or her belongings in. Or they were on their way out. I was in someone's house, but no one's home.

Whoever had decorated this place had only had two colors in mind when they'd painted it: white and off-white. I also noticed there wasn't any music playing, and the people there were scattered into different rooms, each having their own conversations. I wondered if maybe they were just waiting for the DJ to show up. If there had been a DJ playing, Dennis Ferrer's track "Hey Hey" would have been the perfect choice to set the stage for the next scene.

I ended up in what I could only imagine was the dining room area, even though there wasn't a table or any chairs. I looked out the room's window, where I could see out onto the terrace. That's when I noticed him standing there—Leading Actor.

I soon realized he was looking straight back at me. It didn't feel good, so I turned and walked away, heading toward the kitchen. I looked around for a moment and thought to myself, I should find Recent.

As for Leading Actor, I'd had no clue he would be at this place, especially knowing I had left Last at the other club. Usually, if his boys went out, they were all together. If one was there, the others were always around.

Once I was in the kitchen, I made conversation with a guy who was standing by himself. I didn't want to roam around a stranger's home, and I figured this would be my best option to stay out of the way.

He asked, "Would you like something to drink?"

I smiled and said thank you, as the guy handed me half a glass of wine.

He said, "Sorry that's all that's left," as he placed the empty bottle back on the counter.

In mid-conversation, I looked up and noticed Last walking into the kitchen with the rest of his boys. One by one, they all came in. Last looked surprised to see me, and I nodded, rather than saying hello. Like a ghost, he disappeared into another room, and I had no intention of following.

I went in the opposite direction again, thinking I would ask the guy who'd offered me a drink if he wanted to come out onto the terrace with me. I thought it would be the best way to avoid the eerie feeling I had felt on the drive up, which was now back in full-force.

The guy who'd offered me the drink walked in front of me, and I quickly followed behind. Within a few steps, we were out on the terrace, where I thought the coast was clear. And yet, the feeling wouldn't go away.

All the signs pointed to a huge turning point on the horizon. The only thing missing to turn this into one of the worst nights of my entire life would be some type of incident that involved my face.

Leading Actor came out onto the terrace again, this time making his presence known. It would only take a few seconds before the both of us would throw some very serious words at each other, and we all know what words can lead to. Luckily for me, his mouth wasn't a gun, or I wouldn't be telling this story.

It started with me saying something which I knew he wouldn't hear. I was talking to the guy who'd offered me a drink, and he didn't seem to hear me either.

Leading Actor asked me, "What did you just say, Aretha?" Before

I could even answer, he immediately followed it up by saying, "Why don't you go and fix your face?"

At this point, the guy who'd offered me a drink wandered off. Something else must have caught his attention, I supposed. Or maybe he'd sensed what was coming.

Again, even before I could respond, Leading Actor's words became harsher, and he said it all without taking a breath. It was as if he'd been practicing those specific lines in the mirror for weeks. He ended with, "And go take that weave out of your hair, you old bitch."

Immediately, he turned and walked off toward the living room, as if he didn't want to face what I might have to say in return. The last two statements didn't really bother me. The fact that out of nowhere, he'd told me to go and fix my face made me think that even though he made twenty million dollars a movie (for some mysterious reason), he still thought about me.

I followed him to be sure he would hear my response. Then I said what I believed would hurt his feelings, the best way I knew how. Much like I thought he was trying to do to me. "Whatever you say, faggot!"

I do have to admit that was a bad choice of a word for me to use. My mother never raised any of her children to be homophobic. If anything, she encouraged us to never hide or be ashamed of our sexuality, and that if we were too, we would only cast shade on the countless others who are truly in love, while depriving ourselves of it. Her interpretation of the story about Sodom and Gomorrah in the bible was about a couple who'd been given multiple chances to mind their own business and walk away.

Leading Actor turned around and came back toward me. As he returned, I could see he was angry. He was taller than me and stronger. I knew I didn't stand a chance if it came to fists.

After that, everything happened so fast. No one else was really paying any attention and not that many people were in the room. It really came down to just me and him.

He raised his hand and repeated himself, "Like I said, go fix your face!"

Then he slapped me, hitting me directly on my scar. I supposed it was his way of making sure I knew exactly where it was on my face.

My own mother had never slapped me, let alone someone hitting me exactly where he had. I reacted instantly.

I did what I could to protect myself.

I didn't realize it at that moment, but my life was about to take a turn that would affect me for years. The next few moments were some of the most critical I would ever have to go through.

This was not the path I had wanted my life to take. But I ended up going that way anyhow. Because my response was instantaneous, a knee-jerk reaction of self-defense. I was just protecting myself.

And I hit him back.

Only, I forgot I was still holding the wineglass.

It was as if I had no choice. My reaction was involuntary. I didn't have any real aim. Both of my hands went up in the air with my hand still holding the glass of wine. It landed, hitting him behind his ear, and on his neck where it broke.

It was as if my scar immediately knew what to do to protect itself and make sure he didn't hit me again. And Leading Actor certainly didn't hit me again. The blow to the head scared him off so much that he ducked down, turned around, and headed straight for the door.

Right after it happened, Recent found me. Together, we walked out of the house, left the party, and headed toward her car. We got in and we left.

I briefly explained to her what had happened.

I had already taken out my cell phone, and for the first time in months, I called Last. The last time I'd talked to him was about the sale of our condo. I'd never imagined I would be calling him about something as crazy as this. When he answered the phone and said hello, the only thing I could think of was to say his name and then, "He hit me first."

Last responded in a heavy tone, "That's not what they're going to say."

Last hadn't been in the room when the incident occurred, but I already knew he was more than aware something had happened. I understood with this comment that my whole life was about to change, especially because it involved Leading Actor, who could call on several people to tell whatever story he wanted them to.

Although I knew the story he would tell would probably make him look good to the public, when it came right down to it, the lies he told would be his cross to bear. As hard as it would be for me to go through what came next, he had to live with his deceit.

With little more to say, Last and I hung up.

Recent dropped me back off at Vraie's place. When I walked into her house, another woman was still with her.

I told them what happened, from start to finish. Without hesitation, both ladies said they could see how and why events had gone the way they had. Instantly, Vraie declared that she would stand by me, no matter what they had in store. And she did. After spending an hour with them reassuring me, I left her house.

I needed to prepare for the worst.

***

Friday morning started as a blur. When I woke up, I quickly remembered what had happened only a few hours previously. Once again, I asked why in the name of God it had happened to me.

I felt sick inside as I played out Thursday night in my mind over and over. I tried to prepare myself for what was to come next, knowing this was going to change my life. I thought about the words we had said, and how quickly it had escalated. It was almost as if it had been inevitable. I knew it wouldn't matter to anyone that Leading Actor had said what he had and then hit me first.

Everyone's allegiance to him was such that, even if he'd damn near killed me, they would still find a reason to convince the world it had been entirely my fault, even though not one of them had witnessed the altercation.

Most of them had all been stuck in their own conversations, and usually at these parties, no one pays attention to these Hollywood types until after a fight breaks out.

Leading Actor could come up with any story he wanted. He was revered by the world. That made him nearly untouchable. The fact that he was a great actor only made things worse. I had no doubt that if he decided to, Leading Actor could very convincingly play the role of the victim in this situation.

It wouldn't be long before the story broke in the news, and even though I was willing to bet no one had seen what had occurred, each person would have their own story to tell. Then, among all of those versions, would be the one I would give: the truth.

I thought about what it would look like if I were to go public first. Immediately, I pictured a flock of media-hungry bottom-feeders swooping in on me and Scion. The image was so vivid and so horrifying, I didn't want it in my head. I just wanted the whole thing to go away, like it had never happened, despite the fact that I was the one who'd been attacked.

My mother had been the backup singer to some of the world's greatest artists throughout the 1960s, '70s, and '80s. Then she became the owner of a talent and casting agency in the '90s. She'd had her business for over fifteen years, and in spite of that, she hadn't been able to convince me to go on even one casting call.

Striving for that kind of spotlight had never interested me. I also knew my son wouldn't want that kind of attention thrust upon us, for any reason.

I lay in my bed that morning, and just like the Friday in the hospital after my accident, I questioned all the decisions I'd made by going out on the Thursday before.

The decision to get into a fight with a celebrity certainly hadn't been one of them. Finally, I got up and called my third sister back in Toronto. I told her about what had happened the night before, and all the messiness that it would most likely devolve into.

As we were talking, I could see on my call display that Last was calling on the other line. I told her it was him, and I had to go. Obviously, I was curious to hear what he had to say, after what he had told me the night before when he'd implied that they would try and spin the story.

At first, the conversation was calm. He told me they were still at the hospital, waiting for a plastic surgeon who was being flown in from another state. He told me they had done this because of who Leading Actor was. The way he said it made me believe he thought that waiting for a surgeon to fly in was seriously overkill.

He told me that the cut from the glass would have required only five or six stitches for the average person, but because of Leading Actor's profession, he would end up with more. Last did point out that I'd come close to hitting a major artery, which I would have never known without him saying so.

Suddenly, the conversation became heated.

"This is not going to be good, Aretha." Like he was threatening me, he told me about Leading Actor's lawyers, going on about how they were the best that money could buy. How it was their job to make sure he would still get his 20 million dollar-a-movie paychecks.

Never mind the lawyers. I knew there were probably a bunch of other people attached to him whose livelihoods also depended on his future. As some of us know, most people in Hollywood are not willing to give that up. Not for anything.

Once again, I responded, as I had the night before, "But he hit me first."

That's when Last took a tone that was calm again, one that felt like he was trying to soothe my fears. He said the last thing I expected to hear. Last told me that Leading Actor had said he was sorry about what he'd said about my face. Then Last paused uncomfortably.

I took a moment and thought about the statement he had just made. I realized it was probably hard for him to repeat the same words that his friend had said to me the night before.

The entire time that Last and I had been together, my facial disfigurement had only ever came up once. We had been at a barbeque with all his friends. I had been in the middle of a discussion with a random guy who'd stopped mid-conversation and said, "That scar on your face makes you look pretty sexy." He'd said it so naturally, I'd began to blush. Then I walked over to my boyfriend and repeated the compliment.

His response had been just as sweet, "Of course it is, Aretha. Didn't you already know that?"

When Last mentioned my scar this time, it was different. I also wondered why Leading Actor had only apologized for his words, not for hitting me.

I figured either Last didn't want to say over the phone that Leading Actor had slapped me, or perhaps it was because Leading Actor hadn't admitted to everything.

This second-hand apology from Leading Actor was what I considered a white flag of truce, even though I thought it likely to have been coached. At that point, I decided to apologize, through Last, for what I'd said to Leading Actor.

I know how powerful my own words can be, and I had known what I'd said was going to strike a chord with Leading Actor. I just hadn't expected him to strike me. He was the one who'd gotten angry after his words hadn't seemed to do enough damage. It had led to him losing control and lashing out, which prompted my own defensive strike.

By that point, it had been twelve years since my car accident. Just as I never imagined I would have a scar on my face for the rest of my life, I would never have imagined someone would have the audacity to slap my face, while telling me to go fix it.

What Leading Actor had said and done wasn't right.

This was undeniably true.

But no matter how I looked at it, I knew I had to take responsibility for my own actions, too. "You can tell him I'm sorry for what I said as well."

Losing control and arguing with Leading Actor was the worst thing I could have done. I understood that.

Still using his calmest of tones, Last continued, "He's worried that you're going to go to the media and sell the story, Aretha."

Almost talking over each other, I shot back, "You already know I'm not like that!" It was likely he'd had coaching for this part, but I was certain that Last knew that I would want nothing to do with a get rich quick scheme.

A few months prior to that day, my indigo blue two-door Lexus had been almost totaled, when I'd gotten hit on the left side by a Ford Expedition. All I had wanted was for my car to get repaired.

It hadn't mattered to me that this accident had happened in a country where you could sue and get five million dollars for spilling hot coffee on yourself. After what I'd gone through with my previous accident, no way had I wanted to walk into a courtroom for any reason — ever again.

Nothing could have induced me to go to the press with the story about Leading Actor, and Last knew me well enough to understand that as a certainty.

Besides, I still had my brother's voice in my head, telling me it was never good to be a rat. No one likes a tattletale.

After giving my word to Last about not going to the media, or talking to anyone about what happened between Leading Actor and I, he promised Leading Actor would do exactly the same. I knew he was worried that I could tell the story if I went to the media right away and informed the public.

I just wanted the whole thing to go away, and from what I was hearing, it sounded like Leading Actor wanted the same. I thought he should want it to disappear even more than me. Besides, I was told the story he gave to the hospital was that he had injured himself by running into a brick wall.

I ended the call by saying goodbye.

Truth be told, everyone knows a broken heart is blind. For me, it wouldn't be until The Black Keys released a song called "Little Black Submarines" in 2012, that I could fully surrender to the feeling.

Last and I never spoke again.

***

The next day, a slew of different stories hit every media outlet. I was told it was someone who hadn't even been at the party who had given their version. Whoever it was, it would only lead to a bevy of misconstrued and assumptive stories of what had occurred. More importantly it didn't come from me.

The one thing they couldn't do was publicly release my name, since I hadn't been charged, and it was my right to privacy. The day after that, Leading Actor's publicist released another statement saying that I had been aiming for someone else, and Leading Actor didn't even know who I was.

The media went on a feeding frenzy, as they camped outside of my house and banged on my door, trying desperately to get a glimpse of me. Their messages filled my voicemail, asking to find out more. They were constantly trying to contact me.

One message came from a talk show host, who had the nerve to say he'd gotten my number through records of my prior partnership in the condo. I couldn't believe the audacity of thinking he could just pick up the phone and call me when he knew I hadn't given him my number. Any privacy I'd once had was gone. This guy calling only showed how desperate they were for gossip.

Going to kabbalah led me to learn about rechilut from the Torah. "Thou shalt not go up and down as a talebearer among thy people; neither shalt thou stand idly by the blood of thy neighbor." Basically, don't gossip.

Without saying a word to anyone, or getting a lawyer to defend me, I flew back home to Canada a couple of days later. What had happened impacted my decision to leave early. By this point, I was completely done with LA. My son and I wanted nothing more than to get back home, this time for good.

The day after I left (four days after the night of the incident), Leading Actor would give yet another statement, only this time, he gave it to the police. Yet again, it was a different version. It started off with him admitting that he knew who I was. After all, how could he tell a lie about that? He would have had to convince a lot of people in LA to lie, considering how many people had seen us together during the years Last and I'd dated.

Last didn't warn me about Leading Actor's plan to go to the police a few days after I left. Maybe he hadn't known. But over the next two weeks, Leading Actor and his friends produced another four statements supporting his version of the story. Perhaps it was all from the people who handled Leading Actor's press.

It didn't matter, though. His actions merely confirmed that Last and I were enemies now. I would never see him the same way again. I knew for sure my son and I were two people he no longer cared about.

And now that I was out of the country, they knew I would no longer have an opportunity to go to the authorities myself. This time, when Leading Actor told his story to the cops, he didn't tell them I had been aiming for someone else. He also conveniently left out the part of the story where he'd told me to go fix my face and then hit me.

I knew this was his way of protecting himself against any backlash from the public. After all, if it got out that he'd hit me first, there would be a whole lot of people that ride coattails who would feel it. The last thing they would want was for him to lose even a single fan, never mind the millions who might turn their backs on him if they discovered the truth.

A few days after I returned home to Toronto, I took it upon myself to contact the Los Angeles Police Department, after finding out they wanted to speak with me. Once I spoke to the detective who was in charge of the case, my suspicions were confirmed.

The detective told me that Leading Actor had given them yet another story. Only this time, he said I'd attacked him out of nowhere after he had done his best to try and calm me down. There was no explanation given for why I had been upset.

I didn't know how anyone could believe a word Leading Actor said when he kept changing his story at every turn.

I wasn't saying a word to this detective. I told him I would contact a lawyer if I changed my mind and wanted to do so. That's when he informed me that if I came back to California, there would be a warrant out for my arrest. For the first time in my thirty-five years of life, I was wanted by the police. Being back in Canada meant I faced the possibility that I could be extradited.

I contacted what I thought at the time was one of the best legal firms in the US. They had become notorious for defending a celebrity athlete who had been accused of murder. He'd ended up getting off because of a glove, so I figured that if they could help him, they could help me too.

I explained who I was, which I knew would be easy, seeing as it was all over the news. They immediately told me that all my legal bills would be covered if I would go on live television to talk about Leading Actor and explain what had happened. After saying I would think about it, I hung up the phone and never contacted them again.

No way was I going to get up on television and start talking, just for people to ridicule me, all the while a bunch of lawyers are getting paid for playing Make a Deal with my life. Considering Leading Actor couldn't keep his story straight, I figured that me being forced back to LA to tell my side on television would be the last thing he wanted.

More stories popped up in the news. Even though my name couldn't be mentioned in the tabloids, they still made things up with whatever bits of information they had. I still hadn't talked with anyone and especially the media.

By that point, I thought even if I said something, they would only twist it. Or think that because he told his side first, it must be the truth. I also understood that a good percentage of the media is controlled by the entertainment world, and they rarely turn on one of their own. This meant that even if I told my story, they would print it with a spin, which would make him look good and paint me as the villain.

The odds weren't looking good for me.

For weeks after, the media went on a feeding frenzy, and they didn't reserve my story for Thursdays, my unlucky day. I was on every entertainment show, seven days a week for weeks. Trying to get away from the misreported story was almost impossible.

I also had the pressure of my family and friends trying to get me to talk and defend myself. I knew it wouldn't have done any good, not to mention how it would have adversely affected Scion. At almost fourteen years old, he was aware of everything that was going on. Knowing what his mother had told him about what happened, his response was always the following:

"As long as you know the truth, it won't matter what people say."

I did my best to move on. My son's support gave me courage, as we quietly tried to get back into the swing of life. I had to deal with the fact that this wasn't the path I had chosen for myself. Someone else's actions had chosen my path. Leading Actor had told the police a lie, and that had changed the course of my life.

I wish I could say that things got better as time went on.

But they didn't.

A bump in the road was inexorably coming toward me. And this time, it wouldn't happen on a Thursday. The Sunday approaching would be the hardest of my life.

Truth be told, most people probably couldn't bear the thought of it happening to them, let alone live through it.

But I did.

Chapter Six

A WOLF AT THE DOOR + WOLF LIKE ME

I USED TO crack a joke that, as a single mother, I couldn't even afford the luxury of a nervous breakdown. Even as broke as I felt (and as broke as I had been), I knew life must go on. Surviving my car accident took a lot of courage. Moving forward after everything that happened in LA, with what was being said about me in the media, took even more.

By that point, my fight with Leading Actor was worldwide news. Luckily for me, I still had the support of my family and friends, who believed me and not what they read in the paper or on the Internet. I did my best to fall back into regular life and continued to work on building the T-shirt company, as well as getting my son settled back in Canada.

Life goes on. So must we.

When I first returned home to Toronto, I initially stayed with Instant Sister, who was also a partner in the T-shirt company. We wanted to keep up with our vision of being successful by running our own business. As much as I had my friends doing their best to stand by me, they had their own issues to deal with. At the time, my three closest friends (including my instant sister) were going through their own trials and tribulations. We tried to be there for each other, but our own struggles kept getting in the way.

One of us seemed to have it all together: my friend, Happy. He was one of the happiest guys I'd ever met. His smile rarely left his face.

But then life hit Happy, too. His happiness turned into the worst kind of depression right after he lost his job. I'm certain there were other things going on, but that seemed to be his tipping point. Society puts a lot of pressure on us to live up to other people's standards. It can make a person feel extremely unwanted. I knew that for a fact, considering what I was going through.

Happy tried to hide how dejected he felt, but it must have been festering inside of him and I suppose none of us knew how deep his distress was. That's because he did whatever he could to make the other three of us laugh, always acting like nothing was wrong.

The four of us were all very close, living together with our children and sharing the responsibility of raising them. It takes a village. Well, more than that, it takes good people in your village. I had a great group of people to help me raise Scion.

As for Happy, he had never wanted to visit LA when I had been living there, even though I had invited him. He had made it clear that he had no interest in being around Last or meeting any of his friends. When I got back home, after the altercation with Leading Actor, he took every chance he could to remind me, "I told you they were no good!"

After I returned home, and he'd lost his job, the two of us spent most of our time together, doing what we could to keep each other's spirits up.

He would accompany me while I did what I could to take care of the medical condition that had come up when I was still in Los

Angeles. He took me to a Loop Electrosurgical Excision Procedure (LEEP) that was going to take care of the root cause. When we saw what the media was saying about me, he would remind me it was important to keeping the focus on my son. It was the best advice.

For my part, I was there for him when he had questions about God, since I was the only one of the four of us who went to church. The same way he was a life coach for me, he believed I was someone who could teach him about finding his spirituality, despite the fact that sometimes we disagreed. For him to think I could put him on a path to help him find some kind of answer, it made me proud.

If only I knew then what I know now.

But God wasn't giving me a single hint about what would happen next.

***

The next part of my story will be the most difficult part to share. You know my story so far, so you must know how much it means when I say that.

Super Bowl Sunday, February 2006 would be the last time the group of us would all be together. Right after the game, there was a confrontation that would lead to the worst outcome imaginable.

Three of us were in the apartment when it happened: Happy, our closest guy friend, and myself. In the middle of an argument, we watched with horror as Happy suddenly ran for his balcony. It happened so fast that neither one of us had the chance to stop him.

As with all my life's greatest challenges, Happy's end came very abruptly. That single moment has stayed with me ever since.

He was there, and then, he wasn't.

I don't have an answer about why he did it. I never will. It's not my right to say why it happened. Even though his tragedy happened in my story, it isn't mine to tell.

Besides, this book is called Thursdays, not Sundays. If I were to write a book about him, the book would be hundreds of pages about the happiest guy I had ever met. The ending doesn't always tell the entire story. Fittingly enough, listening to the song "Here's Where the Story Ends" by the band The Sundays, is what allows me to put his spirit to rest.

Shortly after he passed, I visited a place I had vowed never to return to, only this time, I didn't take the train. After thirty years, the plane couldn't get me there fast enough. My mother had relocated back to our family's homestead in North Preston, Nova Scotia to take care of her parents, which she did proudly. We had lost my grandmother a few years before, and by the time I arrived, my grandfather was ninety-seven. He had been on kidney dialysis for the past twelve years. He had been hospitalized after having his second leg amputated.

During this time, I didn't attend church. Instead, my mother and I immersed ourselves in the free inspiration that came from reading Joel Osteen's books. My sister-in-law gave me a few of them, with the hope that they would help me to overcome my recent experience and learn how to keep faith. Every day, my mother and I would wake up looking forward to getting our day started by reading from his series Living Your Best Life. Without a doubt, reading kept me moving forward.

Aside from Clark and Scion, my friend Vraie and Deacon Brother were the only ones I was in constant contact with. The two of them kept me occupied as they battled through their own relationships. They were trying to find their identity, the same way I was with mine. Don't we all?

My Deacon Brother had left his wife for someone else. His wife happened to be the daughter of the minister of their church, where I had been baptized for the second time. Parting with his wife and church, and my struggle with Happy's death, kept our talks rooted in comfort, assuring each other that we could start over again. Vraie called me the most. It was encouraging to know that she trusted me to advise her on her marital affairs, almost like I had a gift. Or perhaps it was payback for all the times I'd called her about Last, acting like she could predict things I couldn't. Either way, it brought out the best in us. Sometimes, we talked two or three times a day. Only rarely would we bring up anything about what had happened in California. I don't think she cared. Keeping me away from the past left us with plenty of conversations discussing a brighter future, almost like we were both psychics.

I eventually returned to Toronto, ready to get back to my life. Happy had told me to keep the focus on my son. The last thing I wanted to do was disappoint him by not taking his advice. By September 2006 I had a great job with a notable organization, and in no time, I was a senior manager responsible for a team of five account executives. My job at the time was to make sure each one of them was successful with their conference sales. I loved my work, and I was great at it.

It wouldn't be long before I found my name mentioned in the media again. I had been charged with an assault after the argument with Happy. Only this time, they insinuated that I had been responsible for the death of my own friend while making the assumption that he was my boyfriend. We were never in a committed relationship. From the moment we met we had always remained good friends: His death had been ruled a suicide, with no one at fault. But the media was riding high on a wave fueled by Leading Actor's fame, and this was just something else to feed the fire.

***

Two years had passed after my altercation with Leading Actor before I finally found out what he was claiming against me. The authorities back in California asked for my permission to have a detective fly to Toronto to hear my side of things.

It was in the dead of winter in 2007 when my lawyer and I met the detective in Toronto at a police station close to where I lived.

I'd had several lawyers now, between the civil suit and after being convicted of an assault against Happy. This was Lawyer Four.

Once we sat down in the police station, the detective showed us all of the sworn statements made against me. There were five of them, including one from Leading Actor.

Leading Actor had already given two other statements prior to meeting with the police, and each one made less sense than the last. I would have thought an actor could have come up with a better script. Now, looking at the statements the detective showed me (all from friends of Leading Actor), I could see that each one conflicted with the next. Some of the people hadn't even been at the party.

The Los Angeles Police Department (LAPD) had high hopes that I would give them a statement, which would corroborate at least one version they already had. The detective made it a point to declare that he was only meeting with me to take a statement as an independent witness. He wasn't there on behalf of the so-called victim. As he put it, "I just want to hear what happened to you."

As for me, I still hadn't publicly said a word, and with my lawyer's advice, I stuck to that. The detective flew back to California without so much as a goodbye from me.

After that, the possibility of me being forced back to the US seemed to fade away. I believed Leading Actor wanted nothing more to do with any part of this mess. I knew I didn't.

I just wanted to move on.

The only thing I had done was defend myself after being struck by two men. I dared to hope that was the end, water under the bridge. The past in the past, and my future in front of me. Except, there were a lot more unlucky Thursdays to come, and there's no getting around that day of the week.

***

Being successful at my new job was very fulfilling. I made myself and others a lot of money, and the company's management was exceedingly happy with me. The best part was how supportive the company was of my situation. Regardless of how much money I was making, the way they treated me made going to work feel like visiting family. They were aware of who I was. After all, my situation involved a well-known celebrity. It had made worldwide news. But they also knew the real me.

It was a positive atmosphere for a change. I loved my job. I loved my coworkers. I even loved my bosses. My Australian boss was my favorite boss ever. Right from my first interview with him, we instantly clicked. In all the years that I would come to know him, he never once brought up Leading Actor's name. Hollywood seemed to be the furthest thing from his mind, and he always did his best to keep it out of mine. He even made a promise to his own mother that he was going to make me the best Senior Account Executive he'd ever trained. Within a month of my employment, he kept his word. Unfortunately, my next challenge began while I was working there.

Because it turned out, the past was not in the past, as I had hoped. The State of California came hunting for me, armed with all the statements that had come from Leading Actor and his friends, whom I liked to think of as 'The Wolves'.

After being back home in Canada for over four years, they wanted to extradite me back to the US.

Extradition is a request made by a country to deliver a person accused of committing a crime in that country over to their law enforcement. Because of this, it's handled by the Department of Justice. Based on the treaty between Canada and the US, one country submits a request, and depending on the severity of the alleged crime, the request may be approved pretty quickly.

I never fought extradition. I believed as a Canadian citizen that it was important for me to deal with it directly. I never thought it would happen, but I met it head-on. Initially, I was arrested by the Emergency Task Force in June of 2009, while I was coming home from work, the same way I had been coming home for almost four years. It wasn't like I had been hard to find.

Just like any other day of the week, I had begun my trek home that day by getting on the subway, fighting crowds of people packed on the tunnel's platform.

That week had been a hard one for the entire world. During the same time, The Yeah Yeah Yeahs returned with the release of their song "Heads Will Roll". This time after watching the music video, I knew the song hadn't been written solely for me.

We had just been told that Michael Jackson had died, and it appeared to me as though everyone was in mourning. It was the first time I had ever seen a news anchor cry, admitting that most reporters had given Michael a bad rap, and when it came down to it, they'd treated him horribly.

Even with their brilliance, musicians also seem to suffer at the hands of the media. I can't remember an A-, B-, or C-list actor who has endured the same type of judgmental ridicule as Michael Jackson did, simply for being accused of a crime. This was after he had been recognized by The Guinness Book of World Records for his philanthropic work, giving over a half of a billion dollars to charity. All while he lived in a place called Never Never Land, longing to be a modern day Peter Pan.

After two train rides, and a forty-five-minute delay at Pape Station, I finally made it to Warden Station. There, I caught a short bus ride to my stop. Then I went north up Warden Avenue, heading home to my son and my dog daughter.

As I walked, I noticed a suspicious man sitting in an unmarked car. He was definitely odd and out of place. I could tell he wasn't in his neck of the woods. Back then, I lived in a remote area of Toronto, which was being built up but was still more or less desolate.

The way this guy was situated, and the emptiness of the area, put me on-guard.

I could feel a weird energy as I continued to walk by his car. He was watching me out of the corner of his eye and waiting patiently. I felt something bad was about to happen, but I had no idea what. It wouldn't have mattered, even if my instinctive voice had told me what to do.

Nothing could have prepared me for this.

Once I got past his vehicle and around the corner, I came across another vehicle. It was a small minivan, this time with two men inside. Both of them were also waiting and watching.

After just a few more steps, it all happened. The driver of the minivan quickly hopped out and came toward me. The other man followed.

And there I was, wondering what was about to happen to me.

"Aretha?" the driver asked. "Aretha Wilson?"

I told him that's who I was, and that's when he told me who he was: an officer with the Emergency Task Force.

"I'm truly sorry to inform you," he said, "but I'm here to arrest you on a warrant issued for your extradition to the United States."

The charge was assault with a deadly weapon. No need to explain the rest, because I already knew, but he explained it anyway.

I can't remember his name, but I remember him apologizing. It was as if he felt bad about what he had to do. I could see the look on his face, like he would rather be anywhere but here.

I stood there in shock. It was, by far, the last thing I had expected when I got up for work that morning. While he was reading me my rights, his partner took my bag from my hand. In it was the dinner I had picked up for Scion and I.

That reminded me that my son wasn't far away. I could imagine him seeing this, walking out our door and calling out to me, not knowing what was going on. I didn't want that. It was the last thing I wanted for him.

Thankfully, they put me in their van before that could happen. He put tight handcuffs around my wrists. I kept thinking this couldn't be happening. It couldn't be real.

But it was.

They took me to Vanier Women's Correctional Facility in Milton, Ontario. For the first time in my thirty-nine years, I was now going to experience what my friend, Lock, had.

I was off to jail.

***

It turns out they had sent ten detectives from the Emergency Task Force to apprehend all 125 pounds of me, for something that had happened so long ago it almost felt like a dream.

I can only imagine what it cost the State of California to employ the Emergency Task Force to scoop me up. I was told it cost them five hundred dollars each day they had me incarcerated at the Vanier Centre.

It's good to know what a long chunk of your life is worth.

After spending a few days in Vanier, I was whisked away to High Court. My only chance to regain my freedom was in front of a judge. In High Court, you only have one shot at bail. Of course, you won't be surprised to hear that I got scheduled to go in front of the judge the following Thursday. I was afraid my unlucky streak was going to continue. God knows, I didn't want to wake up next Friday still in the worst place on Earth—behind bars.

Bail hearings are heart-wrenching. Just like a trial's verdict, they can be excruciating to hear. In my case, assault with a deadly weapon was the charge, and in order for the US to extradite a Canadian citizen, the charge has to be for a minimum of two years in jail.

The cost to extradite a person from one country to another is considerably high. For instance, it cost half a million dollars to ship Rocco Magnotta back to Canada. However, he was an accused murderer. Here I was, only accused of assault.

I was transferred to High Court for my bail hearing. Foremost in my mind was the knowledge that if this wasn't done right, it meant no freedom for me. No seeing my son and pretty much no life.

I hoped.

I prayed.

I feared what was to come.

The justice system is a very confusing combination of city laws, provincial laws, judges, crown attorneys, defense lawyers, and the accused with their alleged crimes. On top of that, you have bail hearings and pretrial dates based on courtroom availability.

Courts operate in court time.

In order to begin this crazy process, I knew I needed to get out on bail first. Fighting for your freedom while being incarcerated is never easy. You appear guilty, walking into a courtroom dressed in orange. Believe me, the clothes make the person, especially in High Court.

During my high court bail hearing, I had a cellmate who was being arraigned on a first-degree murder charge. Once she heard the allegations against me, and the potential for extradition, she asked me outright, "Who'd you hit, the president?"

Forget about the president. I was squaring off against allegations that had come from a higher power than that: Leading Actor. I was escorted into the courtroom after a few hours of watching my cellmate pace around the holding cell, pondering her own fate.

Her situation was scarier than mine. I couldn't imagine she had been capable of such a thing. I had read about her case in the newspaper over the previous few months, prior to going to jail myself. Prior to that point, I would never have believed in a million years that I would be sharing a cell with her.

Being in such close proximity to an accused murderer was not a comfortable experience. I was happy when they called my name, and the guards led me out of the cell, even though my stomach was all twisted up in knots over the thought of what would come next.

***

As I was being placed in the courtroom's holding box, I looked around to see who else was in the room. My family filled the audience section, alongside my coworkers, friends, lawyers, and of course, all the media representatives. The knots in my tummy tightened. I realized my life was about to be on display, and that I would be judged by everyone.

A bail hearing usually begins with both the crown attorney and the defense lawyer asking questions to witnesses, who are known to the defendant or the accused. After the lawyers feel they've proved their case, they each rest and end their questioning. Then, the judge might have questions.

My case was different. It was only the judge who asked questions, but it began with the crown attorney making an opening statement. Right off the bat, you could tell he wasn't in favor of my release.

When he began speaking, he made it sound like he knew me and my entire life, although he described a woman whom I myself didn't know. I sat there in disbelief, looking back and forth at my family as he portrayed me as a villain, someone who'd skipped out on bail in California and fled to Canada to avoid prosecution, despite the fact that I hadn't even been arrested in Los Angeles.

I had never seen this man in my life. That didn't stop him from pacing back and forth across the room as though he was on a stage performing for an audience. Then, he started talking about Happy. Not one word that he uttered about the incident was correct, other than the fact that I'd witnessed the death of one of my best friends.

I sat there in the box trying to wrap my head around what the crown attorney was saying. Listening to him was difficult. He was trying to convince the court and the audience that I'd had something to do with my friend's suicide, which wasn't true. Neither I, nor our closest guy friend who was there that night, had any idea of his intentions. If we had known what was to come, we would have done anything we could have to stop him.

My lawyer called his first witness: Clark, my son's father. I felt some relief. Clark was someone who knew me. He would tell the truth. That's what the courts were there for, finding the truth, not for tricking people into believing wild assumptions.

When Clark's name got called, he jumped up and walked through the little wooden swinging doors, up into the witness stand. You could tell he was nervous. His eyes darted across the room, looking at all the authority figures that occupied it, and then at me. He sat down on the witness stand, and we all waited.

Clark prepared himself for questioning by placing his left hand on the Bible. He swore to tell the truth and nothing but. I thought of the few times we had gone to church as a family, when we had still been together. Somehow, the Bible he was holding looked different from the ones we'd used on Sundays. The way they presented this one made it look more like a prop. Something for show. Something unimportant.

"How do you know Aretha?" the judge asked him.

"She is the mother of our son. I know her well," he replied.

I watched as the judge took notes.

She continued her questioning. "How long have you known her?"

By this point, everyone in the courtroom was trying to listen in. The people in the back who couldn't hear made their way up closer to the front. Seated on the wooden benches and scattered throughout the court, I could see some of my coworkers who had come here to support me. Facing them like that was very hard. I was embarrassed and felt horrible.

Clark answered the judge's question by saying, "It's like I've known her all my life. I dreamed about her, even before I met her."

I looked up at my son's father with a sad smile, thinking to myself this must be hard for him, watching the mother of his son go through such an ordeal. I looked at the crowd of people again, and I saw that my son and my third sister were crying. I realized this was difficult for each one of us in so many ways. We were all being affected. They were hurting because of their love for me.

The judge allowed my son's father to continue. It was obvious that he still cared for me. I could feel a bit of the weight leaving my shoulders as he kept glancing over at me, giving me nods of reassurance.

I could almost feel like this would all work out.

He went on with his testimony, saying that I was one of his best friends. He explained that although we were no longer together, our friendship had continued throughout the years, long after we'd broken up.

He explained to the judge how both of us had made it a point to put our son first by making sure he knew his dad and mom were friends. No matter what, we had always been cordial toward each other.

The judge then asked my son's father if he was aware of my assault charge, and the reason for my extradition. She asked him if I had told him what had happened the night of the altercation with Leading Actor.

He said, "From what she told me, they exchanged words. After he said something cruel about her disfigurement, she said something back to him, which prompted him to turn around and come within her personal space. From what I was told, he approached her, and he was the aggressor, hitting her first, on the left side where she is scarred." My son's father made a gesture to show where, by lightly slapping his own face. "I believe her when she says she defended herself with a knee-jerk reaction, after being slapped by him."

The judge seemed to empathize with my son's father, while she jotted down his response. I could see it in her facial expression with her eyebrows knitted, and the way she tilted her head. It's not hard to figure out that it takes two people to argue, and usually, it also takes two people to fight.

Clark took a moment and glanced over at me again, almost like he was looking through me. That was one of the worst moments of my life. By that point, I'd known my son's father for over twenty years. He'd never seen me this low. Nobody had.

The judge asked him about his financial situation, and if he would be a surety by posting my bail. He told her he had saved a bit of money in his retirement savings plan, and that he had a savings account. If he needed to, he would have no problem putting all of it up to secure my release.

Sitting there, I realized how much my son's father truly cared about my freedom, how much he wanted to make sure I would be home for our son.

Normally with a bail hearing, the amount of money being posted is set before you even walk in the courtroom. Or, at least, you have an idea of how much it's going to be. And usually it only requires one person to post it. As I stated before, though, my bail hearing was different. The judge determined the amount as she continued interviewing the witnesses.

After wrapping up her questioning with my son's father, he was excused. He made his way off the stand, and when he walked by me he smiled and whispered, "You're going to be okay, I promise."

I couldn't help it. I began to cry, as I watched him walk away from the glass box where I was sitting. Even though I had so much to be sad about, they were glad tears. Knowing he would do almost anything to make sure I was all right made me feel so happy despite my misery.

***

Next to testify was my boss, who I had only known for about five years. He got up and shuffled his way to the witness stand. On the way, his eyes finally met mine. He gave me a resolute look, and a sharp smile, as if to say, "Don't worry, I got this." I knew he felt terrible for what I was going through, but he'd always praised me for having the endurance and strength to face the obstacles I've had in my life.

Beginning to speak in his thick but clear Australian accent,

Boss talked about the relationship we had. He said he wasn't just my boss, but also a good friend. That we had spent countless hours together, both at the office and outside of work. He even went into detail about our company softball team, and how we played together every weekend. He told the judge that in the five years of seeing me every day at work, and almost every weekend between, he had never once witnessed me being violent or aggressive toward anyone.

As the judge was interviewing Boss, I wondered if she was going to release me at all. I've witnessed these types of hearings before. All it takes is one person to post your bail, someone who will stick their neck out for you. I got nervous, though, especially after my boss offered up his half-million-dollar condo, and the judge still wanted more. My heart raced as he walked off the stand and back to the audience seats. I thought to myself, I'm going to have to go back to jail. Sitting in that cell, next to the woman accused of murdering her boyfriend with an ax.

Everyone in the courtroom sat stunned and silent as the judge looked around, deciding on what to do next. Then she addressed the entire courtroom. "Is there anyone else who would like to speak on behalf of Aretha and perhaps post more bail?"

My heart hit the floor. What did she want? How much more would my friends and family have to give her?

Then a man's hand shot up, and I realized it was my older sister's ex-husband. I sat there in amazement. He was willing to put his neck on the line for me, too, even though he was someone I hadn't seen since I was seventeen. I thanked the Lord that the judge didn't make him get on the stand. The fact that he had offered must have been sufficient for her.

She put her hand up and said, "That's enough."

Right then, it hit me. These people knew me. Whether we'd been close in the past or the present. And all of them cared. Not like the crown attorney, who was just reading off a piece of paper, trying to make me into who he wanted me to be.

Then a miracle happened.

The judge granted the bail. But not before I had to agree to conditions, unlike any I'd ever heard of a judge setting before. She didn't miss a thing.

The judge said she thought I was a woman who, in her mind, was neither a criminal nor a violent person. She even said, "It seems, Aretha, as though you've experienced two very odd situations at the age of thirty-five that are extreme, and otherwise, unfortunate."

She was right. Before all of this, I had had no criminal record. However, that didn't stop her from ordering that I be on a curfew, and in my house, between the hours of 10:00 p.m. and 6 a.m., every day. I was also restricted from traveling. I had to turn over my passport, and I was told not to even think about drinking. I was also warned not to come in contact with Leading Actor (like I ever would, could, or wanted to).

The hardest stipulation was going to be the requirement to sign into a reporting center located in Scarborough, Ontario, every single weekday. That meant a commute of almost two hours Monday through Friday, on top of going to work.

After she read those conditions to me in front of the courtroom's audience, I was returned to the holding cell. There, I waited for both my son's father and my boss to go through the tedious process of being interviewed by the Justice of the Peace in charge of finalizing my bail. Both Clark and Boss would later tell me how they were grilled separately, and then threatened that if I didn't heed the court's stipulations, they would lose every single cent they had put up.

The Justice of the Peace didn't have to warn me, though. No way was I ever going to let anything like that happen. Not when they had put themselves on the line for me.

***

Getting bail from High Court is extremely difficult. Even if you're lucky enough to receive it, while it's being approved, you still have to wait with the women in holding. The ones who might not.

I was put back in the cell with the woman who was looking at life in prison. Her niceness turned into something uglier once she knew I was going free. That was the scariest two hours that I ever had to wait. When they called my name again, I almost tripped as I hurried to get out of the cell.

Eventually, the courts convicted that woman of murder, and she received a life sentence with no chance of parole, until she had served twenty-five years. It was the toughest sentence ever given to a woman in Canada.

Once I was free, I made my way out into the courtroom's hallway. There I reunited with my friends and family, and for a moment we were all thrilled. Then I walked out of the courthouse, through the doors, and out into the street.

That's when the circus began.

So much was going on in court that day, it's no wonder multiple reporters from news agencies and media giants were hovering outside. They were all waiting to hear the outcome of my bail hearing. More importantly, they wanted to get a good look at me. Not just with their eyes, but with their cameras.

There were so many of them. My oldest sister tried desperately to protect me by putting her coat over my head and covering me, but that didn't stop them.

The worst part was I still had on the horrible orange suit. I suppose the powers that be hadn't thought I was going to leave. My clothes were still at Vanier with the rest of my property.

Most people I talk to have taken the time to ask about my story, and what actually happened. They wanted to hear what I had to say. They wanted to hear the truth from me.

However, the media can be ferocious. In my case, some of them were just plain cruel. They created stories manipulated by the truth, alongside an old photo of Leading Actor, that I believe is from an old movie shoot. One where he appears to look as though he'd been beaten up severely. Although alongside my name, at a quick glance the trusting public would be led to believe it as though this was the damage I had caused. With one hit and no real aim, done out of a nervous reaction, I knew the stiches he received were for a small cut behind his ear. According to Last, I'd never touched his face. Although I know for a fact that the altercation happened because Leading Actor had touched mine. Without any official statements from the people directly involved the media made up a lot, filling in their own blanks. I knew they would never provide a good outlet for me. It would always be their twisted words that got printed, and then consumed by the public as truth.

Nothing I could do would stop them. A defamation lawyer can cost twice as much as a criminal one. The average person never stands a chance against the media. Suing them for their lies was out of the question. I had multiple criminal lawyers I already had to pay for. Lucky for me, through it all, I had a good job.

It only cost me $100,000 to hire all those lawyers. I guess that's a pretty good deal. Only $100,000 to pave my way to jail.

Chapter Seven

AIRBAG

UNLIKE THEIR BELOVED celebrities, the media didn't take the time to photoshop any of my pictures to make me appear nice and flashy for their glossy magazines. What appears today, in a simple Google search of my name, is what they chose to portray me as: a monster. They followed me and snapped away, taking pictures of both me and my son. Then they would yell out obscenities or anything to get my attention, so they could capture a shocked or disgusted expression that would make me look as awful as possible.

It was bad. Every entertainment magazine had a different story about me. They even would go as far to print and say that I used a beer bottle as the weapon against the Leading Actor, when I know for a fact my court documents state that it was a glass. Almost everything they wrote was wrong or backward; especially concerning who attacked whom.

For years, as a young woman, I spent a lot of time and money reading entertainment magazines. I also never failed to watch any entertainment news shows. I depended on them to deliver current, accurate updates on all the superstars and their whereabouts, just like they have conditioned us to want... I was swayed by the media into the admiration of the famous. That was, until I read the story about myself in a gossip magazine. A magazine that, at the time, happened to be my favorite. It was within a week of the incident when I read it. This is part of the story where "I am a model" takes shape. Their version of the story claimed I was a model at a party and that after being harassed by Leading Actor all night, I finally got up the nerve to tell him to go and put his di-ck back in his pants (in quotation) and this is what lead to the altercation. I suppose it would only fit their narrative for him considering that's who he usually hangs around with, models. Even though my mother signed me up for modeling when I was a young girl it never went that far. Nevertheless, standing there that night I was the owner of a T-shirt company with the credentials of my CSC and a previous Investment Advisor. I suppose that wouldn't fit their story or they couldn't take the time to figure it out, knowing how important it is to be the first ones to break the news.

After reading the article, and their rendition of what had occurred on that night with the actor, I would never purchase any of those glossy magazines or watch another entertainment program ever again. That is still true to this day. I realized how willing they are to lie. That their stories are almost always fantasy. Every story about me was skewed for dramatic effect. Never in my favor.

Even The Rats newspaper, in my own city, dedicated all of page A2 to me. They wrote warped details about the car accident I had been in, saying that my son was in the car with us when it had happened, as though his dad and I had taken him to the bar with us that night. They even misspelled his name. A lawyer told me the media uses this trick to avoid any backlash from me for printing Scion's name. I couldn't sue them for printing my child's name, because they hadn't actually printed it.

They rushed to print anything they could, twisting psychology reports from my car accident, to be read as though my goal in life was to go around and scar other people in the same way I had been. It was heartbreaking to read. The more they made me out to be a monster, the more money they made selling their lies.

My first job had been delivering The Rats newspaper. I used to get up at five o'clock in the morning, when I was eleven years old, to hand out the daily news to my neighbors. When I think about it now, I'm ashamed I had anything to do with putting that paper on anyone's doorstep. I'll never understand why they did that to Scion, and they will never understand how it affected him throughout high school. Some of the most difficult times came after the newspaper decided to print a picture of the two of us leaving court one day when he was just 15 years old. This would only lead to questions, and odd looks of concern from the students, their parents, and all the staff. Most of them pointed toward Scion.

When I was younger, like most teenagers, I pondered what I would do in the future. I thought about a career based on what I believed it meant to be successful, as well as honorable. I thought about being a doctor, a lawyer, a judge, and of course, a stockbroker.

But back to lawyers. I paid one of my lawyers with a Rolex watch. I gave it to him to represent me at one of many of hearings. It was the only way I could get him to appear and speak on my behalf on such short notice, to get me out of jail and back to my son.

The watch had been a family keepsake my older sister had been saving. I remember the first time she showed it to me. She had been so proud of it. It was an antique watch, and a gift that she wanted to pass on to the youngest of our brothers.

The lawyer said he would give me thirty days to pay him the cash and would hold the watch until that time. When the time was up, I didn't have the money. When I asked him for another thirty days, he said it was too late and kept it. He took the watch in exchange for my so-called freedom. It made me feel as though I was being used. It was as if I was a pawn under the control of someone else, and they would take whatever they wanted from me.

I concluded that some of us will do anything to obtain wealth. A lot of those same individuals only want to become rich, so they can look down on others like they're worthless.

The days following my release became increasingly difficult. I tried to find a new lawyer to represent me, for all my newly scheduled court dates, while still using ten hours of the day to travel back and forth to work. Plus don't forget, on top of that, I had to sign-in five days a week, as one of my court-ordered conditions of release. Which will only add up to more time away from Scion.

The location of the reporting center was in the middle of Scarborough, an area outside of downtown Toronto, very far from where I worked. It was a small brick building right outside of the rapid transit subway station, built underneath a bridge. The building had cameras on all corners of the structure, and a thick metal door with an intercom to request entry. It felt like I was walking back into jail every day.

The officer I reported to on the first day (with my bail papers in hand), asked me about my requirements three times before turning to his partners and saying, "She has to come here every day." It was obvious that the very idea surprised him. I wasn't going to ever forget it. The judge had made sure I would never forget it. Not for the rest of my life.

The officer looked back at the computer on his desk, and for the second time he just said, "Every day." They had never seen another accused criminal that had to report to the center every weekday. So, it wasn't a surprise when his next question was, "Why?"

Most of the officers were eavesdropping at this point. When they heard me say I was being extradited for an assault, and who it involved, they all shook their heads in disbelief.

"No one has ever had to come here every day," the officer told me. "Bet if it were my son, you wouldn't have to come here at all."

He was referring to Leading Actor, and that if I had been

accused of hurting a regular person, things would have been completely different.

I could tell that it bothered him. Just like it bothered many others in authority, who I would have to explain my situation to over the years.

I will say, every time I went into that reporting center, they were always very supportive and polite. Although, I will mention the scariest time I ever buzzed that door was when I arrived right at 9:00 p.m., which is exactly when they close. I had had a late meeting with my new attorney that day, and even though I spent fifty dollars on a cab, I arrived with mere seconds left on the clock. Missing that deadline would have meant throwing my freedom away.

Once they buzzed me in, I immediately went to the thick glass partition, breathless and apologizing for my tardiness. The officer on duty that night got up from her desk smiling, and reassured me, "Don't worry, Aretha, we knew you'd never miss. I would've waited for you."

Then there were the lawyers I had to deal with. Lawyer Five was recommended by a neighbor, who had given him rave reviews. I would later find out that this lawyer had his own issues and had been accused of sexual assault.

I decided to allow him to continue to be my lawyer, especially after he convinced me he had complete understanding of Canadian extradition laws and our treaty with the U.S. government. At his first court date with me, which was an appearance to inform the courts of my new attorney, we walked out of the courtroom and Lawyer Five spoke to me, my friends, and family.

Clark, Boss, other friends, family, and of course, Scion were all there. They always came to my court appearances to support me and keep my spirits up. I was standing there with my arms folded, waiting to hear some kind of expert advice after giving him his retainer. We all wanted to know the answer to the same question:

What was going to happen next?

He couldn't have made it clearer. He told us the same thing, over and over. "Aretha," he explained, "No one ever gets extradited for assault."

Of course, that was exactly what I wanted to hear. I didn't ask questions, especially when he said not to worry. He said he was off to make a couple of phone calls, and I had nothing to get worked up about. A couple phone calls, and I'll be home free, I thought. It seemed like this lawyer knew all there was to know about extradition.

I would later come to find out, after almost paying him $17,000, that he knew nothing. That didn't stop him from promising me or reassuring all of us that no one ever gets extradited for assault. That it surely wouldn't happen to me.

***

I remember the third time he sat me down in his office, which turned out to be my last visit. It was the weekend before my extradition hearing. I usually met him in court, and his office was nothing you would imagine a criminal lawyer would have, especially with the money he was charging.

It was a storefront property away from the downtown core. Through the front door was a dingy hallway. To get to any of the offices, you had to walk up the stairs, because there was no elevator. The floor was unstable and covered with a stained carpet. I could smell the dust that lay over everything. It smelled like old hope. Lost hope.

After letting my lawyer know that I had arrived, the receptionist led me to the boardroom. I never saw the lawyer's actual office, but I could imagine that the carpet in there matched the rest of the place. I sat in the boardroom, looking at all the law books, wondering if they had ever been read, as I waited for Lawyer Five to make his appearance. After thirty minutes of sitting in silence, he finally came in.

I responded, my voice shaking a little from nerves. I knew my trial date was coming up quickly, and I still hadn't been told how this was all going to work. He took a seat across from me, sighing as if he'd had the longest day of his life. I became more nervous while I waited for him to say something else.

When he did, I nearly fell through my chair.

"Sorry," he said, "but you're going to have to go back."

I was scheduled to be in court the following Thursday, and after all the months of being told one thing by this man, now he was saying this? With my heart racing, all I could ask him was, "Is there anything I can do to stop it?" He said no. His phone calls had been with the authorities in LA. I was going to have to take care of this there.

My heart was racing, and anxiety set in. I waited for him to tell me what I should do now. Frankly, I'm surprised I didn't pass out. He was still talking, and I will always remember what he said next, "Try to look on the bright side, Aretha. You'll go back to LA, do a few months, then come out and sell your story for a bunch of money."

I couldn't believe what I was hearing. I knew there was nothing to look forward to in any of that. Jail is one of the darkest places a human can go to on Earth. I understood that from the short time I'd already spent there.

As for the money, I could have sold the story years ago, and I hadn't. I had very good reasons for not doing so, most importantly the repercussions such a decision would have on my son. Not forgetting, I was headed for an extradition hearing where anything said would be used against me in a court of law. Judging from the way the media had been treating my case, I couldn't take that chance. Therefore, I continued to stick to the youngest of my brother's advice, seeing my lawyer never warned me about saying anything either way.

The instructions he gave me were ones I never expected to hear from a lawyer, and the way they came out of his mouth, I was sure they didn't come from any of those law books. "What I would advise you, Aretha, is if you drink, don't do it this weekend."

You would think as my lawyer, he would have remembered that that was one of the conditions the judge had already placed on me.

I sat there with my eyes fixed on him, while my entire body started to go numb. My heart was still racing. I stared at him in shock.

"You should probably spend this weekend in church and speak to your pastor. If you don't have one, get one. You're going to need it."

I still couldn't believe what I was hearing. Words rushed out of me in an accusation, "You waited until yesterday to make all your phone calls, and you're telling me now I have to go back?"

He tried to excuse himself, and the position he'd put me in, "Everyone I've spoken to says the US never uses the two-year treaty, but because he is who he is, you're going to have to deal with it there."

We both sat in silence for a moment, but with nothing else to say, the meeting ended. I could barely get to my feet as he opened the door for me to go.

I walked out of the boardroom and down the dingy hallway, still rocked by what had just happened. As I walked by the receptionist, she called out to me and handed me an envelope.

I opened it up to find another invoice. How much was he charging me for his apology, and his advice to go see a pastor?

Only six thousand dollars.

***

It was around seven o'clock. As I walked through the streets of downtown Toronto, I noticed that it had begun to snow lightly. I could feel the flakes hitting my cheeks. Melting on my skin and running down my face like tears.

The streets became busier, and I continued to wander aimlessly. Suddenly, I realized I had to call Scion. How would I find the words to explain to him what was about to happen to me? I was going to be extradited to California, and according to my lawyer, there was nothing I could do to stop it.

I found an empty storefront to get out of the snow and make the call. After a couple of rings, he answered the phone. He had just made it home from basketball practice and was going about his normal daily routine.

I tried to rush into the conversation, "Just so you know, I'm finished with this lawyer. I'll tell you what happened once I get home." Although I wanted to say the whole thing right there, I still had no idea what I was going to say to him. I was scared. Fear had set in, replacing the anxiety.

"Mom, what did he say?" my son pressed me. "There's got to be something more you can tell me!"

I was amazed at the tone of his response. I don't know who was more scared. Scion at the thought of losing his mom, or myself, at the idea of losing him. I had to tell him something, and the only thing I could think of was to repeat what the lawyer had told me.

"He said, I'm going to have to go back. Probably do a few months, and when I get out, I can sell the story." I tried to make it sound funny, even though I knew it wasn't. Who laughs at something like that?

My son hung up.

I stood there in the storefront doorway, thinking my life was about to be a complete mess. I started to wonder how God would ever get me through all of this. Only this time, for some reason, that instinctive voice was silent. Or perhaps, it was that I didn't want to believe this turn of events could be true.

The snow began to come down hard. I thought to myself, the next person I needed to tell was Boss. I knew he was probably at a bar not too far from where I was, and I wanted to go meet him there. I thought it would be better if I told him in person. After all, he was my surety and very concerned about my freedom, much like everyone else in my life.

I called him first. In the background, I could hear all the people and sounds of the bar. I left the storefront and darted across the street in his direction. At the same time, I tried to listen to Boss on the other end of the line as he talked over the racket. Aside from the noise in the background, and my boss having a thick Australian accent, I was having trouble understanding him.

"What did the lawyer say?" he asked me.

I raised my voice to be sure he heard me. "I'm going to be extradited!"

When I got to the bar the mood was somber. After giving Boss the gist of what Lawyer Five had said, he arranged for a private room. It was an Italian restaurant, which we would frequent to celebrate monetary target victories or other good times. I made my way through the crowd of people and into the private room. With most of my coworkers listening in, I explained it all again.

"The lawyer said, I'm going to be extradited. No matter what." I went into the finer details and ended the story by telling him I might be incarcerated as early as next week. Everyone in the room was shocked, but no one more than me, as I heard my own words leaving my lips. Boss was very disappointed and didn't want to believe it was true.

We discussed how we would break the news to the CEO. He was another person who was concerned about my well-being, and who had given me his full support. I couldn't help but focus on the fact that no matter how many checks my company had cut directly from my salary to pay and retain my lawyers, I was still going to jail.

After giving the news to my coworkers, I left the bar and got into a cab to go home. The only thing I wanted was to be with Scion.

***

We drove across Kingston Road through the slushy, wet snow. I started to remember that, when I had been a little girl, I used to make igloos out of snow banks in early November. That girl had never imagined she'd one day be going off to jail.

This lawyer had talked about it like it was easy, like it was something he had experienced a few times himself. As I sat in the cab, watching the snowflakes hit the window, I wondered if that should be part of the process of becoming a lawyer.

After all, lawyers become judges. If they want to send someone to jail, maybe they should experience it too, at least once. If it was part of their curriculum, and they had to do a few months, they would completely understand what a person felt in their heart when it was their time to go.

My mind bounced around all over the place. I pictured myself going back to jail. It was a horrible thought. One you'd never want to imagine. I just didn't want to picture it. Then it hit me: I might have to spend Christmas with that woman I'd shared a cell with before, who had now been convicted of murdering her boyfriend with that axe.

The thought was so bleak that I swallowed hard, trying to hold it together.

The streets were still busy with cars trying to get through the snow, even though it was evening. It always seems as though people have a harder time driving in the first snow of the year. What should have been a twenty-minute drive, turned into an hour.

When I finally did get home, I dropped my keys on the kitchen table and called out to my son to see where he was. I walked into the dining room, noticing a pile of dishes in the kitchen. I found Scion sitting on the living room couch.

At first, I thought he was watching television, but when he turned toward me, I saw the tears streaming down his face. "I don't care about selling the story," he told me. "I don't want you to go back there." But according to Lawyer Five, I would have to do my jail time in Los Angeles.

I looked at him, trying to hold back my own tears.

Scion and I knew the same thing. This was going to be a tough fight, and we would both suffer when we were separated. It felt like the entire world was against us. And now his mom, his main protector, was going to be taken away.

I sat beside him on the couch and tried to console him. I told him that somehow we would make it through, just like we had before. He may not have physically been in the car accident, the party where the altercation had happened, or the apartment when Happy had leaped to his death. But he had been there afterward for me each time. Now, I was being extradited away from him.

Seeing my son so upset was hard. It was the first time he had broken down since my bail hearing. The idea that he was losing his mom was becoming real.

Sitting beside him, I couldn't help but compare my life to the paper bag that Fiona Apple sings about. I pictured the music video for the song in my head, thinking about how the young boy hands the singer her suitcase. Then he stands there watching her walk away. My heart broke, thinking about how that was going to be Scion and I.

I left the living room and returned to the kitchen to begin doing the dishes; anything to get my mind off my current situation. As soon as I began to fill up the sink, I realized the next person I would have to tell was my mom.

After getting the kitchen straightened up, and my son somewhat calmed, I called my mom in Nova Scotia. I was thinking that hopefully she would be able to get past the upsetting news and help me think. I needed her guidance to advise me how to handle my son, and the difficulties we would have to face, knowing it would all begin in less than a week.

When I called, it was like she had been waiting for me. She picked up on the first ring and listened intently to everything I had to say. After we got past the major points, my mom began by advising me on how to deal with my son, "Whatever you do, Aretha, please assure him it will be okay. Whatever happens, my grandson can always come here."

As I sat in my dining room listening to her, I tried to picture my son in Nova Scotia with my mom. Without me. It was good to know that, along with his father, he had many people to love and take care of him. But the image of my son being without me just didn't feel right.

I made myself a cup of coffee, went back to the dining room, and continued the conversation with my mom. Her next point was that she had spoken to a lawyer in Nova Scotia on my behalf, who had given her the name of someone he thought could help.

He was a well-known lawyer in Ontario. She was adamant that I contact him, but quite frankly, I wasn't interested. I had already gone through five lawyers, spent thousands of dollars, only to end up facing the worst.

I finished my cup of coffee, hung up the phone, and went to bed.

If only I could have slept.

I actually did call the attorney my mother suggested, but I waited until after the weekend and called on Tuesday from work. I was looking out the window at the city, from the nineteenth floor of my office building. I sighed, took a deep breath, and called, despite all my apprehensions. As I dialed the number, I looked out the window again and thought, "God, Toronto is such an amazing city, I wish I'd never left it."

How different would things be if I had stayed?

After a couple of rings, a lady answered the phone. She put me through to the lawyer's voice mail, and I left a very detailed message. I explained who I was, who was representing me at the time, and what had recently occurred. I ended the message by saying, "You're the only person I have left to call."

Lawyer Six called back within the hour. I was amazed that he had gotten back to me so quickly, but I was nervous to talk to him. I had done some research, and one thing I learned was that he actually knew a lot about extradition, unlike Lawyer Five.

He had represented Cathy Smith, the woman who had been accused of John Belushi's death in 1982. She had been extradited, pled guilty to involuntary manslaughter, and only served fifteen months in jail. After reading that, I knew he must be good.

It was perfect timing when the call came in at half past noon. Most of my colleagues had left the office for lunch, which gave me a chance to speak more privately. The office where I worked was a completely open concept, perfectly set up so you could hear everyone's conversations on the phone. It was designed so we could listen to and monitor discussions that our team members had with clients. It also made sure there was a limit to personal phone calls.

The last thing my team members needed to hear was me begging for my freedom once again with yet another lawyer. I was glad they were gone when he called.

Right off the bat, his voice was kind and gentle. It was almost soothing to hear him speak. Still, it was still hard for me to tell him my troubles, and that I was to go back to court on (yes, yet another) Thursday.

Instead of saying it was impossible for him to take the case, he said, "That will give us some time."

I felt a huge weight off my shoulders. Still, there were issues. I had no idea how I was going to pay him. I had used up all my money on my other lawyers.

Then he asked me about my current lawyer, and how I had retained him. I told him that he had been recommended by a friend who'd never told me about his alleged transgressions. Lawyer Six chuckled at the answer. "Don't worry, Aretha, I know him."

My colleagues began to trickle back into the office as I continued my conversation. I knew they were listening in, but I had hope for the first time in a long time, so I wasn't going to just end the conversation yet.

He told me that in order for him to become my new lawyer, I would have to give him permission to contact the current one and stop them from working on my case. He assured me they would do this without hesitation, and that I would not have to contact them directly. Then the discussion came up about a retainer, and how I was going to pay Lawyer Six. By that time, everyone had returned from lunch, my boss included.

Lawyer Six asked if I could come up with at least five thousand dollars to start with.

As I tried to cover the phone with my hand and lower my squeaky voice, I wondered where I was going to get that from. "Looks like I'm going to have to," I told him.

He ended the conversation by agreeing to be in his office at six o'clock that evening. I couldn't believe he would be able to see me so quickly. It seemed like he really cared.

I turned around and whispered to my boss, "I just have to make one more quick call after this one." He looked over at me and winked with a short nod of approval.

I called my CEO, who was in New York at the time. He was another person who I believed could help me. After a very quick conversation with him, he directed me to transfer him to the controller of our company. Once again, he made arrangements with her to issue another check for five thousand dollars, and as usual, she did it the same day. They definitely cared about me.

It was five-thirty when I left work to make my way to the offices of Lawyer Six. I headed down to the subway, through the concourse level underneath the building where I worked.

Riding the subway at this time of day was going to be a horrible trip. I knew it would be completely packed with people trying to get home.

I headed toward the turnstiles. But to my surprise, everyone was going in the opposite direction. I went up to the TTC collector and asked what had happened.

"Someone thought it was a good idea to commit suicide during rush hour," was what I was told. The subway wasn't going to be running anytime soon.

I would have to take a cab to my appointment, but I told myself that I was hardly having a worse day than whoever had stopped the train.

I went outside, surfacing at the corner of Queen and Yonge Street, and called a cab. Looking out the window, I thought about what the TTC collector had said, and then I thought back to a time when I had been fourteen.

It was the first time I had been given permission to ride the subway. Of course, I had been with my best friend, the same one whose father had picked us up from Club Z. We had been on our way to Eaton Centre on the Bloor Street platform when we'd come across a few guys.

They had been in their twenties, and all four of them had appeared to be a little drunk. Stumbling everywhere. Slurring their words. I could actually smell the alcohol coming off them. Even though they had been making a lot of noise, I could still hear the train coming in the distance; getting closer and closer. We had been standing where the platform begins and the train first hits the tunnel.

In the midst of their conversation, one of the guys had turned to see if the train was coming, teetering over the edge and leaning a little too much. As it emerged from the darkness, the train had clipped his head. I'd never heard such a noise. I'd watched his body lift up and fall again, lifeless. He had been dead before he even landed. Both my friend and I had been horrified by the gruesome sight.

My first adult-free ride on the subway had been marked forever by this horrific incident. It had been the first time I had ever seen someone die. Unfortunately, it wouldn't be the last.

It was after six when I arrived at the lawyer's office, but everyone was still there, busy working despite the fact that it was after hours. The place itself was beautiful, warm, and welcoming. The office had a thick, plush carpet. The room smelt like fresh-cut wood. I felt safe as soon as I stepped in. I thought to myself, I bet all the legal books in this place have been read!

I smiled at the receptionist.

She greeted me. "You can take the stairs straight up to his office," she told me. "He's waiting for you in there."

To think a lawyer was actually waiting for me was a nice change of pace. I went up the stairs, and I knocked on the door.

"You can come in, Aretha," he called out.

I opened up the door and walked in, looking to put a face to his voice. Three lawyers stood before me, not just Lawyer Six. He was with two of his partners, and one of them would eventually be the one who I'll call Lawyer Seven. All of them wanted to help me, taking notes throughout the entire meeting. It was as if I got three lawyers for the price of one. And they were some of the best in Canada. For the first time in my lawyer-retaining life, I was in capable hands.

The following Thursday morning, I sat outside the courtroom, waiting for my trial to begin. I noticed the authority in Lawyer Six immediately. I could feel his energy as he walked through the hallways of the court. Everyone had so much respect for him. You could see it in their faces as his colleagues greeted him, had short conversations with him, or offered him little nods in passing. Out of nowhere, the crown attorney came over to us. He stopped to talk to Lawyer Six. I couldn't believe what he said.

"I want to put the case over until January, and we can call her up first."

That would keep me from being incarcerated today or being sent back to LA.

I was ecstatic.

I realized that not only did Lawyer Six's reputation precede him, but it also spilled over to me. It was as if having him beside me meant I couldn't be that bad of a person.

As requested by the crown attorney, my case was heard first.

Without a single question from the judge, my case was put over until January. After all the stress I had been facing, believing I was about to be incarcerated over Christmas, I was suddenly free to leave.

I thanked God, knowing the decision I'd made to fire Lawyer Five had saved me, even though it would only prolong what might be inevitable. I couldn't have been happier exiting the courtroom that day. Now, I thought to myself, if only I could avoid the media circus that was waiting for me outside.

Well, it just so happened there was another special privilege provided to me by Lawyer Six.

We all stood in the hallway together: my son, his father, and of course, the rest of my friends and family — and the media.

Fortunately, Canada doesn't allow any pictures to be taken in any of the courtroom's halls. Therefore, the media always has to wait to try and get a bad shot of people once they get outside.

I turned to the lawyers, who were still standing with us, and asked, "How do I avoid them?"

Lawyer Six leaned in and whispered to Lawyer Seven, "Take her through the basement. They'll think you're just going for a coffee. With her family waiting here, they'll assume you're coming back."

As we were walking, Lawyer Seven looked behind me to make sure no one was following us down the hall. He grabbed my arm, and we made a sharp turn, disappearing through a doorway and down a set of stairs. We walked through a long hallway underground. It was like a secret passage underneath the courtroom, where the media wouldn't be able to get to me.

While we snuck through a series of doors, I asked Lawyer Seven, "What do you think will happen to me?"

He told me that they would start the process of negotiating going back to LA., that most likely I would be extradited due to our treaty with the US and that the allegations against me would qualify for more than a two-year jail stay. At this point they would only be making arrangements with the Canadian Government on my behalf on how and when I was to be turned over to the US.

"I just don't believe Leading Actor will want any of this type of publicity, and he'll never want you or him to end up on the stand."

What he said reminded me of the time when Last had asked me not to go to the media. Surely, there was no way Leading Actor wanted to see me in a courtroom, especially if it meant him taking the stand and being forced to tell the truth.

Lawyer Seven swung the last door open, and we emerged in an entirely different courthouse. We had walked almost a block and a half through the underground passageways, and we'd had ended up on Queen Street West. I walked out of the building onto the street and thanked God that the media circus wasn't there waiting.

I took a deep breath, inhaling the fresh air. I began to walk down the street, enjoying sweet freedom.

Chapter Eight

FISHERMAN'S BLUES +
LET GO THE LINE

THAT YEAR, THE best present I could have gotten for Christmas was my freedom. Not being in jail was an immense blessing, and I decided I was going to do whatever I could to make that Christmas great.

Every December, our company's CEO would set monetary targets for our sales teams to achieve. In turn, it would prompt us to work harder as we worked toward additional Christmas bonuses. As always, I hit my target, More importantly, the work kept me busy and not focused on what was to come.

I couldn't let worries about what would happen in the future consume me. Therefore, I made sure to do the best I could, so that Scion and I would have a great celebration that year.

On Christmas Day, I got up and wandered into the kitchen. I thought I would make breakfast for Scion and my niece, who was spending Christmas with us that year. I couldn't travel, so spending Christmas with my mom in Nova Scotia was out of the question.

For the holidays, my third sister had been kind enough to send me her third child, from the eight wonderful children that she has, and this one happened to be her most comical child. I decided I would make French toast, since I knew it was their favorite.

As I cooked Christmas breakfast, I thought about the presents I had purchased. Getting that bonus sure had come in handy. I spent a good amount of it on my lawyers and the rest I spent buying clothes that I knew Scion would like, not knowing if I would be around the following year to buy him anything.

After we ate breakfast, I went to the closet, where I had hidden some of Scion's gifts. We always had a Christmas tree, but I had always made it a point to never put all the presents under it. Once children realize Santa is really their parents, the best way to keep them excited is to keep the surprise in Christmas.

As usual, it worked. I got him everything he wanted, including a $1,000 surprise package of jeans and other clothes from his favorite store. That morning was the first time in a while that I had seen him truly happy. It made our Christmas very special.

After opening up our gifts, we headed downtown to the theater. Earlier that week, we'd made plans to watch the movie Avatar, which was being released that day. The idea of people living on a different planet in another world seemed very appealing to me at the time. That's probably because the planet I was living on no longer felt like home to me. Seeing Avatar that day seemed like the best place to spend Christmas afternoon.

The next day, we got up and went shopping, looking for some great Boxing Day deals.

We were talking about the movie we had seen. All three of us (me, Scion, and my niece) walked downtown through the busy streets toward the Eaton Centre. We were still reeling from the 3D movie that had taken us on a journey to an entirely different planet.

The air was gravely cold as we walked. The wind nipped at my lips and my fingers. It stung my eyes. Although it had snowed earlier in the month, there wasn't a flake on the ground now. Even with the bitter cold, and the lack of snow on Christmas, it still felt good to be free. I was with my son and my niece. I had a few dollars in my account. And I wasn't in jail.

After leaving the Eaton Centre, carrying bags filled with even more clothes, we grabbed a cab and went for dinner at a restaurant on King Street. We celebrated the last part of our holiday together, eating Mexican food with my niece, always cracking jokes.

Our table was facing the street. I looked out through the restaurant window, thinking about how January was right around the corner. Soon enough, the ground would be covered with a foot of snow. Before I knew it, I would be back in court. All of this would only be a happy memory then.

It was almost impossible for me to stop thinking about it.

***

On the Wednesday night before court, I was in my boss's apartment babysitting his son. My boss's apartment was located on Blue Jays Way, right beside the CN Tower and the Toronto Skydome in downtown Toronto (now known as the Rogers Centre). After putting the baby to sleep, I went out onto the main terrace to enjoy the sight of the city at night.

After a few minutes of sitting, I started to think about how I could be extradited. I found myself looking out at the city I loved, the place where I had been born, thinking how I might be forced to leave it.

I stared out at the CN Tower, remembering the time I had taken the elevator all 1,850 feet to the top. It had been a school excursion with Sir Walter Perry Public School, back when I was in grade three. I marveled at the fact that I had been there in 1979, back when it had still been known as the world's tallest free-standing structure.

Since then, I've always thought of it as a great symbol of the city, and of Canada itself. The tower stands "glorious and free" like the words in our national anthem. The rainbow of colors that light it up at night remind me of the variety of Canadians who live here. The melting pot of people that take pride in this country.

My school gave me a great education about the country I'm from, and the multiculturalism that keeps us so close. While going to school, I never once felt discriminated against. I think that it had a lot to do with the fact that most of the people there, including the teachers, respected that everyone came from other places. We all lived under different circumstances. I come from a very distinctive background with biracial parents, but no one ever used that to label me, or try to make me feel less than I am.

At my school, we sang songs in the morning: "O Canada" and "God Save The Queen." One of our proudest moments was when we received a visit from the Lieutenant Governor of Ontario to celebrate the Queen's Silver Jubilee.

I was so excited that day. I mistakenly thought it was the Queen coming to visit us. My mom bought me a dress that was fit for a princess to wear when I met her. Of course, it wasn't the Queen, but that didn't stop me from wearing it for my class picture.

Then there was my grade three teacher, a Japanese woman. She had been confined to a wheelchair. That didn't stop her from scooting around the school like she owned the place, and not one of us got in her way. As a matter of fact, without any ramps in those days, it was our job at nine years old to make sure she could get over the curbs in the parking lot.

As I said before, at that age, my two best friends were brothers from England. Their mother always treated me as though I was part of their family. From my parents to my teachers, I always thought of Canada as a place where a bird and a fish could make a nest together, and still be accepted.

I wondered why I'd ever left. I slowly rocked back and forth, overcome by anger and frustration. I couldn't help it. Tears rolled down my cheeks.

***

Time flew by, and soon it was January. I returned to court. But this time, it would be different. I already knew what I had to do when I walked in the front door. Lawyer Six had made it clear to me that because of our treaty with the US, I had to sign the acceptance documents for extradition to the United States of my own accord. It was either that or if I didn't show up today, wherever I was eventually, I would've been arrested on the spot and instantly incarcerated. With no more questions asked I would've been brought back to the US and then treated as a person who doesn't show up for the courts.

I had to adhere to a few other rules. This included being incarcerated in the court's holding cells for the day while they processed my newly signed paperwork. It was just a formality in order to have my bail papers re-signed by my sureties. The courts wanted to make sure my son's father and my boss were still willing to put their necks on the line for me, even after I signed.

Providing everything was in order, I would be released again. For now, I would still have to go to jail for the day. I knew all that, and even so, I went into the court with my head held high. I had to forget the media. I was going to face this with respect for myself.

Waiting for the proceeding to start, I was sitting in the courtroom hall when the crown attorney approached me.

He said, "I'm going to call your name first, so that you won't be in the holding cells for long."

I stared at him, amazed by how kind he was being to me now. I offered him a half smile and an approving nod.

When it was my turn, I took a deep breath, opened the courtroom door and entered. As usual, the mood matched the room, with its eggshell white colored walls. I took a seat at one of the many wooden benches for the audience, wondering to myself why the entire place seemed designed to make people feel uncomfortable. I watched the spectators and other courtroom officials bow and tiptoe in and out of the room.

A few minutes after ten in the morning, the courtroom deputy walked in the room, introduced the judge, and stated, "All rise."

The judge took a seat at his bench and after some quick announcements, the crown attorney kept his word by calling my name first. I walked up and stood beside my lawyer at his assigned desk. My legs felt weak. Butterflies fluttered in my stomach, slowly moving up to my chest, a feeling I had now become used to.

I made myself stand there as Lawyer Six made a brief statement to the judge.

He said, "I've discussed today's proceedings with my client, and she is aware of her rights."

I thought to myself, if I had my rights, I wouldn't be in this courtroom at all. Being a Canadian citizen with Métis status, should I ever have to sign a document that would force me to leave my own country?

Métis People, also known as Natives with mixed blood, emerged in eastern Canada in the early 1600s, alongside the arrival of European explorers, Black Loyalists, and other male migrants. My mother had written a book about the beauty of their unions with Indigenous women, titled Mom Suse in honor of my great-grand-mother. One of the earliest Métis baptisms was for André Lasnier, born in 1620 in Port Latour, Nova Scotia. It's probably why my ancestors were religious. To be sure, no Native tribe in Canada has ever signed a treaty with the US to turn over any of our people. As they have since the arrival of those European explorers, others' laws rule the land.

Then the judge spoke to me directly, "It's the court's under-standing that you are fully aware and willing to waive your rights by agreeing to be extradited to the United States." The judge then directed me to approach the bench.

I walked around the table we were standing at and up to the courtroom clerk's desk. She was right in front of the judge.

The clerk slid a paper in front of me.

For a moment, the courtroom was silent while they waited for me to read the document. I didn't. I just looked at it; barely a perusal. I figured there was no point in reading it. I already knew what I had to do. As a Canadian, I truly thought going through with it was the honorable thing to do. This had nothing to do with anyone here but me.

I reached down, signed it, and just like that, it was over.

I could tell by the way the judge knitted his eyebrows that he felt bad for me. I simply nodded in answer to his question. I didn't have to say out loud that I agreed. Obviously, my signature said it all.

The judge looked down at me and nodded as the clerk passed him the document I had signed. "Take this to the high court building and have them process it immediately. I don't want her in holding for more than an hour." The judge smiled again. At that point, I was positive he felt sorry for me. Just like the crown attorney, the judge didn't want me to be in jail. Not even for an hour.

The other security officer in the courtroom walked over and approached me. He then directed me to turn around. "Please put your hands behind your back." He placed the cuffs around my wrists ever so carefully. I was whisked away, back into custody, and as the judge requested, I was out within the hour. This would give me plenty of time to get to Scarborough, where I still had to go and sign in for the day. I did, though I found out that I didn't have to go there on days when I went to court. It didn't matter. I just thanked God that I was free.

Why did I agree to be extradited?

I did it because my lawyer had explained that regardless of whether I fought the extradition, eventually I would lose. Fighting it would simply prolong the process.

I wanted to do the right thing, but I also wanted to be protected by my own government with waivers when I was required to return to the US. My lawyer advised me that I would be allowed to request them.

Now, although I agreed to be extradited, Lawyer Six assured me the process to be transported takes extensive negotiations between the two countries. Even if the extradition judge had ordered a committal based on my signature, the Minister of Justice would still have to consider whether to order my surrender to the United States.

This gave me an opportunity to submit a series of waivers to the Minister. The waivers are assurances or other concessions that are obtained from the foreign jurisdiction (in my case the US), which protect the rights or interests of the person being sought for extradition. The reason for this is to guarantee my human rights and safety throughout the different steps I would face in the American judicial system.

It's a three-step process. At this point, I had endured two of them.

The first was when I had been arrested on charges in the US to justify their intention to prosecute me. As we already know, I had been arrested one year before, back in June 2009, when I had been coming home from work.

The second step was to appear at my extradition hearing, and to sign the waiver saying I wouldn't fight being brought back to the US.

The third and final step was coming next.

In order to begin this part of the process, I would have to appeal to the Minister of Justice in Canada, who would then decide how and when I was to be transported — if at all. In effect, it could potentially take years.

The Minister of Justice, who is also the Attorney General, is the chief legal adviser and a representative of "Her Majesty the Queen in Right of Ontario," also known as The Queen of England. This is the Queen's actual title in Canada and has been since 1952.

Canada is still part of the Commonwealth of Britain. Subsequently, at the end of the day as a Canadian, it is Elizabeth II who would be responsible for executing my extradition. The same Queen I'd worn a beautiful dress for in grade three, hoping to meet her.

Imagine that. My case literally went right up to the Queen! Or her representative, anyway.

There were 150 days from my court date in January before I had to be back in court. At my next appearance, my lawyer was going to request that the judge give me an opportunity to appeal to the Minister of Justice and begin what I thought would be a slow process of negotiating protection waivers for me.

The following days started getting much colder. Every morning's snow would be solid ice by night. By far, February is the coldest month of the year in Canada. Our winters are beautiful, but harsh.

I could feel that everything in my life was changing, although, I still had to continue my daily routine of working, signing in, and going to court. All while trying to raise my son and keep us out of the spotlight. However, there was almost no way of avoiding that anymore. My case was being tried in a court of law, but also in the court of public opinion.

The office where I worked was on the nineteenth floor of a twenty-story office building, right in the heart of downtown Toronto. Everyone in the building knew of me. As I rode the elevator up to my office floor, my case would routinely show up on the monitor in the lift. Once in a while, I would be approached by strangers from around the office building, usually when I went out for a break.

They'd ask, "Was that you I saw in the news?"

I would smile and nod. I certainly wasn't going to lie. The funny thing was that their query was always followed up by the same question: "How do you know him?" They were referring to Leading Actor, of course. My response was always the same. I had dated one of his friends for years.

I hoped that would help people to understand that I wasn't some random girl who'd gotten into a fight with a celebrity. I had been around him week after week. His mother had even welcomed me and Scion into her home.

There were other people I met outside of work, when I was just out and about, who also recognized me. Usually, it was women who had the most passionate response. Once they found out who I was, instantly they would follow up with, "Oh my goodness, I love him!"

It was always weird for me to hear. Some people have a very odd response when it comes to celebrities. For some mysterious reason, they automatically think they know and love them, simply because they saw them play a character on screen.

That's why I would usually respond with, "Why? He doesn't even know you exist."

With that, they would usually get it. Saying you love someone you don't truly know seems far-fetched, especially when true love is a two-way street. Otherwise, it's just infatuation. More importantly, Leading Actor couldn't care less about them personally. He didn't know them.

While my lawyers worked on my case, I passed what little time I had left with the softball team that I was on with my work friends.

We played every Friday evening at different parks throughout the downtown core: Riverdale, Bell Trinity, Stanley Park, and David Crombie. One of my closest coworkers would organize the schedule so that I still had time to go all the way to Scarborough, sign in, and get back before the game started.

Sometimes, Boss would go so far as to pay fifty dollars for my cab, just to make sure I made it to the game on time.

Riverdale was my favorite park, mainly because of the view. The baseball diamond is located at the bottom of a very steep hill, where from the top of it you can see the entire city of Toronto at sunset.

As for my social life, I obviously couldn't have much of one. My Deacon Brother flew in from California to stay with us, and so he could introduce me to his new love. He was so proud and no longer struggling with his identity. We spent the days touring Toronto.

During the evenings, we went to Church St. That way, I could show them where Canada celebrates our largest Pride Suarez, and all the reasons why the CN Tower lights up like a rainbow.

My conversations with Vraie about our relationship predictions continued on over the years. These days, her main concern was if I'd been on a date. When I told her I wasn't going on one, and then she would ask, "Why not?" I would tell her, it wasn't in the cards just yet, and that I didn't mind being alone. Or, I would say things like, "One day, he'll come along." At the same time, I was well aware that trying to explain what I was going through was never going to be easy. Furthermore, I wouldn't drag my own worst enemy through what may come next. It's hard to predict your own future when it is in someone else's hands, especially when they're the ones with a gavel.

Getting out of the house was one thing, but I also had a curfew, which meant I had to be back in by 10:00 p.m.. Some of my friends would come and spend time with me, since I couldn't go out. Some of them did what they could to get me to go out and have some fun, never once worrying about the risk they were taking being seen with me. It's in trying times when you get to really find out who your friends are.

I thank the Lord that I still have a lot of them.

***

One afternoon, after having invited me countless times, one of my four closest guy friends finally convinced me to go out. All four of those close friends wanted me to go to one of their frequent techno house parties, which I had never been a fan of. As much as I say I love music, I still had a lot to learn about that genre. I suppose you could say that I hadn't caught up with the beats per minute and how to dance to them.

I contemplated whether I should go or not. It made me think of a time, the year before, when two of those guys had gone to a concert with me. Neither of them had had much of a taste for the band at the time, but they'd showed up anyway, giving it a try for my sake.

It turned out, the concert had been so good that it had catapulted our friendship to a whole new level. It had started when the show opened with two perfect rainbows in the sky, fitting because the band's new album had been titled In Rainbows, which was initially released as a pay as you want download for as little as a penny. It was the first time I had ever heard of a band being this generous to their fans. This was on top of all the other charities they are known for giving back to.

It had been a perfect start to the best concert I have ever seen in my life. That's saying something. I've been to more than I can list. Wanting to be the girl in a song named "Rio," by the age of eighteen, I had seen Duran Duran four times. I'd met all six original members of the group INXS, after seeing them alongside The Go-Go's at fourteen. Then there was the time when I had gone with the band New Order to a bar called The Big Bop after their concert at Massey Hall, in 1986. Luckily for me, I had been a cashier at the time for a place called Steve's Music Store, where all the roadies would come before a show. They had always been kind enough to leave a few tickets behind.

The concert last year had been so captivating. They had done two encores before the concert had finally ended. The three of us had run around to every vendor buying memorabilia while knowing the band would always give back.

I hoped that maybe I would experience a bit of that same feeling when we went to Sunnyside later that day.

That Saturday, the weather was perfect. I decided to wear jean shorts and a white tank top. It was springtime now. Winter was behind us. I got myself ready and took a cab to Jarvis and Front to meet up with my friends. We ended up at a friend's bar called The Corner Place. We usually met there because it had a great patio, delicious food, and it was always packed with happy people.

After spending a couple of hours there, we left to check out another party, one over by the Toronto docks. My four favorite guy friends knew exactly how to have a great time and take my mind off of what had been going on. And their plans were working.

For the first time in a long time, I let go and relaxed. Before we headed over to Sunnyside, we decided to stop and climb a tree at Spadina by Adelaide Avenue.

Some of us went all the way to the top, while the rest of us only made it to the middle. I found my footing on a sturdy branch. Once all five of us were settled, we called out to people down below. It reminded me of my friends (the two English brothers), climbing the trees to sing "Someone Save My Life Tonight" and "Goodbye Yellow Brick Road".

It was about 6:00 p.m. when we finally got to Sunnyside. Despite the time, the place was completely packed. Sunnyside is a huge pavilion that faces Lake Ontario, and it's outside in the open. The view of the lake, combined with the warm spring air, made it one of the best places in Toronto for events.

At first when I walked in, the music and people seemed to be going a little too fast for me. They all seemed to be dancing as if they were in their own little worlds. Each person had their own style, not caring what the next person thought. It was unlike any of the parties that I had gone to in LA, where everybody tries to do the same dance, to the same music, always worried about what everyone else might think of them.

Most popular music is relatively slow and easy to dance to. Techno is much faster, going at a minimum of 128 beats per minute. Techno DJs are equipped with soundboards and mixers, crafting their music by using the most fascinating sounds. Their music can completely change your energy. For some, it will take you to another level. For others, to a whole new dimension.

Humankind's affinity for music is undeniable. The Bible has an entire book dedicated to music: the book of Psalms. The word

Psalms comes from Greek psalmos. It means song. Humans have always needed music.

After wrestling the crowd and finding a spot that wasn't full of people, we settled in. From where we were standing, I could hear all the different noises, tempos, and sounds. I began to forget all my problems: signing in every day, curfew, court dates, my friend's suicide, car accidents, and the whole mess in LA.

Like everyone else there, I was in my own little world, free from thinking about all my troubles. I began to feel liberated, watching the dusk turn into night. I looked out over the water as I swayed hypnotically to the music, still not really dancing.

As for my four guy friends, that day I would discover something new about them. They could all dance way better than I could and with the DJ now playing Roy Davis Jr.'s "Gabriel" in the background, it appeared as though everyone was in heaven, dancing while they listened to him play his trumpet.

After hours of the music putting off any thought of my dim future, my first closest guy friend said, "Aretha, it's nine-fifteen. If you want to make it home in time for the po-po, we're going to have to leave now." With those few words, I came back to my crazy reality. The party was one of the best I've ever been to, even if they did have to drag me to it.

***

After that day, it wasn't hard to get me to go out. Up to this point, no one had been outright mean to me regarding the LA incident. Most people kept our conversations short. I still ran the risk of a diehard fan potentially attacking me based on the stories in the media. Soon, I realized that my biggest risk would be in the courtrooms.

I feared the date when I would be back in that eggshell-colored room. Not here, maybe, but perhaps once I was extradited to LA, a place where they worship their celebrities. The days began to fly by, at a pace I couldn't slow.

Soon it was June. The extradition request for my return was going to be signed by the Minister of Justice in Canada. Once that was complete, I would then have the chance to appeal to the minister to begin requesting waivers while continuing to remain free. In order for that to happen, my lawyer would have to go to court, in front of a judge, with both Clark and my boss. Only this time, I wouldn't be there.

The stipulation was that I would be required to turn myself in to the Vanier Correctional Facility on June 21, 2010. Lawyer Six would appear in court to request that a judge put my case over until we could come up with an agreement with the Department of Justice. At the same time, my lawyer would also request that I be released immediately from Vanier and be allowed to remain on bail.

The day I had to turn myself in was a Friday. On the Thursday before, I started to become weirdly uneasy. The idea of the next day's events was starting to catch up with me. Something didn't feel right.

I made the decision to call my lawyer while I was at work. I wanted to ask if he could find me a new judge, so that I could avoid spending the entire weekend incarcerated, waiting to see a judge on the following Monday.

Within an hour, he called me back and told me he'd done just as I'd asked.

Feeling relieved, I left work and decided to walk along Queen Street West, going aimlessly in and out of the shops that lined the road. By this time, spring was in full bloom. As usual, Queen Street in Toronto was busy with the hustle and bustle of many different kinds of people.

These days, there's never a dull moment on Queen Street West. Not like when I was younger, when Yonge Street was the hot spot. Back then, everyone hung around Sam the Record Man, as well as The Toronto Eaton Centre. Between the tourists, retail shoppers, students, and other people strolling around Queen Street, it's probably the busiest street in Toronto, day or night. Not to mention that since 2006, Thursdays have become the new Fridays, when most office workers spill out of their office towers and into all the bars.

I wandered into Mendocino, holding the door open for some young ladies. I wanted to look for an outfit, something new to wear for the night.

After speaking with my lawyer earlier in the day, I'd made plans to meet up that evening for dinner with a friend I've known since I was fifteen. He was always great company and would give me an opportunity to pretend to be happy for a couple of hours.

Even though I had a new judge, and I was only going to be incarcerated for an hour or two, feelings of anxiety had started to set in. I thought to myself, What if something goes wrong, and I have to stay there for the entire weekend? My heart raced. For a moment, I saw myself wearing that orange jumpsuit again.

The vision terrified me.

I had to get out of there. Not out of the store, but away from that thought and the feelings it brought with it. I picked up a pair of jeans lying on the wooden table by the front of the store.

Remember, Aretha, you've got a new judge. There's no way any of that's going to happen, I reassured myself.

I took a deep breath and looked at the size of the jeans that were on the tag. Then the price, and reflected back to when I was younger, shopping at the Eaton Centre. At that time, Levi's had been only thirty dollars. These in my hand were three hundred. What made them so special, I wondered?

I put the pants back down and browsed around the boutique. After looking at a few mini dresses, and trying on a blue blouse, I finally left the store. But not without the jeans. Three hundred dollars, to avoid the feeling of wearing that orange suit, felt like a deal.

The restaurant my friend chose was on Queen Street West and Ossington Avenue. It had just recently opened, and my friend said it was highly recommended.

From the moment we walked in, the ambiance in the room

was warm and inviting. The maître d' gave us the most exceptional service. It turned out, I knew him. Throughout the evening, my friend introduced me to different types of truffles, while he drank expensive shots of vodka. As we talked, he kept reassuring me that no matter what, I would be back at home in no time.

Later that night, I went to my older sister's place in East York. I thought it would be the best place to spend the night, considering the next day's events. I also needed to be surrounded by my loved ones. Even though I kept trying to convince myself I didn't have anything to worry about, I couldn't shake the sinking feeling in my stomach.

Scion was at my sister's house, along with a few other family members, including my mother's ex-husband, who was visiting from Lillooet, British Columbia. I'd only spoken to him a few times in my life.

Although I share his last name, he isn't my actual father, but the father of my last three older siblings. My mother married and divorced him prior to my birth. I do have to say, he treated me like a daughter, much like my mom's German boyfriend, who had raised us for eight years.

When I was younger, most of our weekends were spent going to McDonald's and places like Edwards Gardens, a botanical park in Toronto, usually filled with families picnicking. It's where I got to play with my yo-yo, while my older siblings enjoyed the flowers.

No matter where we went, both men had acted like all of us kids were theirs. My mother's ex-husband had been thrilled when my mother gave me his last name because my mother wanted all her kids to have the same name.

When I walked into the house, he was the first person to greet me, embracing me as if I was his own. He said, "Don't worry kiddo, I promise you'll be okay."

I slept at my sister's house that night. I had to be up extra early, so she could drive me to Vanier. I was so glad that I had the opportunity to be with my family.

God knows I didn't want to be alone.

When I woke up Friday morning, the pangs of anxiety began to set in immediately. I couldn't help it. For a minute, I imagined that the truffles had been my last supper, and now it was off with my head!

I was on the phone with Boss at eight-thirty in the morning. The first thing he asked was, "Are you ready for today?"

"Ready as ever, I guess," I responded.

"Good," he said, "Because we need you to play third base tonight."

At the same time, I was being reassured by my boss, I was also trying to comfort myself. Not being able to be in the courtroom while someone else was deciding my fate made me question everything. The worst thing about not being in the courtroom was that I couldn't picture myself leaving it. That also made the picture of leaving Vanier unclear.

I hung up the phone and went to the kitchen so I could make breakfast for my son. His dad was on his way to pick him up to bring him to court. This way, the judge could see the most important reason why he should send me right back home. I didn't eat anything, but I was already on my third cup of coffee when my sister came down the stairs.

Before we left, I took off the chain that was around my neck to give to my son. It was a 14-karat-gold link chain, which I'd worn for years. On the chain are two specific charms: a Star of David, and a Christian cross for my mother's religion.

Even though we went to different churches, I always made each experience fun and exciting for him, breaking down the minister's sermon and putting spins on them, making sure Scion knew that God was great enough to also have humor.

Getting my son to go to church was always easy. Handing him this chain today definitely wasn't. As I passed it to him, I could feel my tears beginning to well up. To keep him from seeing me cry, I put my head down and began to sort through my purse. I gave him the money in my wallet, and I pulled out my driver's license and birth certificate. I would need something to prove my identity when I turned myself in.

"Don't worry, Buddy," I told him, "I'll see you back here in a bit." I gave my son a hug and kissed him on the cheek. I went into the spare room to say goodbye to my mother's ex-husband, and informed him, "I'm going now. I guess I'll see you when I get back home." He smiled and said, "Whatever happens, I'll be there for you." I hugged him, then I walked out the front door behind my older sister.

Once we got outside, she gave me the keys and asked me to drive. Everyone else decided they would go to court and represent me there.

As I drove, I thought about how much I despised traffic, and how I'd really started to dislike it when I'd lived in California. While I'd lived there, most of the highways had been continuously jam-packed, almost twenty-four hours a day. Every freeway from the 101 to the 405, over to the 110 and the I-5 that somehow connects them all, was constantly bumper-to-bumper. Everyone on them always seemed to be in a mad rush.

It made me think of the movie Falling Down, with Michael Douglas. His downward spiral begins by being stuck in traffic, on one of the four freeways I just mentioned.

I would later find out that that segment of the 401 passing through Toronto is not only the busiest highway in North America, but also one of the widest and busiest in the world. On some days, the number of vehicles using it exceeds half a million. I was about to spend the next two hours on that very highway, driving myself to jail.

The ride was quiet. I hadn't even turned on the radio. To break the silence, my older sister said, "Don't worry, Aretha. You're going to be out of there before you know it. As a matter of fact, instead of driving myself back, I'm going to wait outside until you're released."

She'd said exactly what I needed to hear.

I should have remembered that whenever I make those life-altering decisions on Thursdays, they usually don't work out.

Would this one?

Or would I be dragged away from everyone I held dear, forced to face a harsh trial in a foreign land?

In a few hours I would know.

But I wasn't sure I wanted to find out.

Chapter Nine

BODYSNATCHERS

IT WAS AROUND 11:00 a.m. when we arrived at the Vanier Women's Correctional Facility in Milton, Ontario and I handed my older sister the keys to her car. The place where I was going to be incarcerated for the second time. It had taken me about an hour and forty-five minutes to get there. According to Lawyer Seven, I would be there less than the time it had taken me to get there.

The female inmate population had just over 300 beds. The men's side, Maplehurst Correctional Complex, was set up to house 1500. Altogether, the so-called 'superjail' is the same size as one hundred football fields.

For a moment, we sat there, staring at the concrete building and the gate I was about to walk through, which was topped by barbed wire. The facility inside was hidden away from view. The grounds are expansive and connected to the men's correctional center. It also has a separate wing for minors, kids twelve to seventeen years of age. Locally, they call it the "Milton Hilton" or "Muppethurst."

The cute names don't fit the building. It's anything but cute.

Getting out of the car was difficult. The weather was beautiful, and the last thing I wanted to do was spend a minute of that day inside the darkness of a jail. Even though my lawyer had told me it wouldn't be long, I was still not looking forward to it. I told my older sister to go back home, and that I would call when I was ready.

"It's okay, Aretha," she said. "I'm going to wait."

There was nothing left to do except get out of the car and approach the gate. I turned around and looked back at my older sister. I waved goodbye, giving myself one last look at someone who cared about me.

I reached up and pressed the buzzer by the door. A woman answered, asking how she could help me.

"My name is Aretha Wilson. I'm here to turn myself in today."

I received no response, except the loud buzzing that announced the gate was opening. Without looking, I went through the gate and stood in front of the big metal door. Once the gate had closed, the secondary metal door popped open to admit me.

As I walked in, it felt like a cold dungeon. I noticed the dingy, off-white cinder blocks. Ten metal doors stretched away from me down the hall. The cells looked more like cages and were mainly situated on the left. On the other side was one small metal desk. Two female guards were there to meet me.

"For now," one of them said to me, "we're going to hold off on your intake, since your lawyers are in court for you at the moment. We're just going to place you in the holding cell. You can keep your street clothes on."

Hearing that surprised me. I didn't think the guards would be sympathetic to anyone's situation, particularly not mine. God knows, I didn't want to put on that orange suit, and it was a good sign that the guard thought I would be leaving just as easily as I had walked in.

After the guard closed the metal door behind me, it felt so cold in the cell. I knew it was sunny outside. But inside the concrete cage, it felt twenty degrees colder. And damp.

I looked around the small room, trying to avoid reading what was scratched on the walls. I didn't want to read about the other women who had been there before me, and how they'd wanted to be freed. Aside from the endless cinder blocks, there were only a few other things to look at. A pay phone that only made collect calls. A metal toilet bowl, sitting low to the floor, which added to the foul smell in the room. Plus, the bench I was sitting on.

I closed my eyes and pulled my legs toward my chest. Then I wrapped my arms around them to keep warm and buried my head in my knees. The idea of a two-hour nap seemed like a good one. That way, I could fall asleep and wake up to them telling me it was time to go home.

But it wasn't going to be that easy.

Even though I felt like I had been up for the last forty-eight hours, I couldn't get to sleep. Not here.

I stood up and began to pace in the cell. From one end to the other, I counted fifteen steps. In my mind, I was trying to imagine how long the court proceedings would take if they started right on time (10:00 a.m.). I had no way of knowing.

I started thinking back to the advice my older sister had given me after the car accident when it had come time to appear in front of the Ontario Supreme Court and hear the judgment on my case against the cab company. My lawyer had said he would show up on my behalf, so I hadn't needed to be there.

My sister hadn't agreed. She'd said that if I didn't show up to my own court case, then I would be considered just a piece of paper. Without them seeing the scar on my face, no judge would take me seriously.

She had been right. Once the three judges got a good look at me, my lawyer wasn't even asked to speak. I was immediately awarded the money without my lawyer saying a word.

Since that experience, I've realized if someone is going to take the time to judge you, it should be done face-to-face. The same way everyone should have the right to face their accuser. The fact that I couldn't be there in court was starting to make me feel anxious again. I had to take my mind somewhere else.

I got up and walked over to the window. Lo and behold, I found that if I pressed my face to the glass, I could see outside. Beyond the barbed wire fencing, I could see a baseball diamond. Behind that was a highway, and there were a few houses off in the distance.

People on the baseball field were playing in a fastball league. Unlike the open league we played in at work (where we wore our street clothes), these teams had jerseys and coordinated uniforms. With my face pressed against the glass, I began thinking to myself about the game my coworkers and I were supposed to play later that day, under the beautiful sun.

I continued watching them, keeping score in my head. One of the players hit a long pop fly, and when the outfielder caught the ball, I noticed a small, sturdy tree. It was way off to the left side of the field and had been planted by itself, with no other trees in sight.

It reminded me of the peach trees we'd had in the backyard when I was a little girl. Two of them were planted in the garden by the fence, alongside a ton of rhubarb. I was about six years old when my mother gave me my first chore: picking the peaches and taking care of those trees. My mother would preserve the peaches, ultimately turning them into jam and peach pies.

Between the peaches that fell off the branches, and the ones I picked up off the ground to bring into the house, there must have been hundreds of peaches every year. I didn't mind when I found a caterpillar nest that had been spun between the branches, though my mother likely did. Over that summer, I ended up bringing more caterpillars into the house than I'd ever brought in peaches.

I would use mason jars to house the colorful wooly worms, poking little air holes though the metal lids so I could watch them grow and develop until they were wrapped up in their cocoons. Over the season, I would collect countless caterpillars. I waited for them to turn into butterflies, or sometimes moths, which had just as much right to be on Earth as their prettier counterparts. They're just as beautiful as butterflies, in their own way.

A guard calling my name brought my attention back to the present. I was hoping it was time to be released, but instead, she suggested I should call my lawyer. They hadn't heard anything yet.

It was the same guard who'd originally greeted me, speaking to me through the small hole in the window of the metal door. It occurred to me that I had been watching the baseball game and reminiscing over the tree for an hour or so. It was well after noon now.

Maybe the court was in recess, I thought. Maybe there was a delay. I turned and walked to the pay phone. I was starting to get that feeling you get when you know something bad is about to happen. My mind started to race. My heart started to pound so hard, it felt like it was trying to beat its way out of my chest.

I dialed Lawyer Seven's number. As it rang, I wondered if the secretary would accept my collect call, or if she was even aware of my current situation. The last thing I wanted to hear was my call getting rejected.

My call was accepted, and the secretary told me my lawyers had just come back to the office. I have to say that hearing that was a bit of a shock. I thought if they were back from court, they would already be making arrangements to get me out of Vanier.

What was going on?

Waiting on hold seemed to take forever. As I waited, I could hear myself breathing. When Lawyer Seven answered, I could tell he had me on speaker phone. For the first time, I heard his voice crack as he spoke to me. "Aretha, I don't know how to tell you this. Things didn't go the way we thought they would today."

I fell silent. I couldn't believe what I was hearing. I didn't know what to say. Was I going to have to spend the entire weekend in this dungeon?

God, please help me.

After a moment I said, "What happened? Am I stuck here till Monday?"

Another long moment of silence, followed by a long sigh, he said, "No, Aretha, you're not leaving at all." Another long sigh. "The judge we got today rejected our request to appeal to the attorney general, and since you've already signed to be extradited, the judge said you might as well go back."

Again, complete silence.

I was pressing the receiver so tightly against my face that, for the first time in years, I could feel my scar hurting. All I could think to say was, "I don't understand what you're saying."

He sighed again. "Aretha, you asked me to switch judges, and because of that, this is who we ended up with. You're going to have to stay there until the US comes to get you. They have forty-five days to do it, but I would say they should be here within the next two weeks."

Finally, it sank in for me. "So, I'm not leaving at all?"

"No, Aretha, you're not."

***

By trying to avoid staying in jail for the weekend, I had gotten myself incarcerated indefinitely. The injustice of my situation cut me to the core.

What could have been a couple hours was now going to be who-knew-how-long, and all because I had decided to switch judges to avoid the inevitable. Once again, I had made a terrible decision on a Thursday.

Lawyer Seven was still talking, but everything he said was muddy and unclear. Even though I was still holding the phone's receiver tightly to my face, my focus had already begun shifting. I would have to mentally and physically prepare myself for a lengthy incarceration, where I would be stripped of my freedom, my time, my son, my pride…my entire life.

As he was rambling, I heard him say something about calling him on Monday morning, which made me realize I had to call my mother right away.

I interrupted him while he was talking. "I'm going to try and call my mother now. I need to figure out what's going to happen with my son."

Then Lawyer Six said, "Aretha, your friends and family who were in court today didn't take the ruling very well, and yes, I would advise you to get a hold of them as soon as possible."

A sudden vision of Scion flashed in my mind. I saw him standing there in court while the judge ordered my indefinite incarceration. I could imagine the look of devastation on his face. I thought about what this would do to him. How he must be thinking the world was so unfair.

Then I remembered it was my job to make sure he didn't think the world was an unfair place.

I stood there for a moment still holding the receiver, only now I was pressing it into the middle of my chest. After a few moments of just staring at the ceiling, I hung up the phone and went over to the front of the holding cell.

I called out to the female guards and told them what I just heard. I would be staying there. The two ladies that had been there all morning looked up at me from the metal desk, and then prepared to process me. I turned away from the door and walked back to the cell window, so I could look out at the world one last time. The baseball game was over, and all the players were gone.

I couldn't help but feel just like that tree standing out there.

Silent. Still. Completely alone.

***

The intake process and going through receiving is degrading.

The moments went by very slowly, and I sat listening to my heartbeat. Finally, I heard the cell door pop open. When I looked up, there were two different guards walking through the door toward me. One of them had a set of cuffs in her hand. She instructed me to turn around, so that she could place them around my wrists. I was led out of the cell and down the cold hallway with a guard on each side, each holding one of my arms. They took me to an area that was closed off, but visible to anyone who walked by. Once the handcuffs were removed, I was asked to strip off all my clothes to my bare skin. Then I was told to bend over, as they both watched every movement I made.

I was assigned to a unit for women whose charges were violent. On one side was the holding area, for those with serious charges or mental issues. On the other side was the segregation ward, where they keep the women who have behavioral problems. As I was being escorted by the guards, all I could hear was the women wailing and screaming throughout the other dorms.

The one I was brought into had two floors that contained twenty individual cells: ten on each level and one large common area. There was also a metal staircase that led to the second level. The entire unit was open to the view of whichever guard was on duty.

I was assigned to a cell that was at the back of the unit, right across from the shower area. This, of course, was also very open and visible for everyone to see. Once I was released to the guard on duty, she immediately led me to my new home. We walked down the corridor until we got to mine. She opened it up, and I stood there for a moment, looking in.

It was just as cold as the cell where I'd spent most of the day, but it felt a lot smaller. A narrow cot huddled on the right side of the cell, without enough space for another one. Luckily for me, I was being put in a cell by myself. Usually, the jails are overcrowded. Sometimes, two or three women would be assigned to one cell, and it's obvious these cells had never been designed for that. It makes you wonder how much experiences like that contribute to inmates becoming repeat offenders.

I didn't feel like I belonged here.

I wanted out.

Then the guard informed me, "Right now, we're on a lockdown.

I nodded, turned, and walked inside. The guard slammed and locked the metal door before she left. This time, it only took me about nine paces to get to the other side, where again there was one window. I couldn't see out of this one. As a matter of fact, I couldn't even tell if it was day or night.

The moments went by painfully slow. This time, there was no hope of bail. I would have to sit and wait to be turned over to the Americans, with no specific date for when that would happen. For up to the next forty-five days, this was where I would live.

***

After a day of lockdown, I was finally let out of the cell for the first time. I walked out of my cell and into the common area, where our breakfast was now being served. All types of different women, from all walks of life, were strolling aimlessly out of their cells into the area.

I'd spent a couple days here a year ago, and back then we'd also been on lockdown. Before anyone could really see me, though, I had been released on bail. This time would be different. As I started to make my way toward the front of the room, most of the ladies turned to look at me. It was like they could sense my grief at the knowledge that I wasn't leaving. As the new girl, I was ready for questions to come my way.

What I was experiencing was worse than facing one tough judge. In this dorm, there were thirty people judging me, all of them staring me down.

I guess the good thing was, the lady convicted of killing her boyfriend with the blunt side of an ax wasn't there. Not that it really mattered anymore. She had her own problems, so I was certain she wasn't thinking about me. However, the ladies I was looking at now didn't look any softer than she had.

In the front of the room, at the entrance, the women had formed two lines, facing the large thick glass partition that separated us from the other dorms. One of the lines was for retrieving your breakfast, which they served on large metal trays. On each tray was a small portion of fluorescent yellow scrambled eggs, a piece of steamed, rubbery meat that was supposed to be ham, a piece of bread, and one bruised apple. If it looked like that, I couldn't imagine what it was going to taste like. If there was five hundred dollars paid for me to stay here on a daily basis, judging by the food and accommodations, 95% of that money was going somewhere else.

The other line was much longer. I soon came to learn it was for retrieving much-needed prescribed medication. There was no missing that line. The administrator spent about a minute with each inmate getting a pill. It was her job to make sure that every pill was swallowed and taken by the right inmate. Pills are a hot commodity in prison, and like plenty of people on the outside, inmates depend on them for both a mental and pain-free escape.

I hadn't been prescribed anything myself, so I went straight to the line for breakfast.

"Nothing is being served for you here," the guard said to me as I stood there, not knowing what to do next. "Get a tray; I'm not touching it!"

I grabbed a tray, served myself, and turned to sit at one of the metal tables that were bolted into the concrete floor. I wanted to sit at a table that was empty, since they were quickly filling up. It didn't matter, though. As soon as I sat down, I was joined by three other inmates looking for a seat.

One of the ladies sitting down with me was white, and although she wore a hijab, I could see her blonde hair. "What's your name?" she asked me politely.

I thought to myself, something seems different about her. My immediate first impression was that she was a little unsure of herself. She might be a Muslim, but I could tell it was new to her.

I told her my name, and she asked me how I had ended up here. All the ladies were looking at me. They wanted to listen in.

With no reason not to tell the truth, I said, "I'm being extradited to the US for assault with a deadly weapon."

"Did you say you were getting extradited for an assault with a weapon?" Blondie asked me.

"Well, my case involves a celebrity."

"Which one?"

I told them the name of Leading Actor. The ladies looked at each other and chuckled. Then Blondie reiterated, "I meant which weapon."

I laughed at myself. "Believe it or not, it was a wine glass."

Blondie said, "Must have been one heck of a party!"

Then the guard screamed out at the top of her lungs, "You can turn on the monitor now." The guard was referring to the one 24-inch television that was in the room. No way was she touching anything in here.

One of the other ladies sitting at the table asked me, "You're really pretty. Who cut your face up?"

I certainly wasn't expecting that to be the next question. "I was in a car accident many years ago," I told them, "but I'm over it." I leaned in a little toward her, pulling my nose over to the side and exposing the scar that was hidden in the crevice of my nose. Then I pulled the lid of my left eye down, so she could see the scar there. The main one on my face is clear enough for anyone to see, and I was certain that was what prompted her to ask me in the first place.

Then one of the other ladies said something that I thought was weird. "You should be careful. Other women inside might not see it that way."

I wasn't really sure what she was referring to, but it was obvious she thought for some reason that I had something to worry about. It didn't seem like she was concerned about my charges, or the celebrity involved. Those questions I'd expected. It was like she was more concerned with the scar on my face. I had no idea why.

By that point, I figured she had asked enough questions, and it was my turn to ask her one. "How long have you been here?"

"I'm here on an immigration hold," she told me, as if to say that she had been there the longest. The Canadian government wanted her deported after a number of convictions, and they were revoking her citizenship. She had decided that she wanted to fight it. Vanier is a minimum detention center. If you receive a sentence that is no more than two years, less one day, this is where you're sent. Anything more than that, and you go to prison. Hold had been here for almost four years, despite receiving no sentence whatsoever. Her case was in judicial limbo and, therefore, she simply sat in holding at Vanier.

As she was explaining her situation, I was looking around the room at the concrete walls, which seemed to blend right into the floors: bleak and harsh. I was thinking that I couldn't imagine being here for four years.

I couldn't understand why Hold didn't just go back to her country. At least then she would be free. As it turned out, she had been in this country most of her life. After thirty years of only knowing Canada, under no circumstances did she want to go back to Trinidad, where she had been taken from when she was a baby. She also had children now, who had been born in Canada. She wasn't going to leave them without a fight.

A guard screamed out again, "Trays up and get ready for lockdown." I looked down at the barely-eaten food on my tray in front of me, wondering what to do with it. It had only been about fifteen minutes since we'd first sat down.

Blondie told me, "The trays have to be returned back to the stand over there now, so they can count them. Then you go back to your cell, so they can count you too."

Hold told me not to worry. "Tuesday is on its way, which means it's canteen. If you have money in your account, you can order all the candy you like."

I smiled at her, thinking about how strange it was that there was candy in a place like this. I walked over to the stand and put the tray in one of the empty slots. The three of us walked in different directions toward our individual cells.

"Aretha?" Hold said to me. "If we make it out of our rooms again today, I'll see you out here later." I smiled again and walked into my cell. The thought of hanging out with the woman who'd been here the longest gave me some comfort.

Usually in jail, women will completely avoid you if they feel threatened, or if they think you're the target of another inmate. Hold wasn't a friend, but at least she was someone to talk to. I was still puzzled about why she'd made that odd statement about my scar, though.

Once I was in the room, the thunderous slamming of the metal door behind me made me jump, and it was unmistakably locked.

***

Sitting in a cell and not knowing the time, or whether it's even day or night, leaves you with countless moments with nothing to do but think. It's hard. I tried to wrap myself in the thin wool blanket from my cot. It made my skin itch, but I endured it, trying to keep warm.

I couldn't understand how I'd ended up here. Why did I deserve this? I knew deep down inside that Last and Leading Actor both knew I didn't deserve it either. I also knew they weren't going to do anything to help me.

It was the first time I had ever been completely imprisoned. All I kept worrying about was whether or not the US would really come to get me. What would happen once they did? How would this play out? I just couldn't picture myself on a plane, going back to Los Angeles this way, with cuffs around my wrists, linking to other cuffs that secured my feet, like some kind of wild animal.

It seemed so unreal that this could happen to me.

I tried to link all the moments that had led up to this one, reminding myself once again that I was locked in a cell. Then I began to envision myself in court, with Leading Actor testifying against me. I wondered what he would say to get out of this. After five years, and several different stories, I knew he had no intention of getting up on a stand and telling the truth. This meant he would have to lie — again.

I didn't think he could bring himself to do it. After all, it was his idea to never speak to the media, obviously with the hope that the truth would go away. On the other hand, if I went to trial, I would get to testify on my own behalf, and the whole world would get to hear what really happened. I believed a witness stand could provide me with a better platform than the media could give.

Knowing the real truth was a comfort that had allowed me to go through the years of not speaking to the media. More importantly, I knew myself and Leading Actor were the only ones who really knew what had happened. I kept that fact in my pocket. It made me feel better, knowing I would get the opportunity to set the record straight when my case went to trial.

I must have fallen asleep, because I woke up to the loud clanking of the door being opened mechanically. Once again, lockdown was over. Even so, I didn't know if it was day or night.

A small sink in my room ran cold water from its old, chipped tap. A metal toilet was attached to the wall, positioned about two feet off the floor. It was certainly not made for any sort of comfort. The cot rested on a slab of concrete that merged into the cement walls which, in turn, blended into the floor. Everything was the same drab color of confinement. Bricks that looked as though they were purposely painted in teardrop gray.

I'd never felt so alone.

The mirror was the worst of it. Made of some sort of bendable metal, the waves in it distorted your image. It made you feel like you weren't real, with no chance to really face yourself. They couldn't allow us to have glass, for fear we would hurt ourselves, or someone else.

I walked over to the sink and began splashing cold water on my face, as I desperately tried to find my own image in the metal mirage. I cupped the water in my hands, ran it through my hair, and pulled my hair back into a ponytail.

I looked over toward the door and noticed one of the guards must have slid a towel and new linen through the mail slot while I'd been sleeping. I grabbed the towel to dry my face and placed it on the metal shelving bolted into the cement wall. I picked up the sheet and proceeded to make the bed, discarding the old one that had been on the cot for the last couple days. I kept the thin itchy blanket. That small comfort was the only kind I was going to get.

***

When they released me from my cell, I walked out into the common room. This time, the television was already on, but the noise of the women drowned out the sound. Most of the ladies had already come out of their cells and assembled in their respective groups. No one stood alone.

I looked around and spotted a small bookshelf that was hidden underneath the metal staircase that led up to the second level. As I walked toward it, I tried not to make eye contact with any of the women. One false look, and there was absolutely no doubt I would have trouble.

"Hey, Aretha!"

I looked around. It was Blondie calling me. I smiled at her, and she smiled back.

She was already sitting at one of the tables with Hold, as well as two of the others who'd been with us the previous day. I went to the bookshelf, where the books were loosely thrown. There weren't very many choices, probably just forty books in total and mostly paperbacks. I spotted a few mysteries, some self-help, a ton of horror books, and some suspense novels.

I thought about some of the authors I'd liked when I was younger, before I'd gotten caught up reading all those frivolous gossip magazines. Back then, I'd taken a liking to VC Andrews. I think it had had a lot to do with the fact that all of her main characters began with some kind of catastrophic life event, which was never of their own doing. In her books, the characters survived and ended up happy. Her stories always left me believing happiness was possible.

I saw no VC Andrews on this shelf. In fact, there was nothing that would leave you feeling happily-ever-after about anything. I did spot the Bible, though, and immediately picked it up. I thought to myself that this was a book with a ton of stories in it.

Then I thought about when I had gone to church. Someone else was always reading the Bible, putting their own spin on the stories. Except for a few chapters here and there, it was something I had only read a few times.

I grabbed it, turned, and started to walk toward the table where Blondie and Hold were sitting. As I walked by, I smiled at the other ladies and made eye contact. The ones who were looking my way smiled back. They were all obviously keeping a close eye on me, but it seemed as though I was being accepted. Perhaps, it was because Blondie had called me to her table and invited me to sit with her. Or maybe it was because of the book I had chosen.

It looked like I had made a few friends, which included the two most important ladies in the place—Blondie and Hold. The three of us ate all of our meals together, with no one really paying attention to the television. In the following days, I got to know a lot of the other women as well.

No music was ever heard in Vanier. Not so much as a whistle. It was as if the guards knew it would be a type of escape for everyone. There was no way they were going to allow that sort of luxury.

My only real comfort came in the form of the three phones, which we could use to call the outside world, although, only two of them ever worked. It was my only connection to my son, who I called every single day. We made plans for him to come and see me every weekend, which he always did.

I also made it a point to contact my lawyer, my mother, and my boss, as much as I possibly could, constantly making collect calls, so they would know I was still waiting to be retrieved by the United States government.

It seemed no one knew exactly when that would happen.

***

The days rolled by, and I awaited my fate. Each day was harder than the last. But I did have some hope.

Lawyer Six had made arrangements with lawyers in California so that upon my arrival, I would have representation at my initial bail hearing. He even took it upon himself to send $5,000 as a retainer on my behalf so that the lawyers were paid and prepared.

The new lawyers contacted the prosecutor who was directly responsible for my case in LA, and the person appointed by the district attorney to retrieve me. She informed them she was requesting a bail of $60,000 for my release, providing I had someone who was willing to post it. It was a huge sum, but compared to being in jail, it felt like pennies.

In order to secure my release in LA, I had made arrangements with Vraie. She said she would be more than happy to post my bail, and she would allow me to stay at her house. She even offered the keys to her Escalade, once I was freed. Vraie said she would do whatever it took to make sure that I was taken care of.

As for the company I worked for, they also had offices in LA. They were more than willing to make the arrangements so I would be able to work from the office in California and maintain my position as senior account executive.

Everything that was being planned gave me some hope. I started to believe that out of the dark cloud of extradition, there might be a silver lining for me in California.

However, it wouldn't all be sunshine. If I was released, I would have to hide from the media, as well as all the other people in Los Angeles that might give me a hard time. Nevertheless, I would have the opportunity to fight my case, while trying to lead a somewhat normal life.

Most importantly, I would be free enough to know whether it was day or night again.

***

My daily routine became fixed at Vanier. The guards would do their morning count at 5:30 each morning. Once I was up, I would begin exercising with stretches and cardio, followed by jogging in place and knee push-ups. I wanted to stay active. I could see that a lot of the women gained weight by taking advantage of the canteen. Almost like they were trying to eat their troubles away.

After exercising, I would have enough time to read before we were released from our cells into the dorm. It was always the same book, even though I had selected a few others off the bookshelf.

For some reason, the Bible was the book that set me at ease. I didn't start from the beginning. I would just open it to whatever page it landed on and begin reading.

The Bible told me, "If thy right eye offend thee, pluck it out, and cast it from thee." For me, that meant that if I read something that bothered me, then I should skip over it. I would find what applied to me and leave the rest of it for someone else. That way, I could come up with a better ending to my own story.

After a while (reading the Good Book and underlining the passages that I thought fit into my life), I started to remember that there was so much more to my life than jail, or what had happened between Leading Actor and myself.

The days turned into weeks. The only information I had was that the US had exactly forty-five days to retrieve me. My lawyer called it habeas corpus, meaning unlawful detention. After all, I wasn't wanted by Canada, but by the State of California.

Therefore, I could only be held in Vanier for forty-five days before the Canadian government would order me to be released. They would not be able to get another extradition warrant for me without cause, and the only way they would be able to arrest me in the future, was if I decided to wander across the border one day. All I had to do was sit and wait, hoping that no one would come knocking on my metal door.

I began to dream of freedom. Not just in sunny California, but right here in Canada, during the summertime when the days are just as hot.

I was imagining strolling out of the darkness after six weeks. Out into the sunlight, where I could actually feel the warmth on my skin. It became my nightly bedtime story to myself, told as a prayer.

The first thing I always envisioned was me getting off the cot and walking right out the front door to find Scion, my dog daughter, and my family waiting. I would see their smiling faces and tears of joy, when I was finally released.

I swore to myself that the moment I got out of there, I was going to squeeze the hell out of my son. I would promise him nothing like this would ever happen again.

The forty-fifth day of my incarceration would be landing on a Sunday. The Thursday before, I began to dream of being free, thinking I only had one more day to wait. I believed no one would come to retrieve me on a weekend.

Monday morning, my lawyer was going to file the motion to have me released. I thought I would have no problem waiting for a judge on Monday this time. Besides, I would happily stay here for the weekend, if it meant I wouldn't be going to another jail in California.

Thursday morning, I was pacing the small space allotted to me in my cell, and as I did, I prayed. I hoped God would hear my call to change the path the district attorney in California had set out for me. I wondered how it benefited him, costing the United States all that money to come and get me.

Once the cell door opened, I walked out and made my way to the front of the dorm. I got my breakfast tray, sat down, and began to eat with gusto. I had a good appetite that day.

Hold was already sitting at our group's table when I sat down. "Just one more day," she encouraged me, "and you'll be home free. I'll be honest, Aretha. I thought they were going to come and get you."

"Me too," I admitted.

After I ate, I decided I would go for a walk. I wanted to be by myself. Or, as much as anyone could be by themselves in this place. As I walked up toward the front of the dorm to return my tray, I gazed over to the guard on duty. I wondered if she knew anything about what was happening with me, or if she knew my last day could be on Monday.

As I paced around the dorm, I prayed to God. I daydreamed about being released. No more traveling all the way to Scarborough to report. No more endless court dates. No more paying lawyer after lawyer. My hard-earned money would stay mine. No more media. No more jail or being incarcerated. All of it was about to be over. Just a little bit longer, and this whole nightmare would be nothing but a terrible memory.

"Get ready for lockdown," one of the guards yelled.

That was a surprise. It had been weeks since we had been ordered to lockdown. It looked like I would be spending the weekend the same way I had come in. But this time, I didn't mind staying in the cell at all. Come Monday, I would be free.

Once again the door made that deafening noise, and I watched as it mechanically closed behind me once I was in my cell. I stood there looking at my cot and figured I should try to get some sleep. When I woke up, this would all be done. I lay down, resting my forearm across my forehead, and stared up at the ceiling. I fell asleep dreaming about waking up in my own bed.

***

But it wasn't to be.

This time, they actually knocked on my cell, although it sounded more like a baton hitting the metal door. I soon came to realize that some lockdowns we all experienced at Vanier were designed specifically for me.

My heart stopped, and my eyes opened. As I was putting my feet on the floor to get up, the guard opened the door and said, "Roll it up. They're here, and Leading Actor's waiting."

She actually said his name, and then chuckled, hoping to get a laugh from the other guard. Forget the fact that I was being taken out of my own country and away from my son. Forget that I was the one who had been hit by a man because he hadn't liked what I'd said. Forget that this would never have happened if Leading Actor wasn't who he was.

This woman had made a joke.

The other guard didn't laugh.

Maybe this was the reverse of what lottery winners feel. Instead of gaining a windfall, I was about to have everything taken from me.

"You've got exactly three minutes," the guard warned. She turned away, leaving the door partly open.

I could hear her standing right outside, still trying to make conversation while the other guard ignored her. I rushed around trying to put together the few things I had in my room, not knowing what I could take. The term "roll it up" in jail is the guard's way of saying you're leaving and to pack up your cell. Usually, it meant you were going home. That either your time was up or you had made bail. I'd witnessed it a few times with some of the ladies who'd gone home over the forty-three days I had been there.

But that wasn't happening to me that day. I wasn't going home. All of my hopes and prayers had gone unanswered. I was going to be forced out of my own country.

I was devastated.

One of my favorite passages in the Bible that I underlined when I'd first arrived was Jeremiah 29:11-12: "'For I know the plans I have for you,' declares the Lord, 'plans to prosper you and not to harm you, plans to give you hope and a future.'"

As I walked out of the cell, I told myself that although the district attorney had set out this path for me, somehow it was still part of God's plan.

I had to have faith that it was turning out the way it ought to.

I had to have faith that it would be all right in the end.

I had to have faith.

Chapter Ten

MY IRON LUNG

THE GUARDS LED me away from my cell. I couldn't believe it. The thing I had feared most was happening.

I was being extradited.

Aside from the three of us, no one else was out of their cells. It was deathly quiet. Lockdown was still in effect, so none of the women I had been incarcerated with could be there to see me being whisked away.

I took absolutely everything I'd had in my room, wrapped up in a pillowcase. I didn't know what was coming next, or if I would ever see my things again.

"Where is she going with that?" the second guard asked the one leading me away. She was referring to the pillowcase of personal items I was holding, talking about me as if I wasn't even there. "She has to leave that stuff here. She's not taking anything with her."

Dismayed, I asked, "Can I at least leave it for someone else?"

I gave her Hold's name, wanting someone to get some use out

of what I had gathered during my time here. The guard begrudgingly told me I could drop it by her cell door.

It was just as I'd thought. This was the opposite of winning a lottery, and I was going to lose absolutely everything.

Only hours away from freedom, and I'd had it pulled out from under me by a system designed to give all the power to the court. Instead of waking up in a cell for the last time as I had envisioned, and walking out into the sunlight, I found myself on my way to Pearson International Airport in handcuffs.

There was absolutely nothing I could do. I was going to have to face my fate. My life was completely in the hands of the American justice system.

As I expected, I was taunted by the guards who escorted me back to the receiving area of the women's prison. Most of them were mean, and they seemed to get enjoyment out of my situation.

Goodness knows, I would never once consider treating someone that way. I did my best to ignore them. I was too busy looking at the entrance to the visiting area as we walked by the door. I wanted to visualize the last moment I'd had in there with my son because now I had no idea when I would see him again.

Once I was inside the receiving area, I was handed over to the guards on duty, and unlike when I had first been remanded, all of them were unnecessarily mean.

"Step inside," the new guard instructed as she directed me back into that colorless area, where I first came in all those days ago. "Remove everything, and then you can put those clothes back on for now."

She was referring to the clothes I had worn when I'd first arrived. I was going to be able to wear my own clothes, but only for a couple of hours. Then I would have to put a jail jumpsuit back on again.

I stood in front of her, nude, while she ordered me to squat three times. I told myself, Don't worry Aretha; someday this will be made right. I had to draw from the comfort of knowing the truth.

The Bible, which I had left behind, had told me that the truth would set me free.

After getting my own clothes back, the new guard placed me in a holding cell. It wasn't the cell I had been put into when I'd first checked myself in here. This one had no phone, which meant no one was going to know that I was being transferred.

I was in that cell for an hour or so before the guard opened the door again and ordered, "Turn around and put your hands behind your back."

As I turned, I could hear two men talking while they approached me from behind. One of them began speaking to me, first announcing his credentials, and then telling me where he and his partner were from. Then he placed cuffs around my wrists, and informed me, "All right, Aretha, we're going to transport you to the place where you'll be turned over to the US Marshals."

Even though they didn't tell me exactly where that was, I already had a pretty good idea where I was going—the airport. I only got to see what the receiving officers looked like once he turned me around to face them.

They put my driver's license and birth certificate in a little plastic bag. Except for the clothes on my back, they were the only two things I had left with me. The officer handed the bag to his quiet partner, grabbed my arm, and led me out the door.

When I think about it, the only thing they'd left me with was my good name, and by the time I got back to Los Angeles, the media was going to take that from me too.

I was put in an unmarked car. We got on Highway 401, on our way to Pearson International Airport.

As usual, the highway was packed, overflowing with cars going in opposite directions across twelve lanes. We soon took an off-ramp and drove up highway 427, which goes directly into the largest airport in Canada.

The ride was painful, especially trying to find a comfortable way to sit, with tight cuffs around my wrists, and my arms cuffed behind my back. I looked out the window, trying to capture the image of my city one last time.

I kept thinking about all of the moments I had spent in the back of a police car, since this had begun. Then I remembered the Bible, Matthew 5:39, which says, "If anyone slaps you on the right cheek, turn to them the other cheek also."

The problem is I'd already gotten slapped on my left side.

On the way, the quiet cop finally spoke. "What happened with you and him?"

It was like he was reading my thoughts.

A little shocked at the sudden question, I replied, "It's a long story that hasn't ended."

Then he asked, "How do you actually know him?"

"I dated a friend of his for a number of years."

"How's that?" he wondered. "You're Canadian."

I explained that of course I was, but I had stayed in LA, and I had traveled back and forth for years.

He asked me what it was like, and what the people were like, especially the famous ones.

I was just glad to move on from the topic of Leading Actor. I told him, "Most of the ones I've met seemed to get mad whenever they didn't get what they wanted. And it seemed to me they wanted everything all the time."

He laughed. "I can only imagine. They dream about being stars, but I bet most of them turn into assholes."

The quiet one was funny. I thought to myself that this was the difference between the mean guards in Vanier, and the Toronto Task Force. I'm not sure why, but these detectives always seemed to treat me fairly, with respect. Maybe they just had better training.

The quiet one said, "Yeah, I bet you said some s—t he didn't want to hear, and he probably lost his f——g mind."

At that point, I was smiling. So many false statements had been given, but here was this quiet officer who'd gotten it perfectly right. He hadn't even been there!

Although the ride was extremely uncomfortable, both the quiet one and the other officer were nice to me. They cracked jokes about what they thought real Hollywood life would be like. From what I've experienced, they actually weren't far off.

Trying to make myself somewhat comfortable (or at least take my mind off my discomfort), I gazed out of the window. I thought back on some of the actors, musicians, and athletes I'd come across in my life, people that we would consider famous. They may only refer to us as their fans, perhaps a lower form of humanity to some others.

Living in and out of LA, I'd already begun to separate the real from the fake. Not to forget, my mother had been the owner of a casting and talent agent in Toronto for many years, which had given me a front row seat in the entertainment industry. Even though she would explain the importance of it all, she would also say things like, "Nobody is going to be better at being you, than you." Once again, making sure we were all on the same playing field.

A sharp swerve off the highway's ramp brought me back to reality.

We'd arrived at the airport. As we pulled up to the curb, two marshals were already waiting for us: one female officer and one male. Both of them had their credentials displayed in a plastic lanyard around their necks.

Right before we exited the car, the quiet one said to me, "I hope you get to tell your story one day, and that asshole gets what he deserves."

I have to admit that it was moments like these, combined with my faith, which helped me continue pushing through. Even at low moments like this one.

As the task force officers spoke to the marshals, I realized the Americans must have arrived last night. The four of them had previously all met up for drinks. Our Toronto crew had taken them out on the town.

"All right, we can take her from here." It was the female marshal. She took my arm to remove the task force cuffs from my wrists and replace them with her own. This time, at least, they put my hands in front of me. Then she put her jacket over the chain to hide them.

I would later find out they do this so they don't alarm any of the public traveling in the airport. It didn't matter, though. Cuffs or no cuffs, jacket or not, each of my arms being held tight by the marshals made it obvious to everyone what was going on. The airport was busy that day, and I got a lot of looks.

Because the marshals didn't have my passport, we spent an hour getting things in order with the Canadian Border Services Agency before finally boarding the plane. After five years of being away from Los Angeles, I was finally being dragged back. My seat was directly beside the window. I assumed they did that so I wouldn't run down the aisle and try to jump off the plane.

The female marshal asked me if I was hungry, and I told her I wasn't. Even though I knew the airplane food would taste as good as a gourmet meal after all that food in jail, I didn't want to eat. I just wanted to look out the window at Canada, my home, falling away behind me.

As the plane took off and we ascended over the city, I was able to catch a glimpse of the CN Tower, my favorite Canadian landmark. I thought about how different it would be if I had never gone to Los Angeles, I wouldn't be sitting here, wedged in the window seat on a plane, guarded by two marshals.

I smiled at the male marshal. "Is this your first time here in Canada, or is this something you do all the time?"

"Nope, it's my first time even being close to here." He said it as if Canada was on the other side of the Earth, even though we share the longest border in the world with the United States. "Extradition is a very small part of the job. We were just stationed for a while in the Middle East."

No doubt they'd had missions way more important than this one. He then went on to tell me they had gotten the call to retrieve me at the last minute, on their way back to the US after being stationed overseas.

It seemed, someone in US Justice might have almost forgotten about me. I cursed the bad luck that had led to me being remembered just in the nick of time.

***

After a six-hour flight, we arrived in Los Angeles.

The female marshal got up from her seat and informed me, "It will be a minute. We're going to have to wait for all the other passengers to leave the plane first."

It took about twenty minutes for everyone except the flight crew to exit the plane. Then it was our turn. As soon as I got off the plane and walked down the small tunnel, there were a number of officers waiting for us, both LAPD and airport security.

Once the female marshal released me to the LAPD's receiving officer, he grabbed me and drove me face first into the wall. He acted as though he had just caught me in the act of murder.

It was so rough that even the male marshal spoke out in my defense. "I don't know if you're aware," he said, "but it's been five years since the incident. And if you ask me, she's pretty much harmless."

It didn't matter. The LAPD officer continued using what felt like unnecessary force. He rushed me all the way through the airport and into the parking lot, right into the back seat of his car. For some reason, he was very angry with me. Like the crown attorney, he probably only knew what he had read about me on paper. He hadn't taken the time to learn my version of events.

Once we got into the car, the lead detective made sure to inform me that even if I got bail on the assault charge, they were going to place an immigration hold on me. This was the first I had heard about that. They were going to do whatever it took to make sure I remained incarcerated for the entire ordeal. They were determined to punish me, no matter what.

He brought me to their headquarters in downtown LA. By the time we arrived, it was the dead of night, which was probably the worst time to be in downtown Los Angeles.

Unlike some major cities, where the downtown core is the busiest (and constantly filled with people either working or having fun), this place is just the opposite. The people who work downtown completely disappear by five o'clock every evening, getting out as fast as they can. Soon after dusk hits the city center, it's filled with thousands of homeless people, as well as the other castoffs of society.

It looked like a bomb had gone off inside the precinct. It was a complete mess. People and paper were scattered everywhere. Men and women filled the cells. On the other side, detectives and administrative staff talked, moved about, and answered phones. It seemed so chaotic, I don't understand how anyone could know what was going on.

After being fingerprinted and having my pictures taken, I asked the lead detective to explain the immigration hold, and exactly what it meant for me.

"Ask your lawyer, when you get one. Don't ask me anything." His tone made me feel like he was talking to an animal. Or, at least, a person who shouldn't bother to think.

I couldn't understand why he continued to be so mean to me. I figured that if it was up to him, he would have punished me right on the spot just for being accused.

After five years, I was finally booked and charged with assault with a deadly weapon — an extremely dangerous wine glass.

***

The holding cells were on the right side of the station. They looked out into the work area of the detectives. Each one of their desks was piled high with files, and there was barely enough room to walk around, let alone sit.

After an hour, the lead detective came back to get me. Grabbing my arm tightly, he led me down a hallway past all of the other cells that lined the room. As I walked by, someone yelled out to me.

"What are you in here for?" It was a man in one of the male cages.

"Don't speak to her," the lead detective warned, looking straight at me, as if to tell me not to say anything back.

He shuffled me quickly over to his desk, which was also piled high with files. So much so, they were even on his desktop computer, and a few even sat on his chair. He made some space by moving some of the files to another desk. I wondered if they ever got anything mixed up.

I sat in the headquarters of the police station, being interviewed by the lead detective. I kept waiting for him to ask me if I wanted to make a statement, but he didn't. I assumed since I hadn't given one before, he figured why would I bother now? He did have a few other questions for me as he filled out his forms, but my favorite was the one about my ethnicity.

When he asked me if I considered myself black or white, I gave him the only answer I could think of.

"I'm Canadian."

He laughed at me. "Well, what does that mean?"

I said, "It means I'm Canadian. Not a color."

I don't think he liked my response. This time, he didn't laugh.

After a few more questions, the lead detective told me that I would be arraigned in court the following day. Sometime after that would be a bail hearing.

Hours later, I was taken to Valley Jail in Van Nuys, California. This time, the cell I was put in had quite a few other women already in there.

"Hey, where'd you come from?" one woman asked me.

She must have known I wasn't from anywhere around there. She was looking at me like I was from another planet. All of them could tell I was way out of my element, but little did they know just how far. I was also out of my country. Being there was like being in another universe.

All together in the cell, there were six of us. No doubt, there would be others coming and going. When I arrived, I didn't speak to anyone. I just made my way to the phone, wanting to call my family and friends to check in.

Just my luck, I couldn't make a direct call to Canada from their pay phone. No one was going to know where I was. Certainly, they knew I had been shipped to the States by now, but they probably didn't know exactly where.

I was truly lost.

Or so I thought.

The same woman spoke to me again.

"You need help with that phone? I've got a trick. I think I can help you with that. I'm going to call my brother and see if he can hook you up on a three-way call. What number are you trying to reach?"

I wanted to talk to my mother. I wanted her to know I was all right. Besides, she had a landline, and she was always home. She was the most likely person to answer if I called.

The woman helping me began speaking Spanish to someone on the other end of the line; her brother, I assumed. After what seemed like a few pleasantries, she turned back to me. "What's your mom's number?"

I gave her the number, then prayed that it would work. After a few moments, she smiled and handed me the phone.

"Hello?" It was my mother's voice. I had never been so glad to hear her in my life.

For a moment, my mother thought I was free, perhaps calling

from someone's house. It was the first time in a while she hadn't heard my voice come through collect. I was about to ruin her hopes.

"They came and got me, Mom," I said, my throat closing up a little. I took a breath and composed myself, trying not to cry. "I'm back in LA now, but someone was nice enough to make a three-way call for me."

I couldn't hold back anymore. I burst into tears, standing in that cell and listening to the silence on the other end of the line.

When my mom was pregnant with me, she had been a backup singer for Aretha Franklin. The Queen of Soul once put her hand on my mother's belly, and said, "You better name that baby Aretha."

And she did. My earliest memory is of my mother rocking me to sleep while singing "A Natural Woman." It was the first song I ever heard.

Maybe she thought that would put me on the path to being a singer myself. Whatever her dreams had been for me, I know she hadn't named me Aretha with the hopes that I would end up in jail. That was certain.

"I'm so sorry, Mom," I apologized. "I never thought it would go this far." After a moment, I pushed the tears aside and told her the rest. I knew I had to be strong. Breaking down with my mother on the phone wouldn't be good for either one of us. "I'm going to be arraigned tomorrow. I'll try and get bail for myself later next week."

I didn't mention the possibility of an immigration hold. I couldn't tell her that the likelihood of me getting bail was slim. Maybe because I wanted to believe there was still a chance I could get out.

I also didn't want to say too much. After all, there was still a stranger on the phone, who was listening in on this three-way call.

"When will you be able to call again?" my mother asked.

"I'm not sure. Maybe after court, or once I'm transferred to the county jail."

I didn't want her to start asking questions about the bail,

because I didn't really have answers to give her. It was also important for me not to take advantage of the kindness of the woman who had arranged the call. It was international, so it could be expensive.

"Mom, I promise to call you as soon as I can," I said, my voice breaking again. "I love you."

"I love you too, Aretha."

I began to cry again. I tried to fight back the tears, as I handed the phone back. I knew her brother was still on the line.

I realized I was going to have to make some friends quickly, especially if I had to rely on the favors of strangers just to do something simple like make a phone call to my mother.

After a few minutes of talking with her brother, the woman finished her call. Then she came and sat beside me. "Why did you get extradited here?"

"I got into an altercation with a celebrity."

I didn't have any reason not to tell her. Come Friday morning after court, it would be all over the news anyway. The real circus would begin the next morning.

***

After being woken up at 5:30 a.m. by the guards at the Van Nuys jail, all the ladies who were being held were transferred by bus to the inmate reception center. It was called the Twin Towers in downtown Los Angeles. It's where all the people in custody (both men and women), would be sorted. Eventually, they're transferred to their respective courthouses, in the city where their crimes had been committed. In my case, that was going to be the Los Angeles County Courthouse.

That bus ride was depressing. Unlike the bus trips we took as children, going on adventures with our classmates, bouncing up and down in excitement, this journey was grim and dreary. With our hands and feet in chains, no one was smiling.

Every seat on the bus was full, and every woman was chained

to the ones next to her. All seventy-two passengers crammed on the bus were linked, hands to feet, from first to last.

As we pulled away in the direction of the LA County Courthouse, I could see dozens of buses lining up to collect the inmates at the reception center who were waiting to be transferred to their respective locations. That's when I first realized the State of California's courts and jails were a huge and complex system, almost certainly a lucrative business.

After a bumpy and uncomfortably long ride to the courthouse, we finally arrived, and as expected, the madness continued.

While the buses poured out people from across the state, we were all assembled into a cell in the basement of the building. Now I was crammed in with hundreds of other women.

The Superior Court of Los Angeles County is the largest single unified trial court in the United States. It operates forty-seven courthouses throughout the county, and as of 2017, it had an annual budget of $850 million dollars. There were nearly 600 courtrooms in this building alone.

After waiting in the cell for a while, I was eventually transferred to the floor where my courtroom was located, and then placed in another cell with about a dozen women. This was where I would stay until I was called in front of the judge.

This cell had pay phones. Since it was Friday morning, I would finally get the chance to try and contact Lawyer Six in Canada. The operator connected me, and the secretary answered. She actually asked me how I was doing.

"Not good. I was hoping I could speak with Lawyer Six."

"He's not here. However, he knows you've been transferred, and he said to tell you to contact the new lawyer in the States if you called."

"I don't have their number. I was ordered to leave everything behind in Vanier."

She said she would give it to me again, but there I stood with absolutely nothing, not even a pen. I turned and found the woman who had helped me make a three-way call. I asked her if she could help me remember a number. She said no problem.

It was almost like having a friend.

I knew she would help not only because she had helped me to call my mother, but also since after I told her what happened with Leading Actor, she'd started speaking to me like I was a person and not a criminal. Though honestly, I don't think she believed me at first, when I told her who it involved.

I repeated the number to her and hung up quickly. I knew I was going to be called into court soon. At this point, I wasn't sure whether a lawyer would show up on my behalf or not.

I hung up, dialed the new number, and waited for the operator to place the call. After a few rings, there was no answer, just a machine, and the operator hung up before I could even leave a message. I found myself holding a receiver with no one else on the other end. I had no clue what would happen next.

"Don't worry," my new friend told me, "they'll put it over until you can find your lawyers."

I hung up the phone and sat down beside her, trying to figure out what would happen next. I was pretty sure no one would be with me when I stood in court today. It was hard to imagine what was going to become of me, isolated and alone in a place so close to my old home, and yet, so foreign to me.

"Wilson!" a sheriff's deputy called out my name. "Your lawyer is here."

I couldn't believe it.

Someone was here for me!

I immediately jumped up and went over to the front of the cell. I walked out when the deputy told me to and faced the wall when he told me to, exactly as he asked. After placing cuffs around my wrists, he led me into another room that was more like a visitor's area.

The room had a seat and a table, but a three-inch thick partition separated one side from the other. The only way to talk to someone on the other side was a phone setup—one on this side and one on the other.

I waited a few minutes, and then two men came in. They sat down on the other side of the glass. One with long hair motioned for me to pick up the phone. I did and smiled at him, while I waited for him to speak.

"Hello, Aretha. We were sent here by your lawyer. If you remember, we talked briefly on the phone once before."

"I do remember." And I did, too. I remembered how he'd assured me that when he'd spoken to the prosecutor, she was going to set my bail at $60,000. They'd never said anything about an immigration hold. So, I asked him. "What's an immigration hold?"

He paused for a moment, then looked at his partner as he said, "I don't think that's your biggest problem, Aretha. We just came out of the courtroom. I don't believe we're fit to represent you in this particular case."

A ton of bricks falling on my head couldn't have stunned me more than his words.

"What do you mean by that?"

He took a longer pause.

"There's a media circus waiting for you in that courtroom. It's just not something we want to take on. We don't have the capacity for something like that."

"So, I'm going to have to go in there by myself?" I asked, feeling sick again at the thought.

"I will go in and recommend that the judge put your case over for a bail hearing," he offered, as if that was some big favor, "until you can find proper representation. Other than that, there's nothing else we can do."

I could feel my heart pounding so hard I thought it might beat right out of my chest. What these lawyers were saying was sucking the life right out of me.

"What about the five thousand dollars Lawyer Six sent you?" I blurted out. "Will there be anything left for me to find another lawyer?"

"No. Not after today," he informed me. "What I can do is see if we know anyone else who may be able to help you. Perhaps I can send someone to see you once you get to Lynwood."

Lynwood? Now I was going to Lynwood?

He looked at his partner, who shook his head confirming what they both already knew. They already knew I was going somewhere else. Bail was out of the question. I didn't even have a lawyer, and no money left. Plus, I was still facing an immigration hold.

As they both turned to walk away, I ruminated bitterly on how they had just earned $5,000 for a couple of phone calls and a single, brief visit.

After my meeting with the lawyers, I was placed back in the holding cage with my new friend. At first, I didn't say anything. I was still in too much shock. When she asked me if I was okay, I told her how I was going to have to find yet another new lawyer.

"Don't worry," she said. "Someone will take your case. If anything, you're famous. Don't worry. Someone will say yes."

Right at that moment, I looked around and noticed most of the girls had been watching us. Some of them were clearly eavesdropping. At that moment, it was more than obvious that my new friend had talked about my situation while I had been meeting with my newest (and shortest) former representatives.

Although I never went into detail about the night in question, saying Leading Actor's name was enough to get them talking. It wasn't long before they all knew why I was there.

One of the women standing right next to us looked right at me and said, "Someone here has got to be famous." She directed the statement right at me, smiling as if she knew something I didn't.

I guess she must have, because she was one of the women who had already appeared in front of the judge. She had seen the media madhouse that was waiting on bated breath for me out there.

"Wilson!" My name was called out by the deputy again. It was my turn to go into the courtroom.

Breathe, I thought to myself, slowly exhaling. It's going to be okay.

Even though I wasn't sure what okay meant. It was what I had to say to myself in order to keep moving forward.

This courtroom was old and musty. I could smell the residue from when smoking had been allowed in this chamber of a million decisions. I looked around, trying to separate the media from possible witnesses and the looky-loos. I soon realized that I didn't know a single person out there.

But they all talked like they knew me.

"Aretha, look over here."

"Look this way."

"Aretha…Aretha!"

One man gestured for me to smile, hoping for a good photo. Why he thought I would want to smile was beyond me. Who could smile in a situation like this? I turned away, but he snapped the picture anyway. To this day, the first picture that pops up on a Google search of me is that photo. It was one of the hardest moments in my life, captured forever in a picture taken by a man, whose only concern was his paycheck.

Finally, the judge hit her gavel. After a few announcements, and instructions about the media surrounding my case, court was then in session. Once my case was called up, I got my first look at the prosecutor, the person responsible for trying my case.

I stood there listening to what she said. It was obvious she didn't care for me. As for Leading Actor, I would say she was one of his biggest fans.

Prosecutors only have one job: to make sure the person accused is found guilty. When you're dealing with a celebrity in LA, it gets worse. Because of that, justice can't serve you after you've been accused of a crime against a celebrity. No matter how much of the truth comes out, their job is to make sure you plead guilty to some-thing—anything. The more guilty pleas they get, the longer they get to hold their position.

Believe me when I say it; these people have the most control over a person's life once you're in the system. They enjoy making deals with their colleagues in order to reach their goal. As for your life, well, that's not their problem.

I had never seen anything like her before. She was by far the most fragile-looking person I'd ever laid eyes on. Fine blonde hair and skin like porcelain. I watched her send the judge a smile when the case was called.

"The State of California versus Wilson."

Taking her place at the prosecutor's table, I could see in her face how badly she wanted me to be found guilty. I don't think she actually looked at me once. She spoke about me like I wasn't even there. As she painted a picture of what she thought I had done, the judge sat at the bench looking at me while shaking her head. It was as if she also already believed I was guilty.

Then to my surprise, the prosecutor said, "We are requesting one hundred and fifty thousand dollars in bail."

She finally looked over at me with a smirk. I imagine if I could have read her mind, it would be saying, "There's nothing you can do, your life is in my hands until I say otherwise."

I looked away from her. It's hard to look at someone who's trained not to budge while negotiating over your life. I was sure she'd read the statements from those involved. She knew there was more to this than me flying off the handle and hitting a celebrity. I bet she even knew that he'd hit me first.

But none of that mattered.

Her job was to find me guilty.

As far as she was concerned, I wasn't going anywhere, especially since my bail had just skyrocketed. Then, out of nowhere, I heard someone say, "We are here on behalf of Aretha, and we are requesting that her case be put over for the next few days, while she figures out her bail." It was the lawyer with the long hair. He had made his way up through the gallery of people and into the body of the courtroom, past the media storm.

"That's fine," the judge said, "but how is she going to plead today?" Then the judge spoke to me. "You are being charged with an assault using a deadly weapon. How do you plead?"

Everyone in the courtroom had their eyes on me, waiting for me to respond. I swallowed. I had prepared to do nothing but speak the truth.

The deputy standing right beside the box looked at me, and said in a tone that was by no means friendly, "Answer the judge."

In a whisper, I said, "Not guilty."

"Speak up," the judge told me.

I said it again, louder, "Not guilty."

The judge didn't miss a beat. "You will be remanded to the Lynwood detention center until Friday of next week when you will appear here again. By that point, hopefully, we can move on with bail." She banged her gavel again.

The deputy grabbed my arm and ordered, "Let's go."

He led me right out of the box, back into the holding cell, making sure I didn't spend one extra minute in that courtroom. It felt like we prisoners were nothing more than cattle waiting to be shepherded from place to place while the lawyers and prosecutors made deals with our lives.

"How did it go?" my new friend asked when I got back. She was sitting beside the eavesdropper, who was eagerly awaiting my response.

"It was put over until Wednesday," I told her.

"A lot of cameras in there, huh?"

"This whole thing is a mess." I sighed, still unable to understand how it had gotten this far so many years later. I also wondered why that prosecutor hated me. "I don't know how to begin looking for a lawyer here."

"Don't worry," the eavesdropper told me, "There's someone already here who I think may want to help you. You've heard of the case of that football player, right?"

Well, yeah. Who hadn't?

She told me, "The guy who was responsible for trying to prosecute him for the murders of his wife, and that young guy, he's here today."

"I'm not sure I understand what you mean."

"After that whole fiasco with him going free, this prosecutor switched sides. Now he's a defense attorney. When you were in court, I told him about your case. He's helping me with mine, and I'm sure he's still around here somewhere. He already knew about your case, with all the media in the courtroom. You should let the deputy know you want to speak with him. Tell them he's expecting you."

I smiled at her and got up to make my way to the door, where the deputy was standing. I couldn't help wondering about a prosecutor who had switched sides to become a criminal defense attorney. Perhaps, he had the ability to see things from both sides, unlike all the prosecutors I had seen before, who were trapped in the same delusion they wanted the public to believe.

I asked the deputy, "Could you let the ex-prosecutor know I would like to meet with him?"

He told me to wait, and that he would see if the ex-prosecutor was still here. I let myself hope he could help me because I had absolutely no one else. By this time, the lawyers who had declined to represent me were long gone.

When the deputy returned, he told me to step out and face the wall. He cuffed my hands behind my back like usual. Within seconds, I was in the same visitor's room as before. Only this time, the ex-prosecutor was already in the room waiting for me.

I sat down and picked up the phone receiver. I waited for him to speak first.

"What happened, and how did you end up here?" He didn't even introduce himself.

I guess he figured I would know him from the televised trial of the football player. It had gone on for months, after all. Perhaps, he assumed I would recognize him from that one important bit of footage. The one where he broke down after realizing the football player had been found not guilty.

That was probably the moment when he'd switched sides. As I've stated, a prosecutor's main job is to make sure that everyone is convicted of something. There was no room for the possibility that maybe, just maybe, someone wasn't actually guilty. Failing to convict had probably pushed him over the edge.

"I was extradited," I told him.

"I know that," he said. "I mean, what happened with you and Leading Actor. How did you end up in jail?"

I began explaining how I knew Leading Actor, as well as my relationship with Last. I told him specific details, so he would be clear on everything.

After all that, he looked at me with eyes almost glaring, and asked me flatly, "How did you get into a fight with him?"

"We were at a party."

I explained all of that as well, stressing that, to me, Leading Actor was just another guy. He listened to me, nodding his head up and down, as if he truly understood. I told him everything, making sure not to leave anything out. The details were still as fresh as if it had all happened to me the night before. How could I forget it?

"Why did you call him a faggot?" the ex-prosecutor asked. "Is he gay"?

"I'm not sure about his sexuality, and I'm certainly not homophobic," I admitted. "I just thought it would hurt him more than what he'd said to me about my face."

"You must have really pissed him off, saying that."

"It obviously worked. He was angry enough to put his hands on me."

He was quiet for a time before saying, "This should never have happened to you. I'm not sure why the attorney general had you extradited. There's probably more to it than what you think."

I wasn't ready for more bad news, but I was certainly glad to hear a little bit of the truth. I explained my financial situation, and that I had no money left after all the money I had spent on Lawyers One through Seven. Plus, the new ones here who had just walked out on me. I had no idea how I could pay to have someone defend me, certainly not someone as famous as he was.

"Don't worry," he told me. "I'm going to take your case, and you don't have to pay me."

The wave of relief that washed over me was so huge, I wondered if he could feel it. "Thank you," I said, holding back tears. I didn't know what else to say.

What could I possibly say to thank someone for showing that sort of goodwill?

Words simply couldn't convey how much I appreciated his kindness.

Chapter Eleven

THIS IS NOT AMERICA—
IS THERE LIFE ON MARS?

DOWNTOWN LOS ANGELES sure looked different when viewed from a jail bus.

After a horrible day in court, I was finally shipped off with the other female inmates to the Lynwood facility. This side of town always seemed darker, unlike everywhere else in the city, where the sun shined down all day long.

Here, close to downtown, a thick cloud of smog hovered directly over the city's core. It was hard to fathom that it was in the same county as Beverly Hills, a place where you can be fined a $1000 for putting a cigarette butt out on the ground. Of course, some of the people up there own six or seven cars each.

Unlike Beverly Hills, here the streets were lined with waste. The buildings were covered in graffiti five layers deep. A good number of cars, once driven on Rodeo Drive, now looked like they had been abandoned. Most people wandering downtown at dusk seemed to have nowhere else to go.

Nothing had worked out as I'd hoped. Not with my lawyers in Canada, and not with my lawyers in LA either. I don't know why I'd thought I would just get bail and go straight to Vraie's place. Hope is a funny thing. It keeps you going.

The prosecutor had known exactly how to bring me to my knees. Everything from waiting until almost the last day to come and get me, to toying with my freedom. Then requesting an amount for bail almost three times what I had originally thought I would need to pay. And, let's not forget, the immigration hold she had put on me.

I was a Canadian on American soil, charged with assault with a deadly weapon. The immigration hold meant I would have to request a second bail from the federal courts in order to gain my freedom.

As if I didn't have enough to deal with. I pictured the prosecutor smirking while we had been in court. How she had looked at me, almost laughing. The only good thing was that Vraie was still willing to post the bail, even though the amount had increased dramatically. Once again, someone who actually knew me was willing to put support me so that I could regain my freedom.

But even if I was able to post the $150,000 bail, I had a feeling the prosecutor would have another trick up her sleeve, something to make sure my hands stayed cuffed.

And she did.

***

I was going to spend my incarceration within the largest and most troubled jail system in the United States. And I didn't even know how long I would be staying.

Twin Towers is also connected to the Men's Central Jail, a windowless dungeon in downtown LA that has been plagued by a long-entrenched culture of savage deputy-on-inmate violence. As quoted by the ACLU- American Civil Liberties Union.

Unfortunately, it was no different at the women's facility in Lynwood.

The holding cells at Lynwood are divided according to where each crime has allegedly been committed. There are eighty-eight cities within the county of Los Angeles. With a capacity of over 2,000 inmates, it is one of seven correctional facilities operated by the Los Angeles County Sheriff's Department. It's the largest women's jail in the nation. The cells are bursting at the seams.

When leaving the jail, each woman is subjected to a pat down before getting on the bus. Upon returning, though, all inmates must go through a very disturbing and sensitive strip search. Every woman is entirely exposed in front of each other, right down to their bare feet.

This allows the deputies to search 100 women at the same time. Naked, we were ordered to face the wall, with our hands up and legs spread wide apart. They went through, one by one, searching all of us. Nothing could be more degrading, especially because it was done in the bus garage, which made the place feel like it was one of the nine circles of hell. Except for the fact that it was freezing.

After being strip searched and getting re-dressed, I was placed in the third cell of ten, in that particular section of holding. Each one is about 30 x 15 feet. There is absolutely nowhere to sit.

One communal toilet in each holding area (or "tank" as they're referred to), is shared by 60 to 70 inmates. You have to do your business out in the open, for all to see. Not far from where you get to relieve yourself is an area where you can enjoy a peanut butter sandwich and a boxed juice while you wait to be assigned to your cell. This is what had been provided for our dinner as we waited for the deputies to take us away.

Everything in jail moves extremely slowly. The only time there is any rush is when we are in a courtroom. There's never a rush in jail. By the time we got upstairs from holding, it had been almost four hours since we'd arrived.

The hundreds of women who came through the holding cells, from all the different courthouses, were distributed into cells throughout several pods. I was so tired from the day that had been forced on me that I didn't even take the time to count how many women were assigned to my pod.

This pod was at least five times bigger than the small dorm in Vanier. Vanier has 333 beds to Lynwood's 3,000+. When I arrived, the cell I was assigned to was empty, thankfully, so it was mine, alone for now.

Without any rest from the day's harrowing events, I went to sleep almost immediately.

***

The next day, when I woke up and looked out the window of my cell, there were women everywhere. Mind you, the only windows in these cells look into the jail itself, never outside. I was seeing the group of women I was going to be locked up with.

Once my cell door popped open and I was permitted to step out, I realized that, for every cell, there were another two women sleeping in bunk beds in the open area. That meant most women here only had what few things they could store under their bunk.

In other words, most women here had nothing. This was the state's way of updating the jail after it had become overcrowded years ago. They might as well have piled the women on top of each other.

Each one of us had been ordered outside of our cells for the morning count. Like Vanier, this common area was also where all three meals were served, as well as where the women would have the opportunity to gather. As for the bricks that contained us, they were also purposely painted in a teardrop gray.

As long as you were in here, there was no outside. The women in this pod could be ordered to stay here for up to one year without ever once feeling the sun on their skin or breathing the fresh air outside. From one underground garage beneath the courts back and forth to Lynwood's dungeon, we rode on buses with windows that were always locked. No fresh air. Never. That part I thought was odd, especially after my experience with Lock. Never mind leaving prison for two and a half days, we hadn't been given the freedom to go out for a three-minute walk. Perhaps there were too many of us.

Once you're assigned to a pod, that is where you stay until you are released or, depending on your sentence, until you can be shipped off to the next, worse place.

The gym for the pod is the closest you get to anything like going outside. In that room, there are windows that look outside, although they're ten feet off the ground, which means the only view they give you is the smog-filled sky.

As I stood outside my cell waiting to be counted, I began to look around at the other women and their faces. I suddenly realized that a lot of them were already looking at me.

At the time, I didn't know why I was the center of attention. I suppose I should have. Earlier that morning, the LA Times had been delivered to the jail. Of course, my story was big news.

After the deputies were done with the newspapers, they passed them to the inmates to read. The paper was usually given to the inmates who work alongside the deputies. These inmates are known as porters. The porters would in turn pass them around to the ladies who were on the bunks, and by the time the women in their cells found anything out, everyone else already knew the daily buzz.

Within seconds, all of the women in that pod connected the picture taken of me in court to the new inmate standing in their midst.

"Isn't that you in the paper today? I'm surprised you're not in PC."

The girl who said that to me was sitting up on her bunk, looking down with the paper still in her hand, smiling like she knew something I didn't. At first, I couldn't place her accent, but she definitely wasn't American. Her bunk was the first one to the left side of my cell door.

I thanked God I wasn't in protective custody (PC). I had heard on the bus coming here that the actress from Herbie: Fully Loaded was there, and after what happened to me, I didn't want to be anywhere near any other celebrities.

It didn't matter, because I would never see her.

In her case, they'd said the actress didn't have to stay because of overcrowding. Most celebrities that went to jail in LA seemed to benefit from that particular problem.

Finally, the deputy who was on duty ended the count and the daily announcements, allowing us to disperse.

"Feel free to move around," the deputy said. "Don't ask me any questions, unless someone's dead!"

I made a mad dash to the gym, where the pay phones were installed. Several phones were available to use, unlike in Vanier where most seemed to be broken, with only one or two in operation.

This was when I found out that there's only one phone company that provided collect calls for the jail. Trust me when I say they were making a killing from these women. People would do almost anything to speak to a loved one, even for a minute.

The girl with the newspaper got off her bunk and followed me. "You're going to need a calling card to use the pay phone," she told me.

"Is that the only way I can make calls here?"

"Aside from making a three-way, yes."

"Do all of these phones work like that?"

"Yes. Oh, and you have to wait for them to turn them on. Who do you want to call?"

Without any reason to hide it from her, I said, "My son."

"You should get a job as a porter," she told me. "We get to use them all of the time in here."

It was nice to talk about something resembling normal. We talked for a while, and I asked her where she was from.

She told me she was Romanian, which she followed up by saying, "That's why people call me what they do in here." Then she told me her name.

I will call her Romania 1. Her accent reminded me of listening to Dracula in the movies.

"Don't worry," Romania 1 told me. "I already read your name."

I smiled and warned her, "Don't believe everything you read."

"Oh, they might get your story wrong, but they'll always make sure to get your name right."

Instantly, I thought about what the newspaper had done that time they'd written about Scion. She was right. They always got my name right, even when they completely messed up the rest of the story.

Then Romania 1 gave me a warning, "After what I read, you're going to need to call more people than just your son."

That's when I realized that my son must already know exactly where I was. He'd probably seen it all over the news. Standing there, I broke down and started to cry. I didn't care at that point. I was so overwhelmingly sad.

It's not a good thing to be crying in a place like that. The other women don't want to hear it, or be reminded that they should be doing exactly the same. Still, I couldn't help it. Everything came crashing down on me, all the things I had been through up to this point. I tried to wipe the tears away.

Romania 1 put her hand on my shoulder to comfort me. "I'm going to see what I can do about getting you a job as a porter," she told me. "For now, we can use my calling card to call your son."

Even in the darkness of jail, you can sometimes find the light of kindness.

***

A few minutes later and for the first time since the Thursday after I had been whisked away, I heard Scion's voice. "You okay, Mom?" he asked.

Again, I burst into tears. That was my answer.

"Mom, please don't cry."

I tried to contain myself. "I can't help it. I can't believe I left you this way."

Though I was sobbing, he didn't shed a tear as if this was his chance to have strength for the both of us. An opportunity to show me that he could be a man. "You'll be okay, Mom. You've already made it through some very tough times, and we all know the truth. You can't be crying in there, Mom."

"Every time you call," he told me, "I'll make sure I'm here."

"Well, then I'm going to call you as much as I can."

I kept the call short though, not wanting to take advantage of the stranger's kindness.

My son and I said, "I love you," to each other, and I hung up.

With that, Romania 1 became my first friend there. Of course she would be. Within ten minutes of knowing her, she had gotten me on the phone with my son. In jail, that's hard to beat. Along with Romania 1, Freckles, a girl known for having the cutest face, stuck by my side the whole time I was there. It was a relief to have people I knew I could count on nearby.

The next two bail hearings kept getting put off, mainly based on scheduling conflicts between the prosecutor and Lawyer Eight. Romania 1 kept her word. Within the first few weeks of being incarcerated, I had a job. Porters work alongside the deputies and the guards, doing certain tasks, including things like serving food.

Our meals were a combination of beans, peanut butter, and one of four meats. Mostly, it's bologna, which comes marinated in a thick yellowish liquid. I assume this liquid is for storage purposes more than anything, because it certainly doesn't improve the look or taste of the food. I never ate it once.

Everyone's favorite meal was chicken patties on Wednesdays. As a porter, you always had extra to hand out, which got you more friends and favors. Serving food was probably the most important aspect of a porter's role. No deputy here was even going to look at the food, never mind hand it to anyone.

I didn't care about any of those chicken patties. All I knew was that being a porter was the best way to get the opportunity to use one of those phones freely, as long as I had money to buy the calling cards. After a couple months of phone calls, my son and I had racked up a total of $5,000. I used all the money I had left in my savings account.

Hearing his voice was worth all that money, despite the fact that every single phone call had somebody listening in on us. The prosecutor made sure I knew she was listening to me. She mentioned it to the judge in court. That's when I started to believe she didn't just want to put me in jail, she also wanted me to suffer. I think she was sick in the head; planning ways to punish me while she listened to me cry on the phone with my son.

Since we were both porters, Romania 1 and I spent a lot of time together. Whether we were in the gym trying to exercise or going to get one of the three meals from the kitchen, so we could serve the inmates. One day, Romania 1 and I even ended up going to court on the same day, which I guess isn't that rare when you have so many inmates in one place, and a ton of appearances for them to go to.

For Romania 1, that day turned out to be special, because it was deal day. She'd become ecstatic after her lawyers had finally struck a deal for her with the prosecution. This was after she and her co-defendant had been held in jail for almost three years.

They were so happy that we sang on the bus all the way to court. Much like Vanier, there was no music to be heard at Lynwood unless you were singing in church service. Otherwise, the only time we heard music was if the bus driver was nice enough to turn the radio on.

She was hopeful that things were going to work out, although once you're in court, you just never knew what is going to happen. There was no doubt that both she and her co-defendant were nervous.

Believe it or not, Romania 1's co-defendant was a Romanian as well. Romania 2 really stood out. She was a petite, chubby-faced girl about five-foot-two, with a really big smile. She was maybe twenty-five years old, with long black hair that flowed all the way down her back, and bangs that swept across her eyebrows. She kept flicking her bangs off her face, as if she were Cher singing with us on the bus.

She was cute, but by the time we got to court, she was so nervous she was sweating profusely. Pacing up and down the cell, she began biting her nails, while she waited for their names to be called.

Romania 1, Romania 2, and I spent the entire day together in court cells waiting.

"Aretha, I know you trust in the Lord, Romania 2 said. "Do you think everything is going to be okay with me today?"

"Of course. No matter what happens, I promise, He's got you."

Originally, the two Romanians were being offered a deal that would have included three years of dead time, (time already served, plus an additional five-year stay), for a total of eight years of incarceration. As part of the deal, the prosecutor wanted them to plead guilty to kidnapping and theft. At this point, both ladies just wanted to take a deal and get it over with.

Kidnapping is a big charge with a minimum twenty-year sentence. Romania 1 had told me their story, and it began with the two of them giving a woman a ride home one night, after picking her up from walking aimlessly downtown in Los Angeles.

Romania 1 said it had been an elderly Korean lady, and they'd wanted to help her by giving her a ride home. However, for whatever reason, when they'd dropped her off, one of the ladies had decided to keep the woman's cell phone.

Apparently, the elderly lady had left it on the car seat when she'd gotten out of the car after safely arriving home.

On one hand, you would think that giving an elderly lady a ride home is a wonderful act of human kindness. Unfortunately, in the state of California, because they gave her a ride, and then proceeded to keep her phone, they were both charged with theft under $1000. The really serious charge was the kidnapping, even though they left her at her house and continued on to their own place. That part, I didn't really fully understand.

Finally, they got called into court. As I waited for my own appearance, I thought about what they were going through. I had seen Romania 2's desperation when she had asked me about the Lord. It was obvious that this type of faith was new for her, but for some reason or another, she thought it was her only hope. I thought about how happy they both had been on the bus, celebrating how they only had another five years in prison.

When they came back, they were arguing about their case. I tried desperately to calm them down, so I could ask them what happened. It turned out that the prosecutor had taken their deal off the table. They were now asking for twenty years or more, for the kidnapping alone.

Finally, I was able to get Romania 2 to calm down. As we sat together, I tried to comfort her by making promises that somehow her situation would work out.

At one point, she looked up at me and asked, "Is God still going to get me out of here?"

All I could think to say was, "Eventually, yes."

As we waited for the court bus to take us back to Lynwood, we sat together in that concrete room, praying. I was asking God for guidance, while Romania 2 was begging Him for her freedom.

A few days later we were told by the inmates on Romania 2's pod, that on the night when we got back to the jail from court, Romania 2 began to complain about chest pains. She was screaming out from her cell, asking the deputies for their help. She wanted to be taken to the infirmary.

I suppose all the stress from the day had begun to take its toll. We were also told the deputy on duty responded by joking that it was because she was short and fat, all while laughing at her and ignoring her cries to see the nurse.

Apparently, her complaints continued, and after being called an assortment of horrible names, the deputies finally brought her down to be checked by the on-call doctor. As soon as she got down to the infirmary, she immediately asked to go to the bathroom. I read somewhere that when someone is about to die, their body has a need to release everything within it. Who knows maybe this is why it's called passing away?

She had been in the bathroom for a while when it became clear something was wrong. After they couldn't get her to respond, the guards banged on the bathroom door. Eventually, they just opened it up.

I could only imagine her on the floor, leaning against the wall after dying of a heart attack.

The State would never get that twenty years out of her for the kidnapping. Instead, the system took her whole life. All for that phone one of them stole.

Personally, I like to think she's finally free.

***

After six weeks, and several bail hearings that I knew would never be granted, I went to my first pre-trial conference.

That week was a difficult one for me. Thursday, August 12th, 2010, Scion turned eighteen. And here I was, incarcerated, while my baby became a man.

The pre-trial conference is based around whether or not there is sufficient evidence for the case to go to trial. In my case, I wasn't given the chance to contest any of the evidence that was presented. Exhibit 1.2.3 Each color photo is marked for identification and later received into evidence by reference only. Then to be retained by none other than the prosecutor. Who would they even get to testify?

Would Leading Actor show up and actually get on the stand?

He didn't seem like the lying type when I first met him, but hey, let's face it, he's still an actor. One thing I believe, for sure, is some actors are great at being anyone except themselves, even in real life.

As I looked around the courtroom, I thought about all those years ago when I'd read the witness statements presented to me by that LAPD detective. It would make sense that one of the wolves that Leading Actor calls friends would be on the stand today. They would be the vessel sent to begin the process of securing my misery. I thought it could also prove difficult for any of them. I mean, who could remember the details of such a weird and unwitnessed lie? Then again you would think that Leading Actor would've shown up on his own behalf, and especially if that picture that's printed beside my name was the true account of what happened.

To my dismay, the person who showed up to take the stand was someone who, to my knowledge, had not given a statement before. But it was someone I knew very well. He wasn't there to just get on a witness stand and give a statement. It was obvious that he was going to do whatever it took to protect Leading Actor.

He was one of the main wolves, Leading Actor's most dedicated devotee. I knew all about his past sacrifices. He slowly strolled up to the stand. Of course he would do this for Leading Actor. I had known him just as long as I had known Leading Actor. For seven years, I'd watched as he'd moved his family from county to county, in and out of the state. He'd married and then divorced. All because of his commitment to his friend.

Just as I had witnessed in the past, Leading Actor's friends would do anything for him. After all, it's the price one pays in order to sit at the VIP table. Only this guy seemed willing to sacrifice everything. He was loyal, at any cost, right down to giving up his morals.

Now, here he was. About to take his place on the stand at my pre-trial. Whoever had him sent here on behalf Leading Actor, the instructions he had been given were clear to me.

I would only wind up left to struggle with a new lie.

The funny thing is, sometimes the rest of the wolf pack would call this follower useless, a mockery using his real name. He, of course, hadn't even been there when the incident between me and Leading Actor had happened, or at least, he certainly hadn't been in the same room.

He testified that he had witnessed me with a glass in my hand, aiming for Last, not Leading Actor. Then, he went on to say that Leading Actor had simply gotten caught in the crossfire. It was a whole new story. One to add to all the other lies the prosecution had been given.

Last had already given a statement to the police, saying that he hadn't been in the room when the altercation had occurred, that he hadn't seen what had happened at all.

It was hard for me to imagine a human who would make up a story and allow a single mother to go to jail, based on his admiration for a celebrity. Perhaps he thought it would get him some brownie points, a way to show his friend how much he really cared. Personally, I could never get on the stand, look someone directly in their face, and lie.

The pre-trial judge wasn't interested in sorting out the details. They decided that the case would be moved up for trial. It was no concern of the judge that I'd be sitting in jail. Without a doubt, Lawyer Eight had been right: there was more to this. Now they had a new lie to protect. Even if it had been drummed up by their friend they called useless, that lie was very dangerous to my future.

***

After going through the pointless pre-trial, bail hearings, and weeks of court dates, I became sick to death of the judicial system. Every time I was transported back and forth to Lynwood, I was completely stripped, and then searched up and down. I clung to my one connection to the outside world, the pay phone, while the phone bills continued to pile up.

Another court appearance arrived. I had no choice but to hope that this one would finally play out in my favor. Like Romania 1 and Romania 2 had been through before, today was deal day for me. Should I take the deal or not? Should I go to trial and have Leading Actor face me, or should I go home to my son and family now, by taking a deal?

I wanted to go straight to trial. For me, it made the most sense. Besides, everyone should have the right to face their accuser. It's the best way to get to the truth.

The only problem was my regular sitting judge was on vacation. He was the only one who had actually taken the time to assess my case. After reviewing it, his thought had been that none of this made sense.

"Why is she even here?" he'd asked. "And how can we get her back to Canada?" He added, "Hasn't she already been through enough?"

By that point, Lawyer Eight had brought on Lawyer Nine. They had explained to the judge about my curfew, signing in for about a year, etc., all the way up to the time I had spent in Lynwood.

The judge was also aware that I had been incarcerated in Vanier, never mind all the commotion of being uprooted from my life, a stable job, and most importantly, my son.

This was the one judge who believed it was a waste of time and money to have me extradited for an unproven assault. All my other court appearances had been formalities, leading up to what should have been a great day for me.

My goal was to make a deal using my time served. After all, I had already been held for four months at Lynwood.

If I could prove that I had spent enough time already being incarcerated, I would enter a plea of no contest and be sentenced to time served. That would mean I would be immediately released and returned to Canada with no more worries.

My regular sitting judge had instructed that we adjourn for one week while we prepared ourselves. We'd needed to make calls to prove my incarceration and house arrest. Then he would simply finalize my release.

I had spent the whole week on the phone with my lawyers in Canada and the US. They had contacted others who could help prove I had already served the time they were seeking. I even went as far as to contact the officers at the sign-in center in Scarborough, where I had been required to sign in every day. They knew who I was as soon as I called, and they were more than willing to cooperate by stating that I had done everything the courts had asked of me.

As for the state, it was important for them to achieve a guilty verdict, not only to put another notch in the prosecutor's belt, but also to justify the cost of my extradition.

Pleading no contest doesn't mean you are guilty. It just means you don't believe you can win your case, so you aren't going to fight the charges.

With my case, I had started to reconsider after seeing the pre-trial judge had no problem going home every night, while I was in jail. With this decent judge, I decided I would accept the plea deal and get it over with. On the other hand I was looking at the possibility of getting as much as seven years if I'm convicted.

I just wanted to get back home to my son, and as far from Hollywood's self-made hell as I could. Even though I knew the truth of what had happened, I would have to forget about a trial. I would never stand a chance in a Hollywood court.

This was a warning that would come to me from the most unlikely source.

One evening after coming back from court I was approached by the deputy on duty in my pod at Lynwood. She was usually the one who was there with a shift that started from the early morning hours of dawn, and it ended sometime after dusk. She was very pretty, although she seemed a little overworked. Her once bright brown eyes now turned worrisome. I'm almost certain she spent more time with us in that pod than she had with her own family. Nevertheless, she was one of the few who would take the time to show she cared, as much as her position would allow her to. She stopped me on my way as I was heading toward my bunk.

"How was court today, Aretha?" She said to start the conversation.

I began by telling her I was struggling with the decision to go or not go to trial, amongst a new lie and a seven-year sentence. I explained as much as I could and ended it by saying "I'm not really sure what I should do."

I was almost hypnotized by her response, and she said it all without blinking once. "Aretha, he's making 20 million dollars a movie, what's your worth to a studio? They will make sure you're found guilty, and he won't spend a penny." The instant butterfly pounding away at my chest told me she was right.

Another reason why I opted to plead no contest, was because the State of California did not have the justification of self-defense. Even if someone hits you first, if you hit them back and cause enough damage, you cannot claim self-defense.

The only way to claim self-defense, in the State of California, is to kill the other person. I obviously had no intentions of killing anyone.

Come to think of it, no one has ever slapped me, aside from Leading Actor and Last, once. In fact, no one had so much as touched me on my scar since Dr. Lastname's poking and probing appointment in 1994.

At this point, going back to Canada was way more important than getting justice. At the end of the day, Leading Actor and I knew the truth, and he would have to live with it.

At least, that was the plan. But of course, nothing was going the way I wanted it to. Before I knew it, I was in another courtroom because my presiding judge had decided to go on vacation a few days before my final appearance in front of him.

Straight out of chambers, the new presiding judge was unconcerned with anything that had been promised by the previous judge.

As soon as I was moved into her courtroom that day, I could tell she couldn't care two licks about my case. She could barely pronounce my name correctly, and she had absolutely no interest in the details of my case. In fact, if anything, she seemed irritated. She didn't even know why I was there.

The new judge seemed more concerned about getting to recess than anything else. Her only question was, "Is she going to take the deal?" Aside from my case number and mispronounced name, that's all I'd heard from her so far.

I quickly realized that time served was not going to allow me to go home today.. Her idea of me accepting a plea deal would basically mean that combined with the time I served I would have to be incarcerated for at least a year.. On the other hand, if I went to trial and lost, I was looking at the possibility of getting seven years.

Either way, she wanted a decision right away.

Like I said before, you never know what you're going to get once you're in court in Los Angeles. I have no doubt this judge had done the same thing to many, many people.

What happened next would completely change my life.

"Is she going to take the deal or what?" It was the second time the new judge had asked the same question.

Everyone in the courtroom seemed to speak at once. For some reason, they all wanted to make sure I didn't opt to move up to a trial. Even Lawyer Nine seemed to agree with the prosecution, which was a surprise to me.

"You better take the f——g deal," he leaned over and whispered loudly.

As much as I was shocked by what he'd said, it still didn't matter once I realized I would be incarcerated either way. I wanted to take my chances and not take a plea deal after all.

It would almost be worth it to see Leading Actor have to get on the stand and try to lie. After all, we both knew the truth. Him facing me in court would be a lot different from his friend making up stories. I also believed that there comes a time in everybody's life where they must face what they have done and atone, even a famous celebrity.

Through all the commotion, the prosecutor was able to calm the courtroom by asking the judge one question. She walked up to the bench, and on a piece of paper the judge was holding, she pointed to Leading Actor's name. I watched as she slid her finger across the paper, and asked, "Did you see who her victim is?" She said it loud enough for everyone to hear. As if the fact that it was Leading Actor was enough for them all to agree they should lock me up and throw away the key.

The judge read the name, shot me one deadly look, and it was on. My deal was about to be sunk. With no other questions asked, the new judge directed her next statement my way. Her eyes were piercing, like daggers pointed right at me. She wanted me to know that if I gave the wrong answer, it would be the end of my case. "If you don't take the deal being offered, I'm going to send your trial to Lancaster County, where the jury has a 99% conviction rate, and you will get seven years."

What was weird was I hadn't even entered the plea, but for some reason, she wanted me to be guilty. She made sure her threat didn't come across as being idle.

How had this happened? How could this be the world we live in?

She didn't care about any of the details of the night in question, let alone who I was as a human being, or that I was responsible for a young man back home in Canada.

The way she approached my case, it was as if I had been personally responsible for the sinking of the Titanic. It was my fault that Jack was dead. I stood in the glass box looking at her in shock, trying to understand why she wanted to protect this actor that she really knew nothing about.

The truth was of no interest to her, and even if he'd damn near killed me, it would have still been my fault for breathing his air.

I don't think she realized for one second that he was just another human. None of the things he had done on the screen were real. Perhaps, to her, it was more important that I didn't put this beloved actor of hers on the stand, where he would have no script behind which to hide.

It felt like her judgment of me was based on a movie she'd watched. Her twisted view of a celebrity was going to result in me going back to jail.

The final blow came after Lawyer Eight made a special visit to come and see me at Lynwood. The last time I saw him was at one of my first court appearances. Usually, it was Lawyer Nine that showed up in court. The visit lasted about ten minutes, while he ended any of my hopes of what I thought could be getting a fair trial.

After advising me that if I did opt to move to a trial, the prosecution would use the lead detective, their friend they call useless or even Last if they wanted to as a witness, and that Leading Actor would never have to get on the stand. Hearing that Last might show up to testify while the Leading Actor would not have to, slammed the door on me. By that point I knew my lawyer had also given up. Combined with the directions given to me by his colleague Lawyer Nine the last time we were in court.

I realized I don't want to go to trial with any of them. I also didn't want to have to spend the next seven years struggling with a lie that my ex would most likely have to tell on the stand.

It felt as though I was being forced to take the deal.

Within eight weeks, I was off to another place where some of the Manson family had lived, an area known as Chowchilla, California.

After being in a number of jails, I was off to the next worst place in the world.

Chapter Twelve

ALL OF THE LIGHTS

ONCE AGAIN, I was told to roll it up and get everything from my cell, only this time a bus was waiting. After doing another month at Lynwood, I was finally off to start the sentence generously given to me by the celebrity-loving judge.

I was meant to be sentenced to two years with 85% served, the standard for violent felons. The judge made a mistake and offered two years with 50% served. Although Lawyer Nine had warned me not to make direct eye contact with the judge when we returned to court so I could except their deal. I could feel her eyes like daggers on me, as she realized her mistake and tried to renege.

I whispered to my lawyer that if she changed her mind, I wanted to go straight to trial. She signed the deal, though clearly irate about it. I'm sure she went home to her family, and to her own bed that night anyway.

Not me. It had been six months since I walked into Vanier where I had last seen Scion, and I was about to board a bus to the place where there's no rest for the wicked, for at least another six months.

I tried to tell myself that it was all right. That I could look at it as though I was going into hibernation, only to come out better than when I'd entered.

Even Jesus had gone to jail. And I might have made some mistakes, but I was still smart enough to give all of the glory to God.

This moment was where my real transformation began. I finally accepted that life was never going to be the same. This is when I started to see the world from a completely different angle.

I finally began to understand that no one is truly a star, but everyone has a light.

One of the inmates called out to the driver from the back of the bus, "Can you please turn on the radio?"

Like most of the jail bus drivers, he knew it was our only escape and gladly obliged. After going through a few fuzzy channels, he finally came to a station playing clearly enough for us to hear.

No seat was empty on that bus, and once again, each one of us was chained to the next. Even though we were packed like sardines, most of the women were quiet, all mesmerized by the view out of the window. It not only allowed us to see the world outside, the glass also provided a mirror for our own reflections, which some of us hadn't seen in months.

As the song on the radio ended and the next one began, the bus driver turned it up to make sure we heard it. Without a doubt, most of the women knew exactly which one it was. Some of them began cheering. I hadn't paid much attention to the first song, but this one I hadn't heard in years.

"1, 2, 1, 2, 3, 4!" With a few strums of a guitar, the whistling began. Together, they sound like you're being set up for a long, sad journey, which continues for forty-three seconds. As many times as I had heard this song before, I thought to myself there couldn't be a better time to hear it than right then.

Then the verse came in, with a word of encouragement on how to take it slow. It added a bridge of two guitars (that only Duff and Slash could play so perfectly), and in the end, Axle gave us advice with a song called "Patience." Most of the women were looking at the window, and each one of us had our own reflections to sing it to.

The Central California Women's Facility is a lot different from the Lynwood Jail. It was everything I imagined prison would be. Worse even.

It was not for the weak-minded, or for the faint of heart. A woman imprisoned there will either adapt and overcome, or she'll simply die, mentally, emotionally, and maybe even physically, if you're not careful.

***

It was early February, the day I arrived in Chowchilla. Though it wasn't cold, it was still very much winter in Northern California. It took hours and hours of driving, under an ominous gray sky, to get to the place, isolated as it is, tucked away from the rest of the world.

Unlike Canada, where winter is frigid and snowy, here it was characterized by one thing and one thing only—continuous rain. This is the part of the world that experiences frequent fog from November to March. Overcast days are the norm. Once, it rained in Chowchilla for twenty days straight.

The name Chowchilla is derived from the indigenous Chaushila, a Yokut Indian tribe that had once lived in the area. Their name translates as murderers, or so they say. These days, any woman who is caught and convicted in the State of California for murder will live here in the state prison.

Since I was now considered state property, all of my freedoms were taken away. I was considered a non-participating member of society.

I was a convict. No longer fit to live in the free world.

The dreary setting was perfect for serving out my sentence. The area is home to nothing but prisons. There is even another type of prison there.

It's called a Fire Camp.

Although prisoners are no longer fit to be a part of society, after they've been evaluated for their physical fitness, some female inmates are trained at Fire Camp. If they're deemed fit, then they're made fire crew members. Potentials are trained in fire-fighting techniques by CalFire. This included one week of classroom instruction, and a second week of field exercises. In return for training to be a female firefighter, an inmate could get up to four weeks off her sentence.

I was never invited to train at Fire Camp. My crime was considered a violent one, and violent criminals weren't given that opportunity.

Once we arrived in Chowchilla, we were told to prepare for an extremely lengthy intake process, which ultimately took hours. Seventy-five women had come from Lynwood on our bus. A number of other buses had come in from jails all over the state.

Each one of us had been sentenced; now we would start serving our time. Some ladies had one year. Others had three life sentences, with an additional seventy-five years and no chance of parole. I guess this had been ordered just in case the convict died three times, came back to life, and then at the age of seventy-four, took a shot at parole. Clearly, a very likely scenario.

Aside from this new cold and dark prison, I had another thing to worry about.

I'd had my first hint of it when I was in Vanier. Hold had made that statement about the other ladies in jail, and how they might view the scar on my face. I never understood what she meant, and I hadn't thought about it since.

Not until it came up again in Lynwood.

We had been talking about near-death experiences. I'd told the story about what had happened to me in the car accident. That even though my face had gone through the driver's side window, I was still lucky to be alive. One of the girls that night had said, "I was hoping no one did that to your face. You'd get f----d up in here for that." Once again, I thought it was kind of weird. I thought it was odd that someone would purposely do this to someone, but I didn't ask what she meant at the time.

Now here in Chowchilla, the issue came up again. I finally understood what the other women had been trying to tell me.

With all the new women coming in and getting taken out, we kept getting switched from one cell to another as we made our way through the intake process.

After several changes, I barely knew anyone in the cell with me, except for this one woman I remembered from the jail in Van Nuys. The place I had been taken to when I'd first gotten back to California the previous year.

I was sitting by myself and trying not to make any eye contact, when out of nowhere one of the women spoke to me.

"Isn't that a snitch scar on your face?"

Even though she'd asked a question, it sounded more like she was making a statement for the other women to hear. It wasn't the girl I knew who'd asked me. It was one of the girls she was standing with, and now there were four of them waiting to hear my answer.

I replied, "I'm sorry. A what?"

She paused for a moment looking around at the other ladies, then her eyes fixed on me again, and very loudly she said, "Are you also deaf?"

With all of them still looking at me, I started to get very nervous, feeling like a wounded animal being cornered by a pack of lionesses. My eyes started darting between all eight of theirs. My knees became weak, and I felt a lump in my throat. Soon, my heart began to race. I was stuck in a cage, with nowhere to run and everyone is trained not to care.

I was being threatened. I had no doubt about that.

Raising both my hands to create some space, I nervously said to the pack, "If you give me a chance, I promise to explain!" I told them.

I did explain. And mercifully, I survived.

***

Back then, in 2011, CCWF was at 185.9% of its total capacity, with approximately 1700 more women than it had originally been designed for. That's a lot of women I was going to have to face with a pretty severe scar. A scar which apparently spells R-A-T in prison.

Even within the correctional society, there are certain rules people live by. The one about snitching is cause for severe and immediate punishment, delivered, of course, by the other prisoners.

A cut is carved into the so-called rat's face, a slice that extends from the left corner of the mouth all the way to the left ear.

But unlike my scars, which were a sign of surviving something terrible, a snitch scar is given to a prisoner as a sign that the person has turned someone else in. It's a brand of shame. A mark of betrayal. Besides inflicting pain, it serves to warn other inmates that you are a threat. Anyone wearing one is in for daily physical punishment and exclusion, possibly even death.

Sadly enough, the scar from those eighty-seven stitches on my face from my car accident looks very similar to a snitch scar. Ironically, I was more like the reverse of a snitch. I never once spoke out against Leading Actor.

Somehow, at Chowchilla, my scar became a badge of honor. Once they knew the story about how I had worn the scar bravely, through everything I'd undergone, I was viewed as someone who should be entirely vindicated. Not to mention, you would be hard pressed to find a person in there that had love or admiration for anyone rich and famous.

After that, the ladies started to joke around with me. They would ask me, "Did that fool put any money on your books yet?"

The inmates believe that if someone owes you, or if someone's responsible for you being there, that person should be paying for whatever you need to make your stay as comfortable as possible.

***

Chowchilla stunk of mold and sorrow. I was pretty sure that this was where all the smog in California had come to settle.

There were nearly 4,000 prisoners split into the four yards. The receiving yard is where the new inmates all go first. This is for evaluation purposes, to see where you will best fit in. It's also the only yard that's shared with death row inmates.

All types of prisoners are there together, everyone from murderers, to women who were convicted for writing bad checks.

Each unit has thirty-two cells, with at least eight women assigned to each of them. This means that, together, there are 256 inmates of all kinds housed together with only three correctional officers to watch them. In the reception yard, there are 276 inmates per housing unit of unclassified inmates, supervised by only two officers.

Chowchilla houses the largest number of women waiting to be executed on death row, and they're constantly adding more to the list. Part of the problem is, they've stopped executing people in California. The last execution there was in 2006.

However, with fourteen more people added to death row on a yearly basis (men and women), if they were to reinstate executions today, it would take twelve years (at five people a month) to catch up. I bet if they did, Hollywood would find a way to turn it into a television show.

As soon as I got to the receiving yard, I did my best to befriend the deputy, the one who was on duty in my unit, figuring honesty was the best policy. I needed something, and usually a friendly face gets it quicker. Being fresh off the bus, and asking questions of the deputies, would probably get me some sort of response like, "Go kick rocks." But I had to try.

"Hello, sir, I was hoping to ask you a quick question. I just want to use the phone to call my son, and I need to know how to do that."

In the receiving area, there were only two phones. They were only for use by the porters.

To my surprise, the deputy said, "I heard about you. Go ahead. You can call him now. You start work as a porter tomorrow."

I didn't hesitate. I walked behind him, where no one was supposed to be permitted. With a huge smile on my face, I picked up the phone and reflected on how lucky I was as I dialed.

Another aspect of being a porter was the opportunity it would give me to befriend the women I would be living with. In order for me to survive this mess, I desperately needed that.

It was the only way I could make my time a little less difficult.

***

The cells in the receiving yard in Chowchilla were the smallest and darkest I had been in yet. With my own footsteps, I measured the cell to be no more than eight by five feet. In that small space, each cell had two women. All of the cells I had been in were only big enough for a sink, a bunk bed, and toilet installed directly into the floor.

The color painted on the bricks also blended into the floor. Always the same teardrop gray. Here in Chowchilla, there was barely enough room for my bunkie and I to turn around.

Then there were all the little visitors who would come out to see us late at night, as soon as the deputy said, "Lights out." It was deathly quiet, and you couldn't help but hear their tiny nails as they scurried across the concrete floors, going through the unit, looking for whatever they could find. For every woman in the cell, there had to be at least five mice. I stayed on the top bunk, pretending like the mice couldn't get me there.

My bunkie and I rarely slept well at night. I tossed and turned, wrestling with my thoughts. I was filled with despair, entwined with sharp pangs of paranoia. For some reason, I couldn't get the thought out of my head that I might never be released.

Desperately, I fought back with my own imagination, trying to visualize an exuberant family reunion featuring Scion, with my dog daughter pawing at my knees. During those endless nights, I would also try to theorize why fate had brought me there.

Being locked up in a cell, and being sleep deprived, leaves you with endless opportunities to think about everything you've ever done. Every single tiny thing that might have led to this horrible predicament.

At 7:00 a.m., we were led out of our unit by the deputy, into another concrete building where we ate our breakfast. When we left that area, we were given a bagged lunch. It was to be eaten back in our unit. Then again, around 5:00 p.m., we would go back to what was commonly called the chow hall for our dinner. It was the same combination of food I'd had in every jail, except here we always got a side of beans.

It only took about a minute to get to the chow hall from our unit. I soon realized that I had better sit with someone I knew. If not, I might just as well just stay back at the unit, and pray to God that someone would sneak some food out for me. There was no other way I was getting any.

No one wanted a newbie loner to sit at their table. If you tried, you'd be given a look that meant you had one chance to get away. Luckily for me, my bunkie and I got along very well. As soon as they announced two minutes to chow, she was ready to go and usually the first one in the line.

***

Sometimes, we would be confined to our housing units for days. Not because of lockdown, but because it was raining outside. There was no way the deputies were going to get wet watching us walking around, kicking rocks. Spending countless hours in our units also meant a good majority of our time was spent in our cells. However, as a porter, I got to deliver the women all their mail. This allowed me to escape my cell a lot more often.

I went to everyone's cell, stopping at all of the doors. Even if they had nothing in the mail, I would tell them a joke or sing a song. Out of all the 276 ladies in the receiving unit, only one never smiled, no matter what I did to try and make her laugh. She was known as the silent one. I had no idea why she never smiled.

Occasionally, I would get hit on, which was always funny to me. I wasn't used to seeing women with shaved heads and scraggly goatees, with pictures of their kids pasted on their cell walls, dropping pickup lines. Especially when they were directed at me.

They had a term in Chowchilla for women like that. "Gay for the stay, and straight for the gate." Not hard to figure out.

During one of my evening deliveries, I got hit on by a lady asking me, "Canada, you think you'd be willing to take a step in my direction?"

It caught me off guard. For a moment, I thought about what she had said, a giggle wanted to burst out of me that I knew I couldn't let out. The best way to handle a situation that I didn't really want to be in was to say something funny back.

"Ahhh, someone must have told you my secret," I said.

"Oh?" the lady asked me. "Which one is that?"

"That I have eleven toes."

She backed up a few feet looking at me through the cell window, using her left hand to pull at the few hairs growing out of her chin. She seemed to be pondering what I had just revealed.

"That's okay," she finally said. "I think we can get past that. Which foot has the extra toe?"

I shot back, "I have eleven on each foot and believe me when I say, they do come in handy. Sometimes, I use them to sleep hanging upside down in my cell."

We both broke out into laughter.

***

Unlike me, some of the women didn't hesitate to take their relationship to a whole different level, as if they had forgotten about the world, they used to live in. One of the couples I knew in Lynwood got separated when we got to Chowchilla.

Once they arrived, they were housed in the same receiving yard, but slept in different units. They had been in an exclusive relationship since they had been in Lynwood. However, things changed while they waited to be assigned to their prospective yards, which usually took a few months.

After being convicted, one of the ladies was given eighteen years, while her partner had only been ordered back to Chowchilla to finish a four-month parole sentence. Then a rumor started circulating that the one with four months had been unfaithful to the one who had eighteen years. The woman who got eighteen years was pretty upset when she heard the news.

So, the lady with four months decided she would lengthen her stay by stabbing the girl she had been accused of having the affair with. By that point, I was working in the chow hall, and the woman who had been stabbed showed me her wounds as I served her in the line. She lifted up her shirt to reveal her injuries, which had been sealed with a few stitches for each stab.

I served her one scoop of beans, some rice, and then she waved off the rest. They were short little cuts that looked like little, tiny jabs, not really intended to do much damage.

It was like the woman with only four months left had wanted to make a statement to her partner that she still cared and would do anything so that they could stay together, even stabbing the woman she'd been accused of having an affair with, directly in view of a deputy.

She ended up getting the opportunity to stay, all right. She didn't even have to go to court. Once you're state property, if you commit a crime in prison, and you're on their soil, you're basically sentenced on the spot. No lawyers or bus rides required.

The irony is, shortly before her four months became twenty years…they broke up. Love is a fickle thing.

***

I got to listen to everyone's tragedies. They were all true tales of woe. So many women with so many stories, completely different in details but with the same undercurrent of misery and despair.

For me, the most disheartening story was of a girl who got to Chowchilla a year before I arrived, when she had been just eighteen. Her crime was being an accessory in an attempted robbery, and the courts had sentenced her to seven years. This was the one who never smiled when I came around with the mail. The silent one.

Once, we spent the day together in the law library. The library was the nicest room in the whole building. I spent the majority of my time reading and writing whenever I was permitted to go. I always took advantage of the privilege, usually once a week.

Aside from the Bible, I would read everything from James Patterson to Dan Brown. Frank McCourt changed my life with Angela's Ashes. It was the most beautiful, loving story of survival that I'd ever read. The best part was, the story was real.

I found the silent one there that day, trying to find a way to change her current situation. Although, I will say, hers was way more confusing than mine. I can't imagine who wouldn't agree that she deserved a better life than what she had been given.

It was times like those when I realized that no matter what I had been through, perhaps I haven't suffered quite as much as some others in comparison. There's always someone worse off.

"What are you looking into?" I asked, trying to start a conversation.

She didn't smile as she answered, "My case."

"What does your lawyer think?"

Pausing for a moment, she replied, "It's not about my lawyer. It's beyond that."

That made me curious, wondering what she meant. The only way to go back to court is to file for an appeal. Usually, you need a lawyer for that. She said it as if she would be representing herself, but at that point, I realized that even if she doesn't need a lawyer, she needed an advocate to get her case reexamined.

She certainly wasn't the talkative type, and usually in prison, you never ask someone about their crime. That information has to be volunteered. To my surprise, she totally opened up. She started to explain her initial conviction, why she got seven years for being an accessory to an attempted robbery.

When she told me what had happened, I thought, there's no way in this world this can be true. She explained to me that she had three specific tattoos on her body which in the State of California are considered gang-related. If the deputies in prison believe you are associated with a gang, in any way, shape, or form, it's all that's required to carve a chunk off of the remaining free years of your life.

For one tattoo, you can get up to ten more years added on to your current sentence. They made sure to give this young woman every single one of them, turning her sentence from seven years into thirty-seven years.

I understood now why she was silent all the time. The State of California had made sure she had no reason to smile for a very long time. Considering she had only attempted a robbery, you can't help but wonder how she'd been sentenced so harshly.

I was under the impression that our laws on Earth reflected the Ten Commandments. Then again, if that were truly the case, we'd all go to jail for breaking number nine, which would most likely include every judge or criminal I have come face-to-face with. It's always entwined within the other nine. Unfortunately, it's the one sin of man's law that supersedes God's. Some of us lie as easily as giving candy to a baby.

It's hard to believe there's a place in the world where it's okay to punish a human by stealing thirty years of her life simply for having body art. We all know tattoos are a huge part of our culture. It's pretty much accepted in society these days.

I wondered, if she'd had access to laser therapy, and those tattoos no longer appeared on her body, would they set her free? Besides, just having a tattoo doesn't physically hurt anyone.

Then I realized that they probably wouldn't exonerate her because she's not the only one being punished for having them. Hundreds, if not thousands, of men and women are in prison, for what the state of California conveniently calls "gang enhancements."

I like to call it self-expression. A crime punishable by awe.

***

After two months of being in the receiving yard, I was assigned to B Yard, and what they call being "over the wall." Every day, I worked in the chow hall, where I made twelve cents an hour for the food I served.

I prepared meals for the women on death row, as well as the others still in receiving. I interacted with everyone, including the deputies, sergeants, and lieutenants.

One evening, I received a visit in the chow hall, just before I was about to begin my shift. It was a highly ranked official who'd made the special trip up to my yard just to see me.

We were preparing the hall for the hundreds of noisy women that would soon arrive. I watched as this highly ranked official came around the tables and through the sitting area toward me. He was extremely polite; I noticed it immediately, as soon as he asked for permission to speak with me.

Right off the bat, he asked me, "What happened to your face?"

After a few moments of discussing my car accident, he stopped me mid-sentence. "Let's cut to the chase. What are you in here for?" Then he leaned back against the counter with his arms folded, waiting for me to answer.

I started by explaining that Leading Actor and I had had some words, and repeated the story the same way I always did, no matter who was asking. "I only hit him back out of natural defense. I suppose it was a nervous reaction to protect my scar."

The highly ranked official paused for a moment. I could see by the look on his face that he was angry or maybe frustrated. Finally, he spoke as clearly as he could. "If it were me, and it was my scar that he'd slapped, I would've taken that glass and shoved it straight through his neck." He turned around and walked away from me then, not looking back once.

Even though that highly ranked official seemed to empathize with my situation, a good majority of the time, the deputies treated the inmates very poorly. They would go from cell to cell screaming obscenities all day and night. Our mornings began with comments like, "Wake up and do your time." If we asked a question, they usually told us to go kick rocks. It felt like their primary duty was to treat the inmates in a way that reminded us every day that we would never again be fit for the free world, despite the fact that the prisons and jails had originally been created as rehabilitation centers and correctional facilities specifically designed to help reintegrate offenders back into society.

All of the jails and prisons I had been sent to, from Lynwood to Chowchilla, Van Nuys to Vanier, the vast majority of the guards and deputies got off on any opportunity to belittle us.

Treating people with no regard for who they are has to take a toll on any human. At some point, most of the inmates would leave this place. But for the guards and deputies, they are stuck in the system for most of their life. Their own time to serve. For some reason, they passed their time by walking all over the inmates, and even though they were the ones in control, they always seemed to be furious about something.

As for myself, it didn't take long for me to get the picture and stay out of their way. I'd seen what they were really capable of. It was a warning that had come the first two weeks I had been in Lynwood. A male deputy punched a female inmate three times, straight in her face, with her back pressed against the floor. After that event, I'd understood that some of them needed just as much rehabilitation as the people they were in control of.

Sadly, this also included the highly ranked official that had seemed to empathize with my situation.

***

Every minute in jail feels like ten. A day can feel like a week, stretching into a month. Every month that passes by feels like a year. In order for us women to survive the long empty moments, most of us had a set schedule, and a lot of the inmates were rigidly organized.

Even though I had never been on one, I thought this must be what it's like to live on an army base, washing the bricks that contained us, scrubbing them one by one, whenever we were ordered to.

Some inmates would beg a deputy for a broom, then spend countless hours sweeping away the past while preparing for a future that was only a hope in her heart.

Every day, I felt like I was fighting for my life.

Once you're over the wall, you are assigned to a cell with seven other women. The head of ours was very well-known throughout Chowchilla for being the hardest to live with. Most of the women there were point-blank terrified of her.

When we first met, she made me nervous right off with a terse, "Who did that to your face?"

When I told her what had happened, she followed up with the same, "He put any money on your books yet?" Unlike the girls I'd first checked in with, she didn't laugh at all when I said no.

The good thing was we found that we got along. As organized

and hard as she was, I learned something every day from her. I did, however, refuse to let her teach me how to play bridge.

After working in the chow hall every day, the first part of my routine was calling Scion. Even though the phone bills were piling up, thanks to Vraie and a colleague from my most recent job, I always had access to the free world that way. They never refused to do a three-way call for me, making sure I always spoke with my family.

Writing was another way I kept in contact. Members of my family wrote on a weekly basis, and I always wrote back. My closest niece would write letters as much as ten pages long, back and front, giving updates and sending pictures so I wouldn't forget what any of them looked like. I realized that most of the women here had beautiful penmanship, probably due to the volume of letters they wrote.

Our words were meant to be written as much as they were meant to be spoken. Many women here perfected their handwriting with letters to their loved ones, penning their cries for freedom. In so doing, they had developed their penmanship far beyond those living outside those dreary gray walls.

My favorite way to pass the time was working out. My son sent me the money to buy an MP3 player, earphones, and new running shoes. This gave me the opportunity to work out both mentally and physically. It also gave me hope.

The first song I heard after months in receiving was "The Dog Days Are Over." It inspired me. After that, I walked or jogged around the entire yard every day while listening to music. I tuned in to all the radio stations around Chowchilla, day dreaming about the life I desperately hoped I would eventually return to.

I fully intended to live differently. I realized that it wasn't entirely my fault I was here, but there was something about myself I needed to change. I didn't want my whole life's journey to be a waste. Somehow, I knew Florence and the Machine was right: my dog days were almost over.

Aside from the Bible, music was my main encouragement. It

pushed me forward constantly, always teaching me more and more. I learned a lot about Los Angeles from the band The Red Hot Chili Peppers, thanks to their song, "Californication." Their album had been named after the song. If Hollywood were to be made into a movie, that track would be the perfect soundtrack. The band's explanation of the state was almost as powerfully paradigm-changing for me as Frank McCourt's book Angela's Ashes had been.

At night, after saying my prayers, I would lie on my bunk, put my headphones on, and listen to the radio. Then I would dream about the things I was going to do once I was free again.

I listened to musicians like Big Sean and Chris Brown in constant rotation on three radio stations. A song called "My Last" said exactly what I wanted to do the first night I regained my freedom: to live like I never had before. At least four times a day, the same stations would play Cage the Elephant's song "Shake Me Down," which reminded me to keep my eyes fixed on my son. At the same time, the Foo Fighters would give me just enough "Rope", so that I could hold on to my sanity. By that point, I was really looking forward to my sentence coming to an end. With only four weeks left, I began to envision myself doing a moonwalk right out of there as I strolled up "Fascination Street", thanking God for The Cure.

One of the best things we can do is dream. Music became my greatest escape, with lyrics that always reminded me to look forward, to go to a place where I could dance my troubles away, similar to how I'd always envisioned Heaven.

Thankfully, music was one of the few freedoms they couldn't take from me.

Chapter Thirteen

PARANOID ANDROID

AFTER DOING OVER five months at Chowchilla, I was asked to meet with my counselor again. Only, this one wasn't my regular one. Apparently, the regular one was away on vacation. The regular one was detached and avoided eye contact with me. That was actually an improvement on my very first counselor, who'd thought my beauty marks (melanocytic nevus) were gang-related tattoos.

This new stand-in counselor's job was to inform me of my parole conditions for my release.

However, I had some concerns.

She told me that for the first three years while out on parole, I would be required to report every week to a parole officer located somewhere in Los Angeles.

My excitement about getting out of jail and being free suddenly fizzled.

They didn't understand that I was supposed to be going home.

She didn't realize I wasn't from this country. Someone had made a mistake. They were even telling me that I could collect the two hundred dollars they give to inmates upon their release, a benefit that only American citizens receive.

Over the months I had been here, I'd watched as ICE officers, the immigration officials, came to meet with anyone who wasn't a citizen. They would arrive as soon as an immigrant had been sent to Chowchilla. Anyone not from the United States was immediately informed that they would be deported back home after their sentence was done. When their sentence was finished, a bus would be waiting outside to take them to an immigration detention center. There, they would have to wait to be deported back to their home country.

Since we were in California, immigrants usually came from Mexico. Enough of the prisoners were Mexican that ICE visited quite a bit.

It makes me wonder what would have happened if the United States had never taken California away from Mexico back in 1848. Would they still have a huge immigration problem? After all, most people from Mexico who get into the United States, never leave what became the thirty-ninth state. Maybe they should just give it back.

No one from ICE had ever came to visit me. Even though the prosecutor had gone through all that extra trouble to place an immigration hold on me so I couldn't get bail. No one had made arrangements for me to be picked up by ICE after my release.

I sat in the room, waiting for the counselor to go through the State's instructions for me. I thought to myself that the prosecutor must not care anymore about the how, when, or where I was let go now that she'd gotten what she wanted.

The prosecutor had met the State's requirements and kept in line with the treaty agreement between the US and Canada by getting me to plead no contest. I'd accepted the deal for two years, with 50% time served. Even if she'd known I wasn't guilty, her job was complete. She'd earned that all-important notch in her belt. Her job and quality of life were secure for a while longer.

At this point, being released in California would create even more trouble for me, especially with the chance that other people would want to make up their own ending to my story. And that's exactly what I thought would happen if I was dropped off in Hollywood. After all, most of the 'normals' in Hollywood worship their celebrities.

That became even more apparent, once the counselor realized who the celebrity in my case was, the person I had been ordered not to be around for the next three years.

"Am I reading this right? Does this say…Leading Actor?" She stared at the paper as if her eyes were glued on the letters typed on the page. She finally looked up, staring at me.

I waited for a moment, and then answered flatly, "Yes."

She stared at me for a second longer, turning her face into a weird shape. Then she said, "How did you end up in the same room as him?"

The way she said it sounded to me like he was some type of a god, from the planet Hollywood. I was just a parasite, sucking up his air. She couldn't come up with a reasonable way to picture how the two of us could ever have shared time in the same space.

"That's actually not your business," I told her. "I'm not here for that. Matter of fact, I'm in this office because my sentence is over." I waited while she pretended not to hear what I'd said, ignoring me while looking over the documents that were in front of her. It was almost as if she were looking for his autograph in my file.

Squinting, she looked up at me, and asked, "Did you see him at a party somewhere?"

This time, I didn't answer her question. I just stared at her, wondering why she cared so much about a man who didn't even know she was alive.

"You know you're not allowed to go around him for three years."

After hearing that, I realized there was no way I wanted to spend even one moment outside of custody in LA. After this experience, I was more certain than ever that most people were going to give me a hard time. Or worse.

"If you're worried about what I may do when I'm released," I told her firmly, "perhaps you can do yourself a favor and get in contact with immigration. Let them know I'm here, so they can take me back home."

She looked at me oddly. "So, you're telling me that you don't mind going to another jail and waiting to be deported to wherever you're from? Don't you want the two hundred dollars you get when you leave?"

I shot back immediately, "If you weren't only pretending to read my file, you would know I'm from Canada, and no I don't I want the two-hundred-dollar gate fee. I'd rather go to another jail."

I just wanted to go back home.

No matter what it took.

After a few more questions, the counselor ended our interview by telling me she would call immigration as I had requested. I wanted nothing more to do with California. I would rather spend another month in jail than three years on parole in Los Angeles.

I wanted to be actually free, with my feet back on Canadian soil.

I got up and left her office, then slowly made my way back to the housing units through B Yard. As I strolled across the grass, I thought about the fascination we have with celebrities. Most of us have been conditioned by society to idolize them. And it only seems to become worse and worse as time goes on, putting those stars farther beyond our reach with each project they complete.

We are constantly taught and programmed to worship shiny celebrities, through glossy magazines, the news, and the entertainment shows that come on three times a day, seven days a week. We're almost forced to care about who's getting married, who's getting divorced, who is pretty, and who is not. We follow their lives right down to the restaurants where they eat.

We want to know every detail so we can feel important too.

Come hell or high water, we need to idolize them to feel good about ourselves. Frankly, I'm still not exactly sure why. They are never what they seem to be, and they're certainly no better than you or me.

Not to say that they're all bad.

But it seems like anyone in the inner circles of Hollywood is completely exempt from the rules. The same ones that the rest of us must live by, especially the ones who have agreements with the powers that be to make sure none of the bad stuff gets out.

The unfairness of it all festered in my heart.

***

That night, I lay in my bunk trying to fall asleep, but I kept tossing and turning.

The events of the day reminded me of a time when I had been in Lynwood, and I had gone to the only other place we were ever permitted to go aside from court — the Los Angeles County Central Jail Hospital. It was another part of the institution but located off the main premises.

That goes to show you how big the prison system is in California. In Canada, we don't have a single jail hospital, although we do have a health care system that is practically free and designed to take care of everyone.

Going to the Los Angeles County Central Jail Hospital from Lynwood was also one of the only times they allowed men and women to ride the bus together. Even though there was a wire partition that separated us, it didn't stop us from looking at each other.

That was when I had seen the bravest-looking young man I had ever come across. Not just because of the bruises he had been sporting across his face. The word torture came to mind when I thought about what must have been done to him.

I had been surprised he'd been able to even sit up. It had looked as if he was staring off into space, seeing nothing, completely dead-faced. I'd imagined that if I could read his mind, I'd find he was trying to not breathe his next breath of air. Like he could end his own life by just…stopping. But we can't. It's never that easy.

I couldn't look away. Whatever had been done to him should never happen to any human. Not to mention that whatever he had to go back to might be worse. He would have to return to a place where boys don't cry, and a man can't even think about shedding tears, no matter how much pain he's in.

Real stars in the galaxy are huge celestial bodies made mostly of hydrogen and helium. They radiate light and heat from the churning nuclear forces inside their cores.

I believed that this brave young man was as bright and powerful as a star, digging deep within his heart to find the strength to endure whatever he would face upon returning to the men's jail. He didn't have to be on the silver screen to be incredible in my eyes. He was living an inescapable life, with strength and courage. That meant more in my book than some fake person on a screen with special effects enhancing their looks. It's all pretend, usually written by someone else, and always devoid of the real struggle.

Besides, how many attempts does it take for an actor to be one of us?

***

Over the next few days, I became more stressed out as my release date drew closer. I still hadn't heard anything from immigration yet. During this time, B Yard got put into complete lockdown. A few things went wrong, and they put the whole prison on high alert. This would be my last week of incarceration at Chowchilla.

The unit directly beside ours was being investigated due to a death caused by heroin overdose. Apparently, her fellow cellmates had woken up and found her dead. But with eight women in a cell, they suspected that someone had been awake while she had been taking her last breath.

Everything seemed to go wrong that final week. A few days

before the lockdown, the entire yard witnessed the sergeants escorting one of their own deputies off the yard in handcuffs. The rumor was that he'd been caught in the middle of a sexual act with one of the inmates from our yard, and they'd arrested him right on the spot. Then, as if to make a point, they escorted him out in front of us.

Whatever they'd caught them doing, it had been enough for the authorities to close the chow hall down for contamination. That just added to the tension in the air for the rest of us. The place where we were served our meals had to be relocated, all because of the deputy's decision to fool around where we ate.

The last thing you ever want to do is shake up the daily routine of a bunch of humans who are caged. About all we could depend on was our routine.

Not long after, I was getting ready to leave my cell when I heard my inmate number and name over the loudspeaker.

"Aretha Wilson, inmate 56———1, report to the counselor's office immediately."

I had been on my way to meet a friend, and begin my daily routine of walking around the yard for the last time. But after hearing them paging me, I suspected it would have something to do with immigration, so I headed straight to the counselor's office.

As I made my way through the unit, some of the ladies hanging around the common area who knew about my current situation put their hands up for high-fives. With a huge smile on my face, I was glad to oblige as I walked by, responding as I always did by saying, "It's not a high-five, it's four fingers and a thumb."

Then one of the ladies yelled out, "I never saw someone so happy to be picked up by even more authorities and go to immigration jail."

I winked at her as she laughed with some of the other girls, while shaking her head in disbelief.

I got to the counselor's office and noticed my regular counselor was back. She handed me the phone, telling me it was for me.

"Hello?" I said, as my counselor went back to doing whatever she had been doing before I arrived.

"Hi there, am I speaking to Aretha Wilson?"

"Yes, you are now."

The caller told me he was from the United States Department of Homeland Security, and then something about him being in another part of California. He told me, "I understand you've requested to be picked up, and you'd like to be transferred to our Immigration Detention Center. May I ask why?"

"Because you guys brought me here from Canada," I told him. "Now that my sentence is over, it's time for you to take me back home."

"What do you mean, we brought you here?" he asked me. "When and how was that?"

I thought that should be obvious. "Are you serious? Don't your records show that I was extradited, picked up by US Marshals, and brought to California almost a year ago?"

"No, actually, they don't show anything like that at all."

For a moment, we were both silent.

"Well," he finally said, "I have to admit, this is a pretty unusual request. Most people don't just call immigration on themselves."

"That's because the majority of people you have in immigration don't come from Canada. Whether you believe it or not, not everyone wants to be in the US. I'm going to be released tomorrow. Can you please make sure someone is here to get me? I'm concerned about being released in the State of California."

"Why is that?"

"If I'm not from this country, does it matter?"

I didn't want to say anything about my case. I was worried about the media, and what I would go through if they knew I was fair game. I just wanted to go home.

"You got it," he told me. "I'll make sure you're not released, and I'll inform your counselor you want to be picked up by immigration."

Then he asked me for a description of myself, including any tattoos or markings that would make me stand out.

I told him what I thought I looked like, and the tattoos I had, forgetting to mention the one I had gotten while I was in Chowchilla, because it slipped my mind.

Big O was the petite woman who had given me the tattoo with her makeshift needle. She'd worn a tattoo down the left side of her face with pride. She had been in Chowchilla for years, and like the majority of women there, she wasn't leaving anytime soon. On me, she had tattooed an honorary gang insignia, one designed for people they consider survivors.

It looks like three dots stacked as a pyramid, which translates to "my crazy life." It's given to men and women living in the system (usually within North America), mainly kept inside the Latin community. It symbolizes respect among the inmates, for what they've had to overcome. Although I'm not Latina, she'd tattooed my three dots on the right side of my middle finger on my left hand.

I suppose you could say, I'd earned my stripes walking into prison with a scar on my face, after getting slapped on it by a celebrity who didn't like the way I looked. And as much as it looked like a snitch scar, it eventually became obvious to everyone inside that I'd never be a rat. All of it was a part of what seemed to be my crazy life.

When I was done describing myself, the immigration officer said, "All right, Aretha, we know who to look out for, and we'll see you at some point tomorrow."

"Is that for sure?"

"Yes. Like I said, there is an immigration bus. Prior to walking out of the gate, you get on that, and I'll make sure to let them know to expect you."

"Thank you for all your help."

I passed the phone back to my counselor. She took it, and I listened in as she spoke briefly with the ICE official, making sure to confirm my request.

After hanging up the phone, she looked up at me and, for the first time ever, I smiled at her. Then I said, "I'm assuming he confirmed someone would be here to get me tomorrow?"

She looked at me without smiling back. "You really don't want to be released into the city of Los Angeles, do you?"

With my arms folded, I said, "No. Absolutely not!"

"You know most people would do anything to go to LA."

"I'm no longer one of them." I stood there for a moment, while she stared at me with a blank look on her face.

Then she told me, "You won't get the two hundred dollars when you're released into immigration."

"You can keep it," I told her.

After walking out of there, I went back through the unit.

Once again, as I walked by, the same lady called out to me again, "Was that them? They coming to get you now?"

I responded, a massive grin plastered on my face. "You know it!"

I was done with California and its celebrity worship. I wanted nothing more to do with this jail, the counselors, the lawyers, celebrity-loving judges, and everyone else who ought to have helped keep me from being unfairly imprisoned. I wanted to be rid of all of them.

Even if it meant going to another jail.

Once I got out into the yard, I realized what a beautiful morning it was. Warm, bright, and sunny, it was a perfect day for a goodbye picnic in B Yard. I used all the leftover money I had in my canteen account and bought my friends treats to make sure it was extra special.

I met up with up with the two of them. One was a girl who I would call my Chowchilla Sista. She had hair that went down her back, with soft brown eyes and perfect lips. They showed off her glowing personality whenever she smiled.

It was a stolen bottle of shampoo that had put her in there. And even though she had hair like a mermaid, she wasn't the one who'd actually stolen it. Just being with the person who had taken it had gotten her a four-year sentence. Much like me, she, too, had a young teenage son. Our similarities had helped her instantly become my Chowchilla Sista. My other friend was also a mother, only her hair went all the way down to the back of her knees. However, I won't go into her story and why she was in there. It was told to me on a promise to never repeat. As for her sentence, seven years to life.

No one in here was going to counsel us. Therefore, we had all depended on each other to talk about what was bothering us. Three of us spent the day together reminiscing, laughing at all the Hollywood stories I had told them, and a few jailhouse jokes that I had picked up while inside.

We ended our picnic and decided to walk to the gate together the next morning after breakfast. I knew Chowchilla Sista still had two years left on her sentence, and I wanted to make the best mental picture of her that I could, as well as the other ladies who had helped me get through the worst year of my entire life.

The next morning at 6:00 a.m., I was told for the third time to "roll it up". This time, even though my sentence was over, I was actually glad to go to another jail. My fear of being released into LA was still lingering, and the thought of the media being outside only made it worse. I started to imagine all the outright cruel things they'd said, and the unflattering pictures they'd printed of me.

As I prepared to go and meet Chowchilla Sista, and Promise, I packed the few things I had; including the letters that had been written to me from all the ladies I'd met in the other jails. It didn't include Vanier, where they'd only let me keep the clothes I had been wearing when I'd walked in.

The letters I had collected over time meant the most to me, all of them full of well-wishes for a happy life, regardless of whether we ever visited or spoke again. Most people in jail have to face the same truth: the odds of meeting up outside were highly unlikely. After the countless times we were searched, bare naked in front of each other, it didn't do us any good to hide from the truth.

All of the other letters had come from my family members. One of the more interesting ones had come from my closest niece. It was a one-page letter, asking if I'd ever heard of a lady that she saw on an episode of Investigative Hours, who was serving time in California. The show was about a woman and her husband who had duped an elderly couple out of their boat. Then they'd apparently killed the couple by tying weights to their ankles and throwing them overboard. The story had caught my niece's attention, since the woman's husband and my son had the same name.

With over 149,000 prisoners in the state of California, the chances of me meeting a specific one were pretty slim. But as it turned out, that was the woman who'd cut my hair just last week. She was our unit's hairstylist. I told my niece that the money she'd sent me was how I'd paid her. A couple bags of potato chips and a few chocolate bars was the cost of a haircut.

All of the handwritten correspondence I'd received had helped me to keep pushing forward. I made sure to keep every one of them. Everything else I owned, I gave away. I wanted to leave anything that could be useful to other women who I knew would still be there after me. The most important item I left was the MP3 player and earphones my son had sent me. Those I gave to my friend Freckles. Aside from Romania 1, she was the young woman that I'd spent the most time with in Lynwood.

For someone who was twenty years younger than me, she'd coached me through some of my toughest times. The two of us had gotten separated, when I'd been sent to Chowchilla first, and then she came later. It was the best that I could do for her, knowing how important music was to everyone in prison. I thought, just like myself, she could use it to dream of a time when she would also find her freedom.

Once I had everything organized for the last time, I stood there looking around the cell, waiting to be released. I thought about how different this cell was from all the others I had been in. It was the only one that was never empty. I went from being in Vanier, where I was alone in a cell, to Lynwood where porters slept on bunk beds in the common area.

I thought about the last few months that I had lived in here with the other seven women. Sometimes, my roommates would change. But it was always a group of eight women caged up. Somehow we'd made it work—physically and emotionally—in such a small space. Even so, we were a million times more controlled and reserved than any housewives I've ever seen on TV.

It was finally time.

I had served over one full year, even after I'd gotten two weeks off my sentence for good behavior. The only thing I had left to do was go to the detention center in Arizona, and then, finally home.

I hoped my next cell wouldn't be as crowded.

For the last time, I heard the cell door buzz, and we were all released to go out into the unit. I walked straight out, not looking back at anything. I made a beeline for the unit door.

As I walked by, I nodded my head at a few of the girls, trying to keep my goodbyes short. I wanted to make sure not to create any drama now that I was almost out. Some of the ladies knew I was leaving, and some didn't. That's the way you want to keep it there. Boasting about getting out, or giving anyone your actual release date, is the last thing you want to do. It's all part of the etiquette because some of the women will never leave, at least, not while they're still breathing.

Once I made it out to the unit, I looked around and spotted Chowchilla Sista. She was never hard to find. I waved her over so we could go look for Promise and walk out to the gate together.

Already sporting a grin, she beamed, "It's almost over."

I smiled back. "Yes it is."

Suddenly, I could feel my emotions starting to build. I hugged her, trying to squeeze the tears away, wanting to be as strong as I could, for both of us. She still wasn't leaving for a while.

She must have known what I was thinking because she pulled me away from her and consoled me, "Don't worry. I'm going to be fine. I'll see you as soon as I can."

Right at that moment, I knew that out of all the ladies I'd met over the last year, the odds of me seeing this one again were good.

Before either one of us could turn around, Promise was right there with us, urging us to hurry up. It wasn't time to leave just yet. There was breakfast first, but both of my friends were caught up in my anxious energy.

The freedom was so close, I could practically taste it!

As we all walked together through the yard in the direction of the chow hall, I thought about how these two had become two of my very best friends over the last six months. Along with Freckles and Romania 1, they were some of the closest I'd ever had on the inside.

It's hard to think that friendships can grow in a place like this. A place where dreams get locked behind bars, and even the sunlight is stolen from you. But at moments like these, I truly believed that somehow it was all meant to be.

Once we got into the chow hall, we grabbed our trays in a mad dash and sat down by the first table, right beside the exit door, just like we'd originally planned. Once we were seated, we didn't say much to each other. We just sat alone with our thoughts. As I ate, I was so thankful to know it would be my last meal here. No more beans, please.

Of all the jails I had been in, Chowchilla had the worst food. As a matter of fact, in 2011, 12,000 California prisoners took part in a hunger strike to protest the conditions they were subjected to. One of the main issues was the food. The strike lasted twenty days. Even at that point, their food demands were never met. With Core-Civic making billions of dollars annually, I figured the corporate types were all eating steaks while the inmates got by on the proverbial beans and water. Not even proverbial. Literal beans and water.

My Chowchilla sista tried to be funny by saying, "Our last lunch was way better than this shitty last breakfast."

"Well, if it's any consolation," I joked, "I have a feeling there will be twice as many beans in immigration jail!"

We laughed, as the kernel of truth in my statement made it funny. The government knew that beans were filling and cheap, which is probably why we were forced to eat so many in jail.

Even though I knew they were happy to see me leave, I also knew they were sad, because I wouldn't be there with them anymore.

As soon as the exit door was opened by the deputy (indicating we could leave), the three of us jumped up from the table and rushed to discard our trays on the mechanical dishwasher belt.

They walked me out of the chow hall and straight over to the gate, again, mostly in silence. We all stood there, waiting by the door and trying to keep our composure. We acted as if we were simply waiting for a bus, only in this case, I was the lone one leaving. Finally, my name was called. I turned and hugged both of them, and we all said our last goodbyes. As much as we tried to fight it, the tears started to fall.

I walked through the gate and looked back, giving myself something to remember. With one last glance at Chowchilla Sista and Promise, I never looked back again.

I was ready to go, and I only had eyes for the brighter future that lay ahead of me.

Chapter Fourteen

THERE THERE & WHERE I END YOU BEGIN

THERE I WAS!

I found myself on the other side, no longer imprisoned by Chowchilla or the State of California. The worst part was over, and maybe spending time in an immigration jail wouldn't be as horrible as this place. The ladies themselves hadn't been so bad. It was the living conditions that I could have done without.

By American standards, the women I'd lived with over the last year were considered some of the worst people in the world. It makes you wonder, who is actually setting the standards, especially when you have corporations that depend on the billions of dollars being brought in from the prison industry. I have a feeling those people in suits aren't much different from anyone in there, making their living off the troubles of the women and men who are incarcerated. It all seemed to be part of a grander scheme, which would once again allow the elite to ride the backs of others. The rich getting richer.

After going through the gate, I was led into a room in another building, which I soon discovered was the property area. I waited for my name to be called again, so that they could give me my things, although I knew I didn't have anything. Out of the twenty or so women being released that day, I was the second one to be called. The only things I had in property were flat black shoes, a sweater, a tank top, and jeans. As for my driver's license and birth certificate, either they'd been lost or destroyed. I certainly didn't get them back, leaving me with absolutely no physical form of identification.

When I had been at Lynwood, on a few occasions, I had seen women get released from the Los Angeles courthouse. If they didn't have their own clothes to wear, they were given a black garbage bag. It was up to them to poke holes through it for their arms and head.

The bags were given out by the same system that granted them freedom, making the ladies feel like they were still deemed guilty, even during their release. It makes me wonder how with all of the taxes collected from their citizens, they still can't treat people like human beings.

You would think that with all the commotion dragging me to the US, they would have at least kept my birth certificate so I could hurry up and get back out. Although, at this point, I was just happy to be leaving with more than a plastic garbage bag over my head.

The women being released that day all came from the different yards, B, C, and D. Most of them, I didn't know. They all appeared to be happy while patiently waiting to get their things. They were even more ecstatic to receive that two-hundred-dollar gate bonus. A small consolation for reentering society with felony disenfranchisement.

Felony disenfranchisement means that even though convicts are expected to find jobs and pay taxes like normal citizens, the US government can deny them the right to vote in future elections. The Supreme Court of Canada has held that even if a Canadian citizen has committed a criminal offense, is proven guilty and incarcerated, they retain the constitutional right to vote, job or not.

I tried to disappear into an area where I could change, which is always impossible there. No matter where you are, there's always someone looking. The state is so protective of their prison garb, they watch you to make sure they get it all back. That's the main reason for providing the garbage bags: to ensure that none of the state's prison clothing ends up being sold online.

As I changed back into my own clothes, I thought about when I'd first walked into Vanier over a year earlier. How what I'd thought would be a couple of hours in custody had turned out to be more than 9,000 hours of a completed sentence. I still have a hard time wrapping my head around all of it.

"Aretha Wilson?"

I looked up in the direction of the deputy that had called me.

"When you're finished changing, you can head over this way."

I thought to myself, they must be with US Immigration and Customs Enforcement (ICE). After getting my things on, for a moment I smiled at wearing my own clothes again. I then walked over to the deputy.

"Please place your hands in front of you."

I did as I was told, and the deputy placed the cuffs around my wrists, linking them to a chain that connected me to a number of other ladies. Together, we were led by the immigration guards out to the bus, while the American women went home free, but not before being stripped of their dignity and their right to vote, even after doing everything asked of them.

The bus ride was the same as always, which is to say cramped and uncomfortable. This time, we had no radio. We bounced around roughly with every bump, banging from left to right into our handcuff companions. I swear, those buses make you feel every tiny dip in the payment, guaranteeing we didn't have the chance to sleep. No one told us anything, and no one asked any questions. Everyone was too busy speaking to each other in their own languages, which I didn't understand. No one spoke to me. I spent the whole time looking out the window.

Chowchilla must have been their first stop. After two more immigration pickups, our bus was completely packed.

We drove across what looked like an endless desert as I stared out at the sky. I thought about my freedom beyond walls. I thought about the saying, "living outside the box." Then it occurred to me that we all live in a circle. I could look at life from an infinite number of angles, never mind confining myself to four sides.

I had just survived California State Prison without so much as a scratch. Some unnatural force (or perhaps a natural one), had seen me through. My instinct and faith had guided me, as I'd kept my focus on my goal: to survive. I'd used all the advice my brother had given me. He has been incarcerated for the majority of his own life, since being taken away as a preteen. Now he is a Range Representative and Ethnocultural Liaison Worker, who is called upon by the prison guards to mediate when inmates get into conflicts. When he'd told me not to be a tattletale, and that no one likes a rat, I'd listened. When he'd taught me about cards and music, I'd learned. No one would have guessed it, but somehow, he was the one that had set the best example for me. At least, practically speaking.

As I looked to the sky, I thanked God for my son and how he brought purpose to my life. I still wondered what my lesson was in all of this, and if a blessing in disguise would finally be revealed. Although, I will admit having "Cigarette Daydreams" one day will help me to put these moments into a much better perspective. Just as soon as Cage the Elephant releases their next album, the answer will come.

Eventually, after hours of bumpy roads, we finally came to a stop. Wherever we were, it was a smaller detention center in a completely isolated area. Aside from the compound we were escorted into, there were no other buildings or signs of life.

In the distance, all I could see were landing strips and a slew of unmarked planes, without so much as tumbleweed blowing around. The only other thing I could see was, there were a lot more of us (meaning immigrants). Hundreds of them, by my estimate.

Still, out of all the people here, I was the only Canadian, and eventually I was singled out. I was put into a separate room by one of the guards. I still had no idea what would come next, but I could see that my situation was different from everyone else's.

After being placed in this new cell, the guard came back in and gave me a set of their jail clothes to wear. She informed me, "You can knock on the door after you've changed." She walked out, closed the door, and locked it.

After driving for so many hours, I had no idea what state we were in. I told myself I would ask the guard after I changed and she returned. After all, I was no longer in Chowchilla, where I would be reprimanded for simply asking a question.

I changed in the covered area, which was provided in the back of the room. Even though I was putting jail clothes back on, I started to feel better for the first time in over a year. This time when I changed, no one was watching.

Once I was dressed, I walked back to the front of the room to look out of the window, and I knocked on the door. The man outside at the desk looked up at me and smiled. He gestured, as if to say one moment, and mouthed the word, "Please."

Wow, I thought, it seems as though these immigration people are kind of nice. Not at all what I was used to.

Out of nowhere, the female guard appeared again, looking at me through the little window in the door, and smiling as she unlocked it. "You can proceed to the counter over there," she told me.

I walked over to the desk and placed my hands on top of the counter, feeling a little more relaxed.

The guard at the counter lifted his head up from what he was doing and began explaining things to me, "Well, there are some formalities that are required before you are to be transported to

The Eloy Detention Center in Arizona. That's where you'll have to appear at an immigration hearing."

That was news to me, but at least I knew where I was going.

I wasn't aware that I had to be in front of any more judges. I thought it was as easy as rounding a few of us up and escorting us out, only now I found out that I would have to attend one more court appearance, possibly more. I took a deep breath and asked where we were now.

He smiled and replied, "California."

California is actually the longest state in the U.S. All that driving, and I was still here. "How long is the bus ride to Arizona?"

"You'll be flying there."

That was a bit of a surprise, but then I remembered all of the unmarked planes when we first drove in. That's right. This is a business.

He pushed the papers that he was filling out in front of me, and explained, "If you sign these forms waiving your right to fight deportation, it will help things to go through a lot quicker; so you can get back home."

I looked down at the papers with my eyes darting everywhere. I wondered how much quicker it would help things go through, and where did I sign? I bent down, putting my left hand on the page, while using my right hand to pick up the pen he'd placed on the counter.

Just as I was about to sign, in a very stern voice the immigration officer said, "Aretha, where did you get that?"

I looked up at him, puzzled. "Get what?"

"The three dots on your finger. You never told me about that tattoo, when we spoke over the phone."

This was the same man I had spoken with on the phone in my counselor's office the previous day. I looked down at my left hand, realizing my tattoo was exposed.

The gang tattoo I had gotten as a token of respect.

I was caught off guard.

Think fast, I told myself, think fast. I didn't know what to say. I stood there, frozen. Would that small tattoo that I'd been given as a sign of respect end up costing me my freedom?

"What are you talking about? I'm Canadian," I said, after a long moment of silence. It was the first thing that came to mind and my only defense. "If you look closely, it's three stars. Not dots." I pointed at my finger, showing him.

He stared at me with a sharp look as if he knew the truth behind a lie.

My heart began racing. I knew only too well of the other ladies who had been held back, and the years added to their sentences just for having these types of tattoos.

I myself was scheduled for an additional three years of parole, and even though I was on my way back to Canada, I had not yet been released from their custody. Technically, the tattoo could be considered a violation of my conditions. If the officers pushed it, I'd be on my way back to Chowchilla for a whole new sentence.

I thought to myself, I'd better sign this paper, before he makes a rash decision that takes away another three years of my life. Besides, I wasn't lying. They really were three stars, now.

I signed the document as calmly as I could. I didn't want to give him any sign that I wasn't confident in what I had just said. A flashback of the evening before, when I was being released from Chowchilla, came clearly to my mind at that moment. As I was beginning to read over the document, I remembered how adamant the woman who'd tattooed my dots had been that night when we were out on the yard. That's when she said she needed to talk to me.

"Canada, I found out you're being released tomorrow, and the fifteen minutes you spend with me now could save three years of your life."

She told me she didn't want to be responsible for me not going home. She wanted to cover up the three dots she had originally tattooed on my left finger. I didn't think it was a big deal, but for whatever reason, I allowed her to use her makeshift needle and ink to redesign my dots. With a bit of work, she turned them into stars.

For a split second, I thought about pleading my case. As I put the pen back down, I thanked God I'd made the decision to do what she suggested.

I waited for him to respond, and this time as my heart began to race, I thought about some of the best advice I'd been given. Patience and saying less would be way better than doing any more time. Then I heard my inner voice speak. The same one that had been in my head in the mirror when I was back in the hospital after my accident. It spoke clearly and firmly. Be quiet.

It was the same tactic I'd used to get past the guards, the media, the jail term, and the scars. A skill that had gotten me through some of the worst case scenarios of my life.

I realized my words are worth more than their weight in gold, and by the same token, maintaining my silence could be just as valuable.

I could feel my heart as it began to regain its normal pace.

Quietly I waited.

"All right, Aretha," the deputy conceded, "I'm going to give you the benefit of the doubt. In a little while, you'll be headed to Eloy. Until then, I'm going to put you in this cell, where you can make a call if you need."

As soon as he left, he locked the door on my waiting cell, and I made a beeline for the pay phone.

Right away, I knew the best person to call would be Vraie. She would connect me to everyone I would need to talk to, so I could let them know how and where I was. As I waited for the operator to place my collect call, I reflected on all the things she'd done for me, from the night of the altercation, to when I had gone straight to her house, to the times she would visit me in Lynwood. During my entire incarceration, she was the only person in California who had.

She'd even brought her young son with her, just to give me some hope. To remind me that I also had a young man waiting for me back home. During that visit, her son had reminded me of Scion, and of Five and Seven, when I'd first seen them after the accident. Vraie's son had smiled at me with his icy blue eyes, and hummed and sang to himself the whole time while his mother and I talked.

After the operator informed Vraie that I was on the phone, she immediately called out my name, "Aretha! Where are you?"

Smiling, I replied, "Still incarcerated, still in California, but freer than I've been in a while." I went on to explain what the process would be, and how I was still on my way to an immigration detention center in Arizona until they decided it was time for me to go home.

"Who can I call for you?" she asked.

Once again, I smiled. I didn't even have to think about my answer. "My son, if you don't mind."

She put me on hold so she could add my son to the call. While I waited, I thought about the countless times she'd called Canada on my behalf. The numerous calls to all of my lawyers, wherever they were, and never once had she asked for a penny in return. She'd truly been there for me, no matter what they'd had in store. She had been my truest friend through it all, and she kept her word.

"Mom?" It was my son's voice.

"Hey there, buddy."

"Where are you, Mom?"

"Well, you'll be happy to know, I'm not in Chowchilla anymore."

In my mind I saw him grin, as he responded, "Thank God! I'm so happy you're out of there."

Both of us were overjoyed. We talked about all the things we were going to do when I got home, much like we had when he'd been a little boy and I'd been away in Los Angeles.

I could hear how much he had grown over the last year. Everything I had to go through had forced him to become a young man.

We continued our conversation, and I told him about the long bus ride across the empty desert. I told him life would be better, but it would take time to get there.

When the cell door opened again, the guard came in. "Please place your hands behind your back. It's time to go to the Eloy Detention Center."

I had to hang up on my son. I told him I loved him, and he told me the same. I could practically feel his embrace already, and it couldn't come soon enough.

***

Over the last year, I had lived in or been sent to seven different jails. Between Canada and the U.S. there had been the Vanier Detention Center in Toronto, the Van Nuys jail in Van Nuys California, Twin Towers and Lynwood County Jail in LA, CCWF in Chowchilla, and the place I was at now, although, I still didn't really know where that one was. The next one would be Eloy. After that, I prayed that I would never see those drab gray cement walls again.

I had been in almost as many jails as I'd had lawyers, and even though Jesus and all of his disciples had gone to jail, I myself don't recommend it.

Just like the immigration guard had told me, we were flown to Eloy, Arizona. It was an uneventful flight, and by that evening I was incarcerated once again.

Just like the bus, the plane was completely packed with immigrants from all over the world. And then there was me, the one lonely Canadian. Maybe no Canadians were that interested in trying to stay in the US.

As soon as we arrived at the jail, they separated us into different sections based on our sex. This place held 1600 people, all here for the same reason.

Eloy was a little freer, in my opinion, than any of the jails I'd been in before. I don't mean that the people being held here could just come and go as they pleased, but free in a different way.

Just like the place I had been in earlier that afternoon, for the second time in months, I got to change on my own without hundreds of women gawking and three or four deputies searching me.

Unlike what I had seen over the last year, no one was calling anyone names, or being ridiculed for questions they asked. Here they welcomed questions. This was different. This was new, in comparison to what I had been subjected to previously. The type of environment that may have let Romania 2 die because no one had answered her calls for help during a heart attack, seemed to be behind me now.

I was sure a lot of it had to do with the fact that most people here just wanted to go home, even if they might try to get back into the country again next week. Whether they'd committed a crime or not, at this stage, they weren't considered much of a threat.

I was placed in my own cell, and by the time I was situated, it was already lights out. After a long day of traveling across one state, and being flown into another one, I was asleep within seconds.

Thankfully, for the first time in a while, I slipped off to dream with some hope in my heart. Soon, it would all be over.

***

The very next morning, I woke up to find a note slid into the side of the cell door. It was addressed to me about an appointment that had been set up for me to meet with an immigration officer at 10 a.m. that morning.

I hadn't woken up to some awful, loud noise. No deputy screamed at us to get up. Once again, I noted how different this place was—and in a very good way. I looked out of the cell and noticed there were already ladies sitting in the common area. Most of them were watching TV. They all looked like they were waiting for something to happen. I pushed the door open, realizing with a jolt of surprise that it wasn't even locked.

I walked out of my cell, and the other ladies turned to look at me one by one. Twenty or so women were out there at that time. One of them smiled and said hello, breaking the ice. She told me that she was from the Philippines and she had been there for over a year. "Don't worry, I know everything about this place, stick with me."

I was grateful that someone who knew what to do was willing to open up to me, right at the start. The first day in a jail is always like the first day at a new school, only worse. You don't know where to go, or what to do, and you sure don't want to ask the wrong person.

"If you're hungry," she explained, "you might want to clean up fast. The door will be opening soon."

I looked out and saw where I had come in the night before. It looked more like a community center than the bleak, austere rooms I'd been surrounded by in other jails.

I went back to my cell and quickly got ready; washing my face and brushing my teeth, using the bag of toiletries they handed to me when I came in.

When I heard someone of authority yelling to come line up for breakfast, I raced back out. I didn't want to miss anything that would give me an opportunity to better understand where I was. Also, by that point, I was hungry. It hadn't occurred to me until then, but I hadn't eaten anything since my goodbye breakfast in Chowchilla the day before.

As we were led out of our unit, I noticed this felt more like a college campus, compared to anywhere else I had been. The cafeteria was a large room that was bright and airy. I also noticed there were no porters or inmates assisting the guards.

Our food was being served to us by someone other than ourselves. My Filipina friend came and sat with me. She introduced me to a few of the other ladies who were sitting around us.

Everyone was really nice, and I couldn't help but say, "This is definitely different from Chowchilla."

"How do you mean?" one of the ladies asked.

"It seems like everyone here is pretty laid-back. Even the guards are nice."

My Filipina friend looked at me a little oddly. "You obviously don't know where you are right now."

Then she told me that we were in one of the four prisons inside the CoreCivic complex, and that ours had been specifically dubbed "America's deadliest immigration detention center ever." I found out that there had been fifteen deaths there, including at least five suicides, since 2003. Inmates had needlessly died there because of improper medical care and the misuse of solitary confinement.

Great, I thought to myself. I'd just left a place that has the highest number of women on death row in the entire US, just to come to a place known as the deadliest detention center. Just my type of luck.

Seeing the look on my face, my Filipina friend changed the subject. "Did you get an appointment yet?"

I was happy to talk about something else, particularly good news. "Yes, it's at ten o'clock today."

Some of the other ladies were casually getting up and walking outside to soak up some sun, while they waited to be escorted back to their dorms. I got the feeling that most of them didn't mind being here. But there were all those others who had lost their lives trying to stay or get in this country. It felt a little ironic that I couldn't wait for them to hurry up and kick me out.

As we walked back to the dorm, I asked my Filipina friend whether there were any other Canadians in Eloy. She told me she didn't think so, and then she told me something that almost made my heart stop. "Once you meet with the immigration officer today, they'll set a date for you in court. After that, usually you have to wait a few months, depending on where you're going back to."

My eyes went wide. I'd thought I was just about to go free! Now here was the news that I would be spending more months in jail, serving a sentence I had given to myself by asking to be sent here.

Once I got back to the dorm, I sat down on my bunk and stared off into space. It was hard not to wonder if I'd made the right decision by going there. I tried to remember whether I'd made that decision on a Thursday. It didn't matter. I was where I was. Searching through the past wasn't getting me anywhere; aside from being stuck in a painful thought loop.

While I was still thinking, a guard came to get me. After a few ins and outs through the different buildings, we finally came to a stop at a visitor's section much like the one in Vanier, where I'd last seen my son a year ago. Off to the side were private rooms.

I was checked in by the transportation guard, and then placed into one of the private rooms. I was free, without any cuffs, and totally ready to meet with this new immigration officer.

I waited eagerly, wondering what type of person they would be. The paper appointment slip only had their first initial and last name, the building number, time, and the date.

Finally, the door opened, and in walked a lady who had more of an air of authority than any of the immigration officers I'd seen yet. She sat down in front of me and immediately identified herself, saying she was an ICE officer from Homeland Security. "Once I found out what had happened to you," she reassured me, "I wanted to get working on your file immediately."

I couldn't begin to understand what she meant by that. It sounded more like she wanted to help me, rather than make me sit here for months on end. Even some of my lawyers, to whom I'd paid thousands of dollars, had never seemed thiseager to help me; aside from the best ones, Lawyers Six and Seven.

She explained that her daughter had just arrived back in America after being on a two-year tour in the Middle East, and that she was supposed to start her holidays today.

"Are you serious?" I was stunned. She had given up time with her family to be here and work on my case? "Do you know what I was extradited for?"

She said she did, and that she'd read all about it online. Great. If she'd read about it online that probably wasn't good, because any search on Google had nothing good to say about me. My closest niece had told me about what she read online. All the cruel things from the news, blog posts, and of course, people's half-baked, uninformed opinions, which is treated about as highly as fact on the internet these days.

According to Proverbs 19:5, "A false witness will not go unpunished, and he who breathes out lies will perish." I can only pray that those people spewing hate online have found a way to forgive themselves.

I hoped that this woman had been smart enough to read between the lines.

"I can only imagine what the Internet told you about me."

"I don't believe everything it says," she revealed to my great relief. "Besides, my official position is that there's always more to someone than the news story tells. I'm on your side. Do you want to tell me what happened?"

I relaxed in my chair a little, and then I told her about everything I had gone through, starting with why and how I had been extradited. I ended it all by saying, "I just want to go home now."

For a moment, she stared at me with a blank look on her face. It was as if she was trying to take in everything I had endured. Finally, she broke her silence by saying, "I'm going to do everything in my power to get you in front of a judge this week. There's no reason for you to be here. I'm really sorry you had to go through all of this."

"Do you know how long I'll have to wait, before there'll be enough Canadians to fill up a plane and go back home?" That was the real question. After all, it had to be worth the money for the US to ship me out.

"I'm not sure," she told me again, "but I'm going to do what I can to get you back as fast as possible. I'll be in court with you this week, and I'm sure we can get on the schedule for this Thursday."

For a moment, I just sat there, wondering if this was really going to happen. Thursdays were never kind to me. "Aren't you supposed to be on holiday for the next couple weeks?"

She looked at me and shook her head, "Not as long as you're in here."

For the first time, in a very long time, I felt a complete sense of relief. She wasn't going to be fooled by what those Google searches said, nor would her mind be swayed by the fact that I was a convicted felon. I thanked God that there were still good people in the world even though I hadn't been living in that world for a year.

Later that night, as I lay in my cell, I prayed to God, asking Him if this would all work out. That instinctive voice answered me with an emphatic, "Yes, you better believe it."

Here comes that true faith. To believe beyond a shadow of a doubt that not one of those other bad days would matter. Finally, something wonderful would happen for me on a Thursday.

Say what you will, but the Law of Averages can work to your benefit, if you give it enough time.

Chapter Fifteen

CLOUDBUSTING

I MADE IT. That's what I thought to myself, as I stood waiting for my mother's ex-husband to pick me up. I held my release papers in one hand, and my bag of letters in the other. I could feel the sun shining on my face. Frankly, I don't remember a time when I'd ever felt better. I was finally free and back on Canadian soil. If not for the care shown to me by that ICE officer from Homeland Security, it might not have happened. Or at least, it could have taken weeks or months more off of my life.

It didn't help that my identification had been thrown away. I had to have one of my Canadian girlfriends named K who was great enough to write a letter to the Canadian embassy on my behalf, saying that I was who I said I was. The ICE officer had contacted the Canadian government to make sure they'd issued me travel documents so that I could finally, at long last, go back home.

A number of things had had to be put in order so that I could be released, and I'd be willing to bet that my case was different from many other immigrants leaving that immigration detention center in Arizona.

It had all begun with the judge agreeing to set a date to finalize my immediate release as soon as I waived my right to fight deportation. This had happened within a week of my arrival.

Over the following two weeks, there had been a couple more court dates. To be honest, I hadn't even paid attention to the proceedings. A few days after my last court date, I had been woken up at 5:00 a.m. and quietly taken back to the same airport, where I boarded a special chartered flight to Seattle. I was the only passenger on the Boeing 747, accompanied by twenty transportation guards.

I have to admit, it did make me feel special, knowing I was the only one there. No longer chained to anyone else. Once I got to Seattle, I was retrieved by another Homeland Security officer. Believe it or not, they were also supposed to be on holiday that same week. Instead, he'd driven in from another state to take me home. He drove me all the way from the Seattle airport to the Vancouver border. Bless him, he talked the whole way there.

"I have to admit it, Aretha," he told me, "I had a good look at your file. Your case is definitely…different."

I asked him why, expecting him to say it was because of Leading Actor being involved.

Instead, he told me, "This is the first time I've ever seen an immigrant get convicted of assault with a deadly weapon, but not get banned from the country."

I didn't understand what he meant, so he was only too happy to elaborate.

"It's standard procedure when a foreigner gets convicted on our soil for them to get banned from coming back into the US. For some reason, with your case, there was a motion to dismiss your removal hearing on the grounds it was improvidently issued. That means the courts should have never accepted your case. Let's put it this way: if you want to come back and visit us tomorrow, you can."

"I doubt that's going to happen." I almost laughed. "I have no intention of coming back."

"You never know." He chuckled. "You may want to come and go shopping one day."

After everything I had been through, nothing could make me want to come back to the United States. Ever. Not even if it was a free round-trip ticket. I was a proud Canadian, and I wanted nothing more to do with the US. I was done.

I was a bit bewildered by how friendly he was with me. Like he said, I was a convicted criminal. A foreigner who had been accused of hurting one of America's darlings. Yet I was still being treated with respect and kindness by one of their law enforcement officials. I guess it just goes to show — people are people all over.

After a three-and-a-half hour drive, we arrived at the US-Canadian border and were asked to pull over so that I could be checked back into my own country. The two of us got out of the car and waited for the Canadian Border Services Agency. An agent was coming out to meet with us.

I stood there, looking around for a moment, asking myself if it was all real. With my hands and ankles no longer cuffed, I smiled as the wind caressed my face. I breathed in the sweet scent of the trees.

After I was turned over to the Canadian authorities, the border patrol agent led me into the building. He asked me to take a seat and wait for my name to be called. I did as he asked, nervously looking around.

Less than five minutes later, I was called up to the desk, "Aretha Wilson."

I quickly made my way to the woman who'd called my name. By far, she had the thickest German accent I'd ever come across, but since she was an immigration official, I knew she was just as Canadian as I was. And she was just as friendly as any Canadian.

"I heard you were dropped off by the US officials. What happened over there?"

"I was extradited for assault to the US. I just finished my sentence, and now I've come home." I rolled my eyes, shrugged my shoulders, and smiled at her as if to show that I couldn't even believe what I had just said.

"Well, there we have it! A little trouble here, a little over there. And now you're back home in Canada, where you can turn over a new leaf." She smiled warmly at me, "Welcome home, Aretha."

Those were just about the loveliest words I'd heard in a long time..

"Thank you," I told her. And I meant it, with all my heart. "I'm not sure who's coming to get me, but if we could call my oldest sister in Toronto, I'm sure she'll know."

She took it upon herself to make the phone call to my oldest sister, so that I could listen in, putting the phone on speaker mode. After identifying herself as Canadian Border Services, we discovered it was my mother's ex-husband coming from Toronto to Vancouver to meet me.

That's when I found out that he had instantly jumped in his car and driven for three days straight as soon as he'd learned where I was going to be released.

My oldest sister offered up his cell number, and the officer dialed him next. He answered after a few rings, and after identifying herself, she asked him if he was on his way to pick me up. I heard the excitement in his voice as he exclaimed, "You have her with you! I'll be there in about twenty minutes!"

He was true to his word. Maybe even a couple of minutes sooner.

***

Once that was settled, I was free to go.

Without any hesitation I turned around, and went straight out the door. I hurried right out to the end of the parking lot and just stood there, beaming with joy as the sunshine kissed my skin. I stared out at the trees, which seemed to go on forever. I wanted to be the first person my mother's ex-husband saw when he arrived.

As I waited, I thought about the last time I had been in court with the ICE officer from Homeland Security, just before I had been flown to Seattle. The media had found out where I was and had shown up.

One man in particular had found his way in, looking to get a quote from me. The look on my face when I found out who he was must have said it all, because the media man was escorted out without being given any further chance to bother me. No way was the ICE officer going to let him cash another check off of my sorrows.

Without any media here, there I was, finally standing on my own. No more guards, deputies, judges, lawyers, prosecutors, crown attorneys, cops, or detectives. Even though the last few I had encountered hadn't been as bad as some of the others, I was still glad to be free of them all.

Good people can be found in every profession. After everything that I had witnessed I can still say that, even about law enforcement. I'd told the ICE officer from that day in court that if I ever wrote a book, I would include everything she had done for me.

Her response had been, "Feel free to use my first and last name." I would never forget it, as I would be forever grateful for her help.

She'd arranged everything, including having me escorted out of the country and being told I could come right back. Of all the women I have had to deal with, from Dr. Lastname's assistant to the counselors at Chowchilla, she showed that she truly cared about my situation.

My sliver of light that broke through that seemingly impenetrable wall of darkness.

A tap on my shoulder brought me back to where I was, still standing in the parking lot. I turned around and found myself face-to-face with my mother's ex-husband.

"Hey kiddo," he said casually, already smiling at me with his arms open wide. He was clearly waiting for a hug.

I wrapped my arms around him, overcome with joy to be home.

Even though I knew I was free, the hug made it feel so much more real. I bet most people who walk out of jail are never sad about it. Freedom is a must, and boy, did it feel good to be back on my native soil.

"Where's your stuff?" he asked.

I shrugged my shoulders, showing him the bag of letters I had in my hand. "This is it."

Still smiling, he shrugged too, "That's okay. We can go get you some new things now."

We walked to where his car was parked, but before we could leave, I looked at my mother's ex-husband. "I'll be right back." I told him.

I headed back to the building and went inside. I stood there for a moment, trying to make eye contact with the kind officer on the other side of the room. Finally, I just shouted to her, "My dad's here!"

She smiled at me and shouted back in her thick German accent, "Of course he is!"

I'm not sure why I did that. It's not like she'd asked me to. Maybe it's because I was so used to reporting everything I did to authority figures. It had become a natural reflex for me. Or maybe it was the feeling of pride you get when your dad picks you up. I felt like a kid again, being picked up after sports practice.

Either way, it was the first time in my life that I had ever called him dad. It felt really good.

Later that evening, he drove me to the airport so that I could catch the red-eye to Toronto. We talked about some of the things I would have to look out for in the future, being a newly released convict that was still a figure in the news.

"It won't be easy, kiddo, but I know you're going to be okay. Something good is going to happen." Then we talked about the rainy days in Chowchilla. I told him how it never stopped raining.

And about all the mice that came out at night. I could see that it bothered him, knowing that he couldn't protect me from any of it.

He had coached me through some of my toughest moments, always giving me great advice. Importantly, he provided wonderful guidance after losing my friend Happy.

Then there had been the phone calls, where we would spend all our time talking about John Coltrane. How he was the greatest saxophonist the world had ever heard. He would start scatting, as if he was a jazz musician himself. No matter how I tried to interrupt him, he wouldn't stop his "scilly-dapaodou-pido" scat singing for a solid two minutes.

Once we got to the airport, I checked into my flight. Before leaving, I wanted to show my appreciation to my mother's ex-husband, "Thank you for coming to get me, along with everything else you've done."

"Anything for you, Aretha," he told me.

He had been the last person I'd hugged the day I'd turned myself into Vanier jail. Now after driving for three days to come get me, he was the first person to hug me a year later, when I finally got back out.

I never saw him alive again after that day. But when I look back now at all the times he had been there for me, it's probably the real reason why I told the kind officer he was my dad.

***

Thursday, June 30, 2011, I was in Toronto, standing in front of my son once more. We were back at my oldest sister's house. The two of us couldn't have been happier, seeing each other for the first time in a year.

I knew I had to leave the past behind. To do my best and try to lead a normal life. We started making plans to get our lives back on track. I made arrangements for my son to get a job with one of my favorite guy friends while my son waited for the HVAC program to start at George Brown College. It was what he'd decided he wanted to take in order to have a future career in building operations.

I wanted to put my life back together too, starting with returning to work. Prior to getting out of jail, I'd made arrangements with the last company that I'd worked for. They were going to allow me to go back to my position there.

Unfortunately, the management had changed, and for some reason or other, they stripped me of all my seniority. I still wanted to give it a try and start again. I accepted the job, telling myself I was lucky to have it.

To celebrate my release, I met up with my four favorite guy friends at our friend's bar, The Corner Place.

After that, I went on another techno adventure. This time, with another guy that I had known for years. He'd become like a brother to me after convincing me to listen to an entire album from start to finish. The album had turned out to be for the same concert that was the best one I'd ever seen. The one with two rainbows in the sky. His favorite song on the album was "Jigsaw Falling Into Place." Our friendship solidified once we realized I'd been dancing to 166 BPM the whole time.

I ended up hanging out with him and a couple of his friends with whom I was familiar. One of them took it upon himself to make sure he stayed with me the entire time, as if he were my knight in shining armor. Treating me as though I were the "Lady" that the group Modjo sings about. This guy knew everything there was to know about techno and house music. He'd been going to raves and industry parties for more than twenty years.

The Comfort Zone was his favorite dance club in Toronto. When it came to dancehall and reggae, Jah-know, he would know everything. If there was going to be anyone to teach me how to really listen to music, this would be my guy. He could hear all the different sounds, while keeping the beat of tempos shifting from allegro (109-132 BPM) to presto (168-177 BPM). If I am thinking about it now, he's best described as "Genius of Love." By The Tom Tom Club.

We decided to go to Cherry Beach on Toronto's Lake Ontario. Much like Sunnyside Pavilion, it's by the water. It also hosts some of the world's best techno/house DJs. Only this place was free to get into, and we were so close to the lake that we got to dance in the sand, with a forest of trees on the other side. Everyone was moving, as the day turned into night, and the sky filled with stars. People danced like they were the hounds of love, literally howling at the moon.

I noticed most of the lyrics of the tracks being played at these parties contained simple instructions, leading you to feel positive, full of love, and best of all, free. Hearing songs like Green Velvet's "Lalalala," you can't help but relate to every word. Almost like he was the pastor, and we were in church. I may have been afraid before, but this time, I let go.

Lots of people I knew were there, and as with most of my good friends, we were all brought together by music. These were people who had all stood by me, but I knew there was a chance that others might be jaded, opinions twisted by the news coverage surrounding my case.

I faced a few other challenges when I got home, even on days that weren't Thursdays.

Upon returning, I had made a doctor's appointment to get myself checked out. When I got the results, I found out the LEEP procedure I'd had years ago didn't quite work out. It had actually become a lot more serious than I could ever have imagined.

I was still developing a growth which had become more and more visible, especially during the many strip searches I'd had to endure while I was at the Lynwood facility. They had actually sent me to their infirmary, but I'd refused to have treatment for it while in the US. Never mind at the Los Angeles County Central Jail Hospital. I would wait until I got home.

After a biopsy, my physician referred me to the head of Gyneco-logic Oncology at Princess Margaret Hospital, who was known for being a remarkable doctor. He wasn't just the head of one hospital, but of three. The others were the hospital I had gone to the night of my accident, and the one where I had been born. I was informed that even with surgery, there was a 99% chance I would still have to undergo chemo and radiation treatments. Unfortunately, my plan to go back to work didn't last long enough to even really get started.

It wasn't just because I would have to take more time off for my newly discovered medical situation, but my new manager's attitude was degrading and difficult to deal with.

I had worked alongside her as a Senior Manager for years, but now she acted as though she was terrified of me, somehow forget-ting that we had once shared bottles of wine. Not to mention the many times I had fallen asleep at her house. She had no reason to be scared, but she was. And so, for both those reasons, I left.

I would soon come to realize that leaving the job would come back to haunt me. The darkness of what I had gone through would continue to cast a shadow over my professional life.

The power of the Internet is like the ocean, deep, wide-reach-ing, and uncontrollable. It felt like Google had handed me another sentence, only this one was a life sentence. It would afford me no opportunity to lead a normal, happy life again.

Even though I'd pleaded no contest, served my time, and did what was asked of me, people will always think what they want. It certainly doesn't help that a Google search of my name comes back with millions of results, and yet, not one word directly from Leading Actor or myself.

All the information is added to the Internet by strangers, and then recycled by others with their own narratives. This makes it near impossible for me to find a job and keeps me trapped in the past, all while other people pretending to know my story make a profit.

Having an honorable occupation was important to me. I took

positions that I thought would make others happy, while providing a service, which included making them money. However, by this point my entire understanding of how and why we earn money had changed. If I'm to quote one of my grandfather's favorite bibles verses, 1 Timothy 6:10 "'For the love of money is the root of all evils.'" From what I've seen, and after spending a good chunk of my life's earnings on lawyers and seeing what the gossip magazines and prison industry make from the other side of the camera, I wanted no part of any of that lifestyle ever again. Besides, I'd always had more fun sharing the money I'd made. I've never been a fan of the get rich quick scheme. For my future, I wanted to look for opportunities where I could give back. Shine a light emotionally, as opposed to monetarily, on those who need it most.

***

Treatment of my condition, one of the world's most malicious and deadly diseases, doesn't work for everyone. My heart weeps for those who have succumbed to it, and the loved ones who lost them. Fortunately, I didn't lose my battle.

"Dying of cancer would be the easy way out." That's what I said to Dr. Remarkable, when he first gave me the grim diagnosis. I wasn't going to let it be the end of me.

"Aretha, you're taking this pretty lightly," he seemed surprised.

But I wasn't. "God has a lot more for me to go through," was my unwavering response. This time, my faith was so strong, I didn't even have to question my inner voice.

My surgery was done at the same hospital where I had been born. A few weeks after that, I had a major mishap, where my delicate stitches were ripped right back out one by one. There were a few other minor surgeries so they could remove other tumors around the area. In the months following, Dr. Remarkable informed me that reconstructive surgery would likely be the next step. I didn't believe any of the negative prognosis, and I was declared cancer free about a year later.

I even avoided the chemotherapy and radiation treatments. However I'm meant to leave this world in the end, it wasn't like that.

Then, without getting another stitch replaced, each one of my wounds naturally healed back up. I actually turned out better than before.

It was all because I had been placed in the best hands at The University Health Network. In one of my many follow up visits with Dr. Remarkable, he confided in me, "Aretha, I have to say you are a living anomaly."

I responded with, "And you've saved my life, so what does that make you?"

Both of us just smiled at each other. There was nothing else that needed to be said. We were grateful.

***

This was more reassurance for me that life would go on. Even though I went through so many twists and turns, I always believed there were better times up ahead for me. This was not the end.

Surviving was another beginning, leading me to another Thursday, and another decision to go out. My Radiohead friend called me and invited me to his friend's birthday party. After beating cancer, this was just one more reason to celebrate life.

Turns out, it was the same friend who'd had taken care of me that night a year ago, when we'd all gone to Cherry Beach. I knew there was something familiar about him, and it only confirmed my suspicion when he said, "You may not remember it, but I first saw you once in an elevator when I was fourteen with some friends." Once I was reminded, I recalled the moment, even though we'd never said a word to each other at the time. However, I did over-hear him ask someone else if they knew my name, and remember it as being the first time in my life that I ever felt pretty. A chance encounter in the '80s, and twenty seven years later, we'd found ourselves meeting again.

We spent the night reminiscing while listening to music, going through the different meaningful songs in our lives. By the time Friday rolled in at midnight, we had already made plans to go back to Cherry Beach the following Sunday.

Lo and behold, this would be one of the best decisions I ever made. I went out on a Thursday, and finally the tide turned. That Thursday led me in a positive direction.

I found true love.

First and I have now been together for more than ten years. We've gone to see some of the best DJs in the world, from Danny Tenaglia to Dennis Ferrer, with countless others in between. Not to forget some of our hometown favorites, Christina Barron, a musical mistress who will have me dancing to my own name, and Tyler Hill, who creates sound transitions that are so smooth, together as + One, they can make anyone "Move". Then there's Kenny Glasgow, who aside from the youngest of my brothers, is the only other musical mathematician I have come across. My feet have never been happier. Best part is we can usually find any one of them spinning inside Toronto's Wiggle Room.

I must admit, our relationship feels like the Stardust song, "Music Sounds Better With You". And unlike when I had been with Last, First and I can "Enjoy the Silence" while listening to Depeche Mode.

Falling in love was the last thing I'd expected to happen, especially with my history. But despite everything that was being said about me, he didn't care one bit. Instead, he made the effort to get to know me for himself. The only time it ever came up was when he said to me, "Aretha, I have to admit, I did google you. Those pictures that come up do not do you justice."

I've lost count of how many times throughout the years that First has told me I'm beautiful inside and out, along with the multitude of I love yous that I receive from him daily. Hearing encouraging words like these from him every day taught me not to harbor any resentment or anger about what I'd been through. With him, I learned to love myself, which is the truest kind of healing.

It takes a great amount of control not to respond to a stranger who sends you unwanted emails, or to ignore the blogs filled with heartless statements all based on lies. But I managed it. Though sometimes, it was difficult not to pull my own hair out. I can't help but think that God placed First in my life for a reason.

He even had a daughter, named after my favorite country, aside from my own. Much like her father, she's not swayed by what others may think. She's truly helped me to focus on what's important: the love of family, and keeping a host of friends.

Vraie came to visit me in Toronto, again bringing her son. He has now turned into a lyrical master, becoming a self-taught musician. I'm also happy to report my Deacon Brother has been with his husband for seventeen years now. Goes to show that love shines in a rainbow of colors.

My mother is still gracing me with her ways. Now I know why she sang Aretha Franklin's song, "A Natural Woman" to me. It's not that she expected me to be a singer, it's how I made her feel. Even though I'm not much of a singer, I sang the same song to my son in my own womb to help set the tone. Since then, I have gained the admiration of my son, who will always encourage me to reach for the sky, even when I'm drowning.

He does this with the love of his father, Clark, who continues to be one of my best friends. The kind German border agent had been right. After 45 years, I sought out and found my loving Native Aunt, so I could see what was on the other side. I turned over a new leaf, and discovered I'm the eldest of another brother, two sisters, with three uncles and aunts, all connected to the Aslin/MacDonald clan. A clan that's also filled with cousins, nephews and nieces. As for my older siblings, they all respect the fact that I've got a lot of experience now.

For my family still stuck in the system, I sing "I Say a Little Prayer" for you.

***

In spite of it all, I'll never have control—nor do I want to—over what people believe or say. However, I can have control over myself, and I can make it a gift. It's like being in prison: you learn to live with it. Much like I have with the consequences of my car accident. Besides, another one of my mother's wise phrases was, "If someone is talking bad about you, you should be happy, because they're leaving someone else alone."

Still, there was a truth I had to face after thinking about all my decisions and the changes I needed to make. The lesson I needed to learn had always been there in black and white, inside of me all along. Turns out, Morrissey was right: bigmouth does strike again and again. I'm responsible for all of the words that have left my own mouth, and I've made a number of poor choices.

Hollering back at the cab driver, after he cut me off, certainly didn't get us where we wanted to go, regardless of how much I love my scars today. I knew insulting Leading Actor was going to strike a chord, and I had to take responsibility for provoking him.

Without a doubt, there are certain words that can trigger an instant slap in the face. The 2022 Oscars is a perfect example of this. Personally, I don't recommend saying any of them. Nothing good can follow. That is, unless you're the type of celebrity where they don't charge you with a crime and still give you an Oscar, even if you hit another actor on live television, during an awards ceremony.

As for my friend Happy, I wish I could say more. I do look forward to a time when I will see him again. I have faith that day will surely come, the same way I knew cancer would not be the end of my story. One of the most important lessons I learned was by reading The Power of the Spoken Word, by Florence Scovel Shinn. With faith, say it, and it becomes yours. Your instinct (otherwise known as the slight pang in your chest), commonly called butterflies, will guide you along the way.

Our ability to speak is our power. All wars start through words. Anything that inspires happiness comes from our lips, especially when a smile is included. I love the New Testament of The King James Bible, John 1:1, which reads, "In the beginning was the Word, and the Word was with God, and the Word was God." I believe God gave us the ultimate gift, which is to speak. It's one of the things that sets us apart from the rest of His creations.

After all, my dog is never going to call me Aretha. Yet it knows it's a dog, because we gave it that name. Without saying one word back, they will listen to all of our commands. A diamond ring that is presented to another means so much when coupled with the words, "Will you marry me?"

Learning how to control my own mouth was a change I needed to make and where I would find the blessings in disguise through all of my past mistakes, eventually even granting me the courage to write about my experiences. It certainly hasn't been easy, but I'm very grateful to have made it here.

At times, it has been difficult to continue to move forward, but somehow, I've always managed to do it. Although, I don't think any of it would be possible if not for all of the books and the music that have shaped my life. And, for me, the Bible brings it all together, keeping me on the right track. The righteous track.

Beyond the smog-filled skies of California, I see a silver lining in those clouds. The ones that hovered over me endlessly while I was in prison. This was where I first realized that I would have to truly surrender to the will of God, especially once I knew no judge or lawyer would have the answer. And I certainly couldn't put my faith in a celebrity. Besides, mercy, along with justice, can only be granted by the one who honors it.

Going to jail gave me the opportunity to realize there is more to life than just seeing day or night. It's knowing there is also dusk and dawn, and the freedom to view the world from many angles. We don't exist in a limited, four-sided box.

Being confined to reading the Good Book led me to believe there was a reason for each season. A purpose for my presence. And it nourished me with plenty of food for thought. It allowed me to cultivate a relationship with God in which I could happily surrender all my faith to Him. I suppose, if I were to describe this part of my life's experience with a psalm, Echo & the Bunnymen's song "The Killing Moon" would be a good metaphor for how it feels. He does wait for you to give in to Him, until you feel forgiven. Even if you tell Him to get lost, He's not leaving. To me that includes those moments when you find yourself talking to yourself with the hope that someone else is listening. Or when that inner voice in your head gives you the courage to look in the mirror, and say out loud, "It will get better. It's just going to take some time."

Poor, rich, famous or anyone in between, every one of us has purpose. We can become superstars in our own lives. We can find a way to love ourselves despite scars, the suicide of a loved one, and jail cells. We can find the willpower to not respond to what others say, and that will make a huge difference. We can challenge ourselves to never make the same mistakes more than once.

Telling the truth does set you free. I believe that honesty should always be the only policy. Not just the best. It feels better, and it's our ultimate challenge when using the gift of words.

At this point, I'm convinced each one of us is a good book. Like Biggie Smalls says, we've all got a story to tell. And I'd bet each person comes with a great soundtrack.

Besides, every generation has been told to keep our own diaries, much like those prophets and disciples have, with the hope that someone else can relate to it. Eventually.

Every day you have an opportunity to be real. To live outside of the box that's been programming us. Although, it seems to me, it's the music in the background that keeps us glued to the TV. One commercial could leave a song stuck in your head for an entire lifetime.

Currently, I'm reading Aaron Tabors' 365 Interactive Devotions: Jesus Daily, and The Diary of Anne Frank. Personally, I would rather read or listen to music than watch television. I can hear a young lady named Koffee with a song called "Toast" that will encourage anyone to get through the day. Or, I can immerse myself in Earth, Wind and Fire's song "Fantasy", which allows me to escape to freedom and claim victory for myself anytime I choose to put it on. When I look back at all the caterpillars I collected throughout the seasons, it turns out the best one I ever caught was a song by The Cure. It reminds me that I can be beautiful inside and out, whether butterfly or moth in a flicker of the dark. I've also learned when singing the song "Swamp Thing" by The Chameleons at a karaoke bar, you might be surprised to discover, you're not the only one.

Music has always been my vessel of hope, guiding me through my entire journey, even when I could only imagine it in my mind. I can always find a melody swimming in the back of my head. With or without lyrics, it is the most relatable connection two humans can have, good or bad. It can make you feel like someone understands you. I'm also certain that most of us would agree that the best way to create the atmosphere in a movie is through its soundtrack. It leads us to empathize with a character, creating a world of emotions with (or without) anyone on the screen. The beloved writer Hans Christian Andersen was credited for saying, "Where words fail, music speaks."

It's for all the reasons why I'm completely mesmerized by Charlie Chaplin's ability to entertain us while dancing through an entire silent movie, simply using a hat and cane.

I suppose if I'm to question anything as real and relatable, music is the answer, with words sung "As" in the key of life. It's forever and a day that I will be grateful to Stevie Wonder, who taught me what it means to love at the age of five.

Over the last few years during the covid pandemic, there have been no parties to go to, no concerts or DJs to be seen live. Not even the angelic voices of a gospel choir to be heard in a church because a good portion of the world was on lockdown. Most of us were confined to our own homes. It was not until last year, in 2022, when we were all slowly released to migrate back into the public. Not being in community has taken its toll. And yet, I tell myself it's all right. From my experience, you have an opportunity to come out of hibernation better than when you went in. Besides, I'd much rather take the inspirational advice that comes from CamelPhat and Jake Bugg's song, "Be Someone." Or I could close my eyes and put myself on a "Hillside" with Chronic Law.

"Speak only if it improves upon the silence," is what Mahatma Gandhi once said. And these days, much like when I was in Chowchilla, I'll say just about anything to put a smile on someone's face. The truth is, only good can follow kind words; creating the best of feelings in even the worst situations.

As for it being Thursday, no matter what I would have done yesterday, or even last week, I ended up exactly where I am supposed to be. I'm not only lucky to be alive, but it's a miracle every day that I wake up with air in my lungs.

In conclusion, I would say that it's best to leave the past where it belongs, behind you. Embrace what you can't erase, choose your words carefully, and you will find that everything has always been in its right place. Eventually.

You just have to have "Faith" by being "Optimistic."

A short note with a long list of the Toronto DJ's, Promoters, and our Frams (The family of friends who are true supporters) that I've had the opportunity to dance amongst. Each one of you has lent a hand in helping shape so many lives throughout our great city - mine for certain.

To the Dj's: whether it be a roller/ice skating rink, a club, a bar, a stage, on the beach, in a studio, or in your house, it has been a gift to be in your presence; where if only for a moment, one could feel like they've touched heaven.

In my world, you are all musical ministers- And blessed are those who will know every heart needs a beat.

Carl Allen Chico Umengan Sherwin Lamando Andrew Gater DJ Nostrabrammus Tony Duncan The Sunshine Crew DJ Sol Basil Campbell Edward Melia Mark Oliver Ty Hale DJ Marcus Rob Anderson Rob Daboom Jojo Flores Peter Primiani Steve Primiani Starting From Scratch Joe Rizla Kingdom Dre Noel D'Layne DJ DTM Manzone & Strong Gio Cristiano Michael Valenti Anna Elmendorf Ali Black Flipside Kwame Younge (Knowledge Keeper) Kimmo Hyytianen Rogelio Bayaton Adam Fairhurst Dwayne Anthony Joey SoundQuest Shawn

Grant Ron Nelson Tyrone Solomon The Assoon Brothers Andre Silva Brad Nelson (Goldfinger) Danny Henry Dat So DJ Yogi Davidson Elie Eric Planethouse Paul Dela Cruz Earl DjLazy Dave Campbell Matt C Forrest Kendlbacher Marco Frekkls Fleming Gene King Jackie Spade Jules Worth Kevy Kev James Cox Keenan Bittner Jerome Andrews Anthony Donnelly Jason Clarke Joseph Navarro Jay Moher Ticky Ty Tricky Moreira Junior Palmer Manolo Tavares Miz Megs Jay Force Justin Corrado Melanie Sutherland Deko-ze Amalia Leandro Mark Kuffner Demuir Paul Lopez Hubert Kowlaczyk LeBaron James Amir DJ Ron Jon Jellybean Benitez Ritmo Collective Greg Gow Jay NuFunk Mark Zeldan Pedro Mondesir Mark Poludnikiewicz Neil & Noel Shaun Hudson Morry Weisfeld Iced Misto Ron Allen Corey Dawkins Nicole Rodgers Nigel B Wade B Rick Nurse Carerra & Tavares Basil Ellis Roberto Palacios Dirty Dale Roland Gonzales Jason Palma Sasha Sakic Nitin Mr. Haze Trevor Le Caviier Ivan Palmer Jon Chetty DJ Shannon Terry Demopolous Dino Demopolous David James John Jinga Hal Perry David Marchione Tim Sidvak DJ James Kouvarakos Kosta Bolontzakis Mark Scaife Maves Marrs Barrs Jack Declared Mike Gleeson Lesley Bernardi Jonny Lopez Kenny Pounall Arcadia Gsine Chico Pacheco (Percussions) DJ Lazarus Matt Patrick Nick Holder Jonny Dac Andy Roberts Chris Vench Paul Revered Steve Glass Jason Rumball Johnny Lopez Loopity Goofs Mario Castillo Chris Larson Douglas Carter Sleepy Freeman Kosta B Joseph Berardi Anthony Berardi Sean Romans Mark Foreman Katie B Zoe Thorn Jenny Boo Jamie Kidd Mike Gibbs Ryan Wiley Nour Bawab DJ Ritchie Nathan Barato Takin Steve Oh Sam Caravella Andy Cue Simon Jain Sean Starr Joee Cons Johnny White The Art Department Rudee Nik Tyler Hill Christina Barron Kenny Glasgow.

To DJ's/Musicians that I've missed, don't know or the ones that I will come to, continue to create. Music is the sustenance needed for our souls, as with food that gives us energy and the water that quenches our thirst.

Eddy Kaay Balance Gino Ralph Lindsay Lodenquai Stephen Beltzer Gathurin uf Soulz Joel Norton Gavin Gerbz Rissa Dee Mike Jones Monique Proulx The Geary Ave Warehouse Chantelle Lelliott White Labe WLP United Soul Yunaverse Cy Campbel Gavin Merritt Fun Boys tINI Roland Gonzalves Roman Jay Coombs Norbert Ricafort (Photog) Hot Stepper Productions Karl Wint Enza Ruscillo Sonit 1LIV1 Kat Lovebrigade House of Wayne (Photogr) Anthony & Stephen Phillips Industry Charles Lewis INK B&A Associates Jaclyn Wilson Richard Hollywood Ted Clarke Moe and Dean Paul Alfano Phantom Adam Spencley Pradeep & Sasha Sweet Touch Foundation Gogo Knecht Bespoke Experience Knudles Pat Boogie Joga Olivier Charles Jonathon Mcneil Joey Tdot Box of Kittens alienInFlux Bridgette & Sophia Deerr Apollo MiMi Calma Harvest Jeanette Newhook Jenne Turcotte Denise & Leslie Jenn Starr Steven De Francesca Soraya Haick Summer Daze Ded Pixel (Photog) Virgil Teixeira Robyn Alexis Terri-Lynn Moe & Dean Eugene Mcintosh Byron Dill Ford Medina The Wiggle Room The Assoon Brothers Footwork The Comfort Zone-1 & 2 Junior Williams Vertigo Bedrock The Tony Ruscillo Family Michael Holtzman Laila Childe Charles Khabouth and the late Johnny K. Sound-Hugh, Andre, Sasha, Tryfon, Neil and Noel.

Cheers to all the people and places that have lent a hand in helping to shape many countless beautiful souls. Each one of you is an attribution, while taking us on some of Toronto's finest free loving musical journeys.

To the dawn disciples and angels that I've lived with here on Earth: Michael Mark Peter John, Tommy Brett Bruce Andrew & Ghost Matt Steve Will Alan Ice, Michael P, Roger, Vince, Delio, Greg, Kyle Jimmy & Deb Brian Derek Hank Kareem Stuart Michael G Mikey D Lucan Jamie Rick (Artist) CJ Tammi Cassandra Bray (Artist) Michelle

Krista Becky (Artist) Zoe Queent Red Princess Colleen Anestie Adam Screech Mpho B Mit & Mel BM Hem Joanna Tony Leh-Lo DJ Ezii Scott Rueben Marcus Lauren Nessy Joseph Sally Norman Sarah Elyse Minty Chef-Jenny Kathie Jysse Kenny & Dean. Walking with Ghost by Tegan and Sara, you discovered me going through The Bridge School Collection, where I was once lost. Subsequently it's After The Gold Rush written by Neil Young covered by Thom Yorke that best describes the love I have for each one of you now that I've been found. I'm humbled. Thank you for always making sure I feel like I'm right at home. I'm grateful for the seventeen years you've spent helping raise me, while making sure I always got back to my own home.

Rest for the angels: Johnny Mac, Big Bob, Richard McNielly, Chris Melia, Jason Ulrich, Rudy Gan, Kimmo Hyytianen, Joee Cons and Tommy, along with so many others, who will one day be one of us.

To my best friends, Betty Jo, my instant sister (Martha), my cousin Shantelle, Lucy, SheriAnne, Shani, Lana, Denvil, Byron and Mariaah. I was once told that friends/relationships are like seasons; they come and go, wilter and grow. I have no doubt that God has strategically placed each one of you in my life at the perfect time with a purpose, to bring out the best in me, and it's what I believe true best friends are made from.

To the youngest of my best friends Breana, also now an angel. Forever your beauty and honesty will be etched in my mind, as I remember you performing the song Bohemian Rhapsody at the age of five. Almost as if the song was written just for you. Regardless of how, when and why you left this Earth, alongside your angelic voice, you continue to be a blessing to many lives, much like Freddie Mercury, who also had a purpose. And don't we all.

If not for the guidance of Raicheal Fuller (Copy-Editor), alongside Chad Allard (Final Editor), Jeffrey Kenneth Hodgins and my Deacon Brother David sharing my truth never would have been possible.

Helping me decipher such an odd and twisted journey is your gift, to understand that each and everyone of us has a story to tell.

With an extension of gratitude to my reading group. Christina Laflamme, Donna Saunders, Mary Kargus, Japhet Bower, Lindsay Lodenquai Sasha Bear and Hilary Syme. All who would all take the time to read those painful drafts, alongside Geoff Micks who would also help me to discover all the reasons for why my book has its name.